BUREAUCRATS and BLEEDING HEARTS

Indigenous health in northern Australia

Tess Lea

To my family, for enabling me to breathe

A UNSW Press book

Published by
University of New South Wales Press Ltd
University of New South Wales
Sydney NSW 2052
AUSTRALIA
www.unswpress.com.au

© Tess Lea 2008
First published 2008

National Library of Australia
Cataloguing-in-Publication entry

Author: Lea, Tess.
Title: Bureaucrats and bleeding hearts: Indigenous health in northern Australia/
    author, Tess Lea.
Publisher: Sydney: University of New South Wales Press, 2008.
ISBN: 978 1 921410 18 5 (pbk.)
Notes: Includes index.
Subjects: Aboriginal Australians – Medical care – Northern Territory.
    Aboriginal Australians – Northern Territory – Government relations.
    Medical care – Northern Territory – Citizen participation.
    Community development – Northern Territory.
Dewey Number: 362.849915

Design Josephine Pajor-Markus
Printer Ligare

This book is printed on paper using fibre supplied from plantation or sustainably
managed forests.

BUREAUCRATS and BLEEDING HEARTS

Associate Professor Tess Lea has operated as a senior bureaucrat in both federal and Northern Territory postings. She established and now directs the School for Social and Policy Research at Charles Darwin University, which aims to drive applied work with an intelligent edge. She is known for *Learning Lessons*, her landmark review of Indigenous education (1999), and for undertaking a Churchill Fellowship exploring means of improving school-based education in 2006. Born in the Northern Territory, Tess Lea returned to Darwin in the mid 1990s and was immediately struck by the tremendous heartache of public health and other forms of social service. This book is a testimony to the challenges of that service.

CONTENTS

ACKNOWLEDGMENTS

This book has emerged from a long period of tutelage in the magical and arcane arts of being both a bureaucrat and an academic, for which I have many people to thank. Gillian Cowlishaw remained the most insistent of supports, unshakable in her commitment to both anthropological analysis and the importance of this work. At the deepest of levels, she is my guiding light. With Hal Wootten, Gillian provided a warm place to think in my sojourns to Sydney and, with Franca Tamisari, supplied inspiration to think with. The book has been a while in the making, and over the years, others have provided much-needed encouragement, including Donald Brenneis, Ian Buchanan, Emma Kowal, Andrew Lattas, Stephen Muecke, Beth Povinelli, Nicolas Rothwell, Marilyn Strathern and Paul Torzillo.

I owe much to many I cannot acknowledge. This book is based on an ethnography of Territory Health Services, the real name of a real organisation, but of course all contributors have been renamed, unless they are well-known public figures and appear in that capacity. Territory Health Services has itself experienced a name change: it is now the Northern Territory Department of Health and Families. But keeping its former name here treats the organisation as I do the subjects, which is in keeping with a key message of this book – namely, that the bureaucracy is peopled. *Bureaucrats and Bleeding Hearts* focuses on the people who generate forms of bureaucratised agonising about Aboriginal welfare in the north: the professionals, practitioners, researchers and policy officers who are usually faceless in analyses of government policy. It argues that while the issues surrounding poor Aboriginal health are undeniably real, how bureau-professionals formulate this as a dominant problematic is undeniably cultural.

To the unnamed – or renamed – regional officers who took the risk of letting me shadow them so that I could produce an insider's account of being a bureaucrat and bleeding heart, I owe my deepest respect. I am especially grateful to the woman I call Marlena, for taking a risk on a person she didn't know, on a project that sounded vague, at a time when she was in the thick of having to sort out her own new beginnings. Her willingness to experiment opened other doors by establishing a precedent others could reference. Peter Plummer and Katherine Henderson were the bureaucratic conduits, while the plight of the late Bob Collins paradoxically rescued some of the convoluted thinking. Bob and I journeyed together on an explosive tour of Indigenous education that still has me inveigled in the complicities and deep personal risks of honest and muddy interventionary work.

The original ethnographic research was funded by a grant from the Carlyle Greenwell Bequest, through the University of Sydney. A less developed version of Chapter 5 appeared as 'A Benign Arithmetic: Taking Up Facts About Indigenous Health' in *The UTS Review: Cultural Studies and New Writing* 7(1), May 2001: 59–73 (now *Cultural Studies Review*). The Centre for Research in the Arts, Social Sciences and Humanities (CRASSH) at the University of Cambridge generously provided the space and time for rethinking the manuscript, and the steadfastness of colleagues in the School for Social and Policy Research at Charles Darwin University made retreating for writing amidst all other demands a possibility. The dynamic Naomi Tootell provided excellent editing advice and a sensitive appreciation of the arguments. I am also grateful to the publication team at UNSW Press: to Heather Cam for her expert guidance, Ella Roby for timely advice, and to Sarah Shrubb for a copy-editing exchange that was both exhilarating and enriching.

Finally, the love, forbearance and wisdom of my children, Daniel and Elise, supported by my partner, Gregory Moo, fundamentally sustained this work from beginning to end.

ACRONYMS

ABS	Australian Bureau of Statistics
ANU	Australian National University
ATSIC	Aboriginal and Torres Strait Islander Commission
CDU	Charles Darwin University
CGC	Commonwealth Grants Commission
CRASSH	Centre for Research in the Arts, Social Sciences and Humanities (University of Cambridge)
DLG	Department of Local Government
HDI	Hospitals Development International
HIPP	Health Infrastructure Priority Projects scheme
MEDLINE	Medical Literature Analysis and Retrieval System Online
MSHR	Menzies School of Health Research
NGO	Non-government organisation
NT	Northern Territory
NTMS	Northern Territory Medical Service
NTU	Northern Territory University
OATSIH	Aboriginal and Torres Strait Islander Health
RDH	Royal Darwin Hospital
SWSBSC	Strong Women, Strong Babies, Strong Culture
THS	Territory Health Services
VOQ	Visiting Officers' Quarters
WHO	World Health Organization

PROLOGUE

This is an anthropological study of the culture of public health governance in the Northern Territory (NT) of Australia, a site for ongoing national anxiety. Given all the goodwill, money and effort thrown at interventions, why do Aboriginal people die 17 years younger than their white counterparts? What will it take to 'close the gap'? This book takes a fresh look at these longstanding issues, shifting the anthropological lens away from Aborigines and onto planners, policy officers and professionals operating inside the Northern Territory's health bureaucracy. It asks what it takes to become a helping white in Australia's postcolonial frontier – someone who passionately cares about and resolutely strives towards improved health for Indigenous people – and how such determination to help is sustained in the face of a self-declared history of failure. As the final version of this book was being prepared, the reverberations of the Australian Government's national emergency intervention in the Territory, introduced by former Federal Minister for Family, Community Services and Indigenous Affairs, Mal Brough, in June 2007, were still being felt by targeted communities. Citing the rape of small children, violence against women, closed communities, uncontrolled grog running and X-rated pornography, Brough unleashed a suite of 'drastic measures'. Compulsory health screens for signs of abuse in children; leasehold changes and a disbanding of the permit system for Aboriginal townships; privatisation of home ownership; removal of Indigenous tenancy organisations; suspension of the Community Development Employment Program; compulsory school attendance tied to forms of welfare sequestering; and more.

Readers will find this work both one step removed from that federal intervention and a haunting mirror of its genetic pattern. For insofar as it appeared to be an extraordinary time, it was also very ordinary; it was no more than a radical eruption in a continuum of interactions between the liberal settler state and its margins. Viewed anthropologically, there is much that is repetitive in the drama of these events. Take, for instance, the nature and style of public concerns about whether or not the Australian Government's interventions can secure their desired effects. Some asserted that the emergency measures were destined to fail. Others argued that the situation for abused children remains so dire that drastic actions are required immediately: sure, mistakes will be made – that's inevitable – but to not act is unconscionable!

The unifying aesthetic of failure in these cycles of argument and debate, point and counterpoint, is essential to the culture of remedialism, which is the subject of this book. It is a culture which – like all organic forms – is unconsciously geared towards its own reproduction. The rhetoric of failure is grist for its reinventing mill. Things are bad today because of past policy failure (such as a lack of 'good governance' in the organisational forms set up in previous remedial efforts). If, in the future, aspects of the current national emergency measures are deemed a failure, many will claim it was due to the poor quality of the implementation effort: perhaps a lack of nerve on the part of the NT Government (Brough's argument); or perhaps some kind of fatal undermining by 'naysayers' (Noel Pearson); or perhaps because of its heavy-handed methods (the bleeding hearts).

The tropes of interventionary necessity are always underwritten by the promise of one day getting things right. The cunning of remedial logic lies in the ever-present allure of precisely this promise of an abstract future perfect. Incantation of the certainty of mistakes simply feeds the muscle-bound faith in the power of external intervention to amend and improve, operating as a spur to proceed with more of the same.

The sad verdict revealed in this book is that failure is not only integral to the bureaucracy's self-replicating process; it is created and nourished within the cultural bloodlines of service delivery. With new dollars to be chased, it becomes impossible to ask: What exactly is failure? What is success? Instead, notions of success and failure are measured against a yardstick of under-conceptualised and idealised western cultural abstractions. Such is the case in the imagining of what a good life is and what it takes for an Aboriginal person to have one.

The reform imperative underlying many interventionary efforts is the restoration of statistical equality. In this book, for instance, 'success' in Indigenous health will have been achieved when current statistical differences, such as gaps in life expectancy, are removed. Health professionals and community advocates alike are necessarily vague about the opportunity costs of this promised life and what kind of physical and cultural body the 'institutions of care' have in mind in their irresistible talk of health equality (Povinelli 2006: 57). We never quite grasp what else is up for grabs if the ordinary nature of black life in this country – the thick sociality that includes early infections, overcrowding, chronic disease and premature death – is to be fundamentally transformed. An accurate discussion of what forms of cultural meaning people are being asked to sacrifice or covet in adopting the prescriptions for cure cannot be had. It would take long and complicated, hard and intelligent discussions which are not possible when program determinism and genuflecting to the simplifications of agreeable and inarguable Indigenous health solutions are the order of the day.

Analogously, key architects of the remedies promulgated in the current crisis are equally vague about what else might be lost and/or unexpectedly catalysed in the bid for statistical equality. From national emergency influencers such as Helen Hughes, who has turned her sharp but curiously blind eyes to the 'socialist experiment' of remote Aboriginal communal living, another new-old equalisation prescription is pressed: work, mortgage, tax, privatisation and market enterprise (Hughes 2005, 2007). Such words might sound more prescriptive than the friendly talk of collaboration and relationship-building among public health progressives, but they are equally vague on the fine print of the remedial contract. Fine print is always worth reading. Simply follow the world news on any given day for a reminder that the flourishing black market of administrative rorts, carpetbaggery, blackmail, nepotism, violence, bootleg and illicit trade is organic to our economic forms. We prefer the comfort of seeing these as atypical scandals, but viewed without the moral screening, they are always all around us – virtually in the air that we breathe – and they are essential to productivity and its profits. There's blood and mud at the end of most money trails. And yet the reappearance of the seamier side of economic opportunism in the Indigenous domain is deemed a problem created by sentimental previous policy and Aboriginal naivety in the face of modernity's demanding requirements (problems which more social programming will amend).

For those who would uphold faith in the power, logic and rationality of liberalism's grand schemes for good development, I have some bad news. These 'corrupt' relationships are the equally natural and expected entailments of our governing forms. Far from being aberrant, they are in fact constitutive of the good, the bad and the ugly of our 'real economy'; representing, dare we say it, a true sort of normalisation. As Marx reminds us, capital makes no moral judgments; it is the great human leveller, caring not a fig for the high-minded principles argued in its name. And, in the same way that corruption and principled governance are both constitutive of the fullness of our societal formations, policy perfidy is just as likely as rationality within our bureaucratic operations. When we talk of the seamier side of human relations, aren't we acknowledging this very inextricability?

Of all the mirroring of the cultural assumptions that underpin the Howard Government's national emergency and the arguments of this book, perhaps the most disturbing is found in Chapter 2. In this chapter, we venture behind the closed doors of state officials in the Northern Territory to witness live policy in/action. Back in 1999, the hot policy issue that had bureaucrats working round the clock was the imminent privatisation of public hospital management throughout the Northern Territory. Saving Aboriginal lives was part of the justification then too. The chapter begins with a story of Territory health bureaucrats hovering attentively, eagerly awaiting a federal government Cabinet decision that would determine the next priorities for their activity. The privatisation plans were unexpectedly cancelled, after almost two years of their absolute necessity having been promoted, leaving the officers with the task of churning new rationalisations of a vindicatory kind – for the most crucial part of their job, after all, is to create irrefutable logic out of arbitrary policy flurries.

Fast-forwarding now to late June 2007, when senior bureaucrats were dramatically called to the national emergency briefing rooms to be told of the federal government's radical plans for intervention into Aboriginal communities in the Northern Territory, we can imagine a similar scene. Though the bureau-professionals in Canberra would have known from their incessant environmental scanning that something was brewing, the exact content may have taken them by surprise. As news zapped through the inner coterie, those involved would have felt suddenly enlivened by the adrenaline surge of early policy mobilisation. Just as in the case of the last-minute ditching of the privatisation plan, the senior bureaucrats would be simultaneously appalled and excited, at once cynical yet eager to be at the table, for being there supplies proof of one's superior access to the putative centre. They have been called upon to *make a difference*. Their harried phone calls to and from journalists and other privileged outsiders, their confidential production and consumption of the raft of artefacts marked strictly for internal circulation, and the around-the-clock work of producing information kits and briefings for variously situated powerbrokers within and without the network, all feed the sense of imminent change that is the essence of the state's own myth of monumental effect.

Those at the heart of policy emanation truly believe in the centralist power to change the external environment by mandating its shape through statements of intent (whilst also insisting that their interventionary targets are the true authors of the declarations). And true enough, regardless of whether they are antagonistic or amenable to the pronouncements, Aboriginal spokespeople bargaining for position and helping whites of the sort featured in this book all uphold this magical belief. To illustrate: since the federal government's announcement of the emergency intervention, NT officials have been telling each other that, despite the intervention's clearly under-conceptualised initiatives, if any good at all is to be extracted, Canberra will require their full-bodied assistance.

Flying to meetings to bargain for money, mining the semiotic cracks identifiable in the first round of announcements for positioning advantage, they found themselves in possession of a very strong bargaining chip. Recall how the compulsory checks for sexual abuse announced in June 2007 were swiftly retitled as comprehensive child health screens by July? The new euphemistic phrasing gave hint of the policy path being cut through the legal and medical quagmire generated by compulsion without parental permission and screening without diagnostic efficacy. But the switch to child health screens in turn activated a suite of other medical and ethico-legal considerations, including the requirement to follow up any abnormality the doctors might detect. Nobly offering to take responsibility for responding to referrals once the volunteer cadres of imported emergency response doctors return home, officials from the NT Health Department seized the opportunity to press for an increase in funds, ostensibly for the delivery of community-based primary health services.

To be sure, the issue of referral and follow-up in the context of the latest round of intervention into NT Indigenous lives is a matter of no small consequence. For far from being overwhelmed by evidence of sex crimes, the emergency 'child health screens' have been (re)revealing other health issues that infuse ordinary, everyday Indigenous life, such as endemic hearing problems and dental cavities. These cruddy sorts of issues have been such a commonplace part of NT Indigenous life that locals are snickering at the aghast tones of southern discovery. Yet their widespread prevalence also means that the vast majority of referrals are for specialist services that are in short supply nationally: ear, nose and throat doctors, and dentists, for a start. Accordingly, the bulk of federal funds awarded to the Northern Territory for addressing the health side of the emergency intervention into child abuse will not go towards providing sexual health, primary health or even family support services. Instead, they will be used to import new fly-in-fly-out specialists to attend to these ordinary issues via (legally required) follow-ups; follow-ups that, in the case of hearing at least, are unlikely to assist, if we refer to the Commonwealth's own guidelines (see OATSIH 2001), which emphasise the relatively small role that specialist surgery has in Aboriginal ear disease control.

Back at the negotiating table, amidst the jostling for funding advantage, such paradoxical issues (sometimes called the 'unintended consequences of policy') may be discerned, but they cannot be held in focus for very long, given both the shared interest in maintaining the mirage of policy rationality and the pressure to minimise talk of contradictions within agenda-setting meetings. Such brinksmanship and circularity are played out at every level imaginable, for it is the bureaucrat's and bleeding heart's job to seek program funding opportunities. A NT senior official tells me that in their part of public sector, the money-extraction plan entails pretending not to have data the federal government needs to track those who are to have their welfare payments quarantined, purely in order to demand a heavy administrative subsidy for fulfilling the data request.

Should we condemn such self-interested milking of the emergency discourse? The Northern Territory is utterly dependent on federal subsidisation for its economic survival and the national intervention offers multiple bartering slots. Aboriginal organisations are similarly recruited into vying for funds. Whilst complaining most emphatically about that gravest of insults in black institutional politics – the lack of consultation – there is also judicious praise for aspects of the intervention and alignment for the seemingly bountiful money flashed in and out of government announcements. At some point in the predictable discourse of institutional regeneration, there will be a belated recognition that the money is not hitting the ground where it is needed but is instead simply creating more administrative and professional positions ... perhaps that criticism has been aired already? Such are the little practices of authorisation and abrasive recognition through which the legitimacy of statecraft is upheld.

Indigenous communities do not directly match the monstrous images of rape and daily carnage sweepingly projected onto them all. Nor do they need to, for here is the point about the bureaucratic emanations of the developmentalist state: such emanations have a magical relationship to the worlds that they simplify, distort and describe. Exact correlation between 'rhetoric and reality' is not required. Beginning with representations of the world that may be somewhat tangential and oblique to on-the-ground realities, and actively seeking to change that world for the better, government pronouncements conjure reactions from the subjects of policy regardless of the extent to which those pronouncements match the worlds those subjects live in. 'What works' for processes in the discursive political realm always bears a contingent relationship with 'what works' in the paddock. In any case, it is not analytically productive to dwell overlong on the difference between appearance and reality in the hope that a policy corrective lies in the latter, for symbols and simulations have impact too (see Baudrillard 1988).

Yes, yes, but how will Indigenous lives improve, if not through these measures? For me, in this book, 'what works?' is not the question to be answered – it is the question to be understood. It is the motivating imperative behind the continual press of the state into the lives of those it seeks to govern. This book explores the conditions of possibility for the repeated emergence of the question 'what is to be done?' and the generally entangled, circular, self-perpetuating and co-constitutive nature of bureaucratic processes that this question activates.

My approach is always anthropological and always biographical. As an intervener, I too worry about making things work and make no pretence of being 'free of normative impulses' (Brown 1995: 3). As an anthropologist, I know that concentrated human effort is required if any of our cultural constructions are to approximate the idealised purposes we ascribe to them. The state may be an artifice, but it is still one of human making, and principled stands need to be adopted here as much as anywhere. Nihilism won't shift our structures in any kind of direction. It is this dual condition, as both the worried white and the anthropologist, that makes me one of the naysayers on the current 'state of emergency'. Without more complex analyses of the nature of bureaucratic inertia, of the barren thinking and circular logics, of the inefficient practices in policy design and program delivery, of the redundancies embedded within service delivery frameworks – and without greater intellectual expertise applied to solving complex implementation and sustainability issues in the mundane, messy realities of life on the ground – there will be little change at all for those at the butt end of welfare. Mandating just doesn't cut it. Nor do little bleats emanating from the critical sidelines about the dissembling fast switchback moves in the announcements or the disrespectful lack of consultative processes. Clever brokers who mediate the distance between high-minded policy rationalities and the vicissitudes of community action are vital to any effect: perhaps we should be working out how to identify and support these players (see also Lea 2008). Evidence, and the application of intellectual rigour and accountability within policy, might also help.

Like a mutating virus, the emergency intervention is at once new and different and yet the same as all that precedes it. Inhabitation of this self-replicating cultural form is the subject of this book. It is not a book that offers answers, but it does proffer explanations. At a time when Indigenous people are under new forms of siege and overnight policy experts are pronouncing remedies on a daily basis, a detailed anthropological account of the circular culture of public health remedialism, and how this reproduces itself from the inside, seems especially to the point.

While the focus is on the organisation formerly known as Territory Health Services (THS), the narcissism of governmentality is universal.

Outline

Bureaucrats and Bleeding Hearts is organised in three main parts. The first covers the bureaucratic setting in question, Territory Health Services; the second how bureau-professionals learn about and then attempt to execute their vexed responsibilities; and the third considers how life is viewed once bureaucratic modes of apprehending the world are fully incorporated.

Chapter 1 introduces the tools of analysis that help us approach this field anthropologically. Chapter 2 explores the social dynamics that energise the production of policy, braiding two concurrent events together: the formulation of a new corporate plan for the organisation; and a mad scheme to privatise all the public hospitals of the Northern Territory in one hit. In Chapter 3, interrogation of the Health Department's structure and operations reveals the paradox that coordination creates more fragmentation, which only more coordination can solve.

Part 2, Absorbing and Delivering, deals with institutional sociali-sation, focusing on the kinds of things professionals learn to say and do when they contemplate the problems of Aboriginal health. More particularly, Chapters 4 and 5 explore how health professionals become institutionally ordinary when they consider themselves to be doing such unorthodox and radical things as travelling to isolated communities, dealing with dramatic issues of ill-health and poor living conditions. The most theoretically complicated part of this book is also its heart. Chapter 6 looks to the social life of health facts in an organisation founded on the ideological principles of science and evidence. Turning the focus away from the accuracy of health facts, this chapter explores the moral imperative of information sharing by posing two simple questions: 1) how are health facts transmitted? and 2) what do facts do? Intriguingly, while lots of information is made available about Aboriginal people and their states of health and wellbeing, little is known about how they inhabit themselves. For instance, does urinating feel different if you have chronic renal failure? Who would know?

This is not a flippant question, for it is an important feature of the cultural life of policy bureaucracy that aspects of the personal are strategically removed from view. It helps upholders of the goodness of the state to imagine it as an omniscient and benevolent presence, marred only occasionally by a bad apple. (Much as the disavowal of intrinsic corruption and nepotism enables us to posit western economic forms as inherently benevolent.) In Chapter 7 I show how attempts to make programs appear fair and anonymous actually transpire – in embodied interactions between health professionals and their Aboriginal clients and project partners. Such encounters typically have both a surface normality and a surreal lack of engagement.

Reiterating my personal involvement in the ill/logical repetitions and mythical constructions presented in previous chapters, Part 3 reminds us that there are no saints or enemies in this work – only people trying to do their best for the people they want to help. But, in this most worthy of pursuits, the heavy emotional dependency of bureau-professionals on those they prefer to see as dependent tends to be obscured. The subtleties and rationality of this deception constitute the magic of intervention.

PART I

THE SETTING

INTRODUCING THE HELPING WHITE

Searching the mudflats of Shoal Bay for crabs, part of an induction tour designed to teach something of the land and the people we've been employed to assist, only one of our party of neophyte government health employees is able to retrieve the camouflaged mudcrabs from the soft, dark silt in this dense tangle of mangrove roots and stalagmite suckers – and even then only after the tell-tale signs are patiently pointed out by Pat Gamanangga, our Aboriginal teacher-guide.

'This one now – you see im?' she asks, and oh, how eagerly we strain to distinguish the kind of hole a mudcrab would make from the many seemingly identical pockmarks cratering this mangrove swamp. We are anxious to please, keen to know how to see, to acquire the skilled vision and cross-cultural canniness promised in the aims and objectives listed for this special public health orientation program (see Box 1.1).

What mudcrabs teach bureaucrats

Pat's dillybag bulges while the newcomers' remain empty, but she shares the bounty. 'M-mm-mmm,' murmurs Katrina, a resident clinic doctor on Bathurst Island, 90 kilometres north from us here at Shoal Bay. 'We got big mob now. I can see 'em roasting on the coals already, 'ey,' she says, patting the bag Pat has given her, her simulated bush talk purpose-

Box 1.1 Cultural orientation (THS 1998)

Primary Aim of Activity

To introduce participants to Aboriginal cultural activities such as: hunting and gathering, the preparation of various mangrove foods, basket weaving and cross-cultural communication.

Key Objectives

To achieve this aim the following objectives form the basis of the session:

1   provide an awareness of the different varieties of mangrove foods and their preparation;

2   introduce participants to the collection (hunting and gathering) of natural foods in the Top End coastal regions;

3   teach participants the processes of collecting raw materials (plants) which are used to produce certain bush crafts;

4   to share with participants the role of Aboriginal men and women in hunting and gathering exercises;

5   to encourage participants to learn from one another and getting to know and understand each other in a relaxed and informal manner;

6   promote and assist participants in ways of survival.

built to establish her connoisseurship of bush tucker and, by semantic entailment, her ease and familiarity with Aboriginal people.

In the tacit way that much bureaucratic knowledge is conveyed, Katrina had established her cross-cultural credentials early into the excursion. On the bus ride out, we had collected unripe cheeky plums from old trees near a petrol station on the highway. They were astringent, face-puckering fruits the size of olives and the shape of nashi pears, and most of us spat them out immediately, repelled by their immature bitterness. Katrina had been the exception. 'Delicious!' she had declared emphatically, going on to collect more handfuls, accepting the eager donations of others. On the mud flat, Katrina's enthusiasm for the task of foraging had been dutifully echoed by others ('It's great, isn't it!'), each participant expressing their appreciation of this unique opportunity to learn about and gather authentic Aboriginal tucker, maintaining the public secret of obligatory pleasure in authorised race relations.

The same sense of polite duty accompanied our dreary return trek to the picnic area, some 40 minutes distant from the crabbing fields, in the glaring midday sun. With itchy grey socks of drying mud on our skin, and our hessian carry bags weighed down with water bottles, sunscreen ointment, cameras, crabs and *long bums* (sea snails) Pat has collected for us, we trudged in desultory step upon the inch-wide ripples left behind by the outward tide, the tepid tropical sea a good mile offshore. The oppressive March air was sticky, still and hot; so heavy it pressed down our tongues until even talking took too much energy. We marched in silence, monitored by the rhythmic slap, slap of jandals agitating out of the hard suction of wet sand, refusing to complain.

At one stage Kathy, a British nurse sojourning temporarily in Darwin during a working tour of Australia, stopped us and pointed seaward. Past the harsh silver light glinting off the baking sand ridges, curiously close to the shore in shallow brine that was milky with suspended sediment, a fin appeared and disappeared, reappeared and disappeared, over and over again. A dolphin maybe, or perhaps a shark. The glare and heat quickly evaporated idle speculation and our trudging resumed, the small fin mystery unresolved. Carrying a large water container, I had been conscious only of its weight, shifting it from my left to my right hand, now up to my shoulder, then to my head, then back down to my palms, where the wire handle imprinted a reddish pink rivet, no matter how it was held. No position remained comfortable for long.

Hearing distant shouts from a second group straggling in our wake, we turned as one and squinted back at the small figures so far away. They were waving, shouting and pointing, we think perhaps at the mesmerising fin.

'Yeah, yeah – we've seen it!' we shouted back, uselessly, our voices muffled by the hot damp wind, before grumpily turning our backs to sand-crunch on, resentful at being forced to pause yet again in the glaring heat.

Finally, among the spiky Casuarina trees lining a small saltwater creek, the campsite slowly materialised. Back in the shade at last, over-eager bonhomie soon returned in a loudly appreciative gush of eating cooked crabs, hastily rolled out of coals the moment inner crab juices spluttered out of calcified eye sockets – this was the sole indication of readiness. Between gritty mouthfuls of crab and crumbling damper bound by a sand-encrusted, thickly charcoaled rind, Ross, a research doctor in charge of public health programs at the local medical research institute, proclaimed: 'We should be oriented like this every few months – for stress release!' We laughed agreeably, our mutual assent conscripted by the necessity of enjoying our time in the scrub learning about Aboriginal bush tucker and augmented by the relief of being at the tail end of a mildly arduous event. We were bonded by the overweening desire to prove our lack of racial ineptitude.

'Wish you'd dropped that bloody water bottle. We were yelling and yelling at you to "DROP IIIIITTTTT!!!"' the stragglers panted to me as they joined us under the trees, collapsing wearily onto the thorny sand.

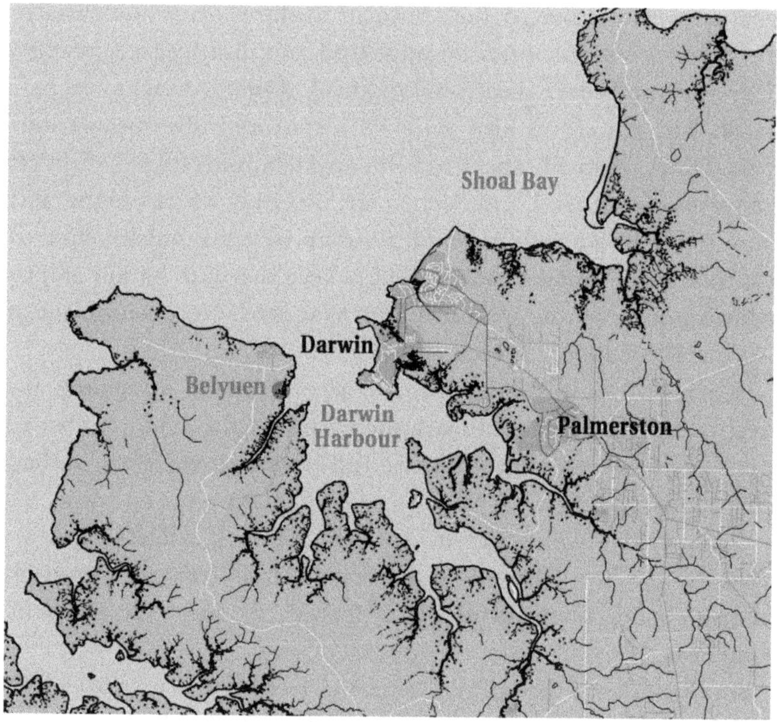

Figure 1.1 Map showing Belyuen in relation to Darwin coastline

Entanglements

> What surprises many fieldworkers in Australia, including me, is
> not simply that culture and economy meet, but that they meet in
> ways that disturb our sense of the boundedness of cultures and of
> the compatibility of different kinds of cultures ... On fishing trips
> Dreamings surge from beneath motor-powered dinghies; over a
> campfire meal heavy-metal music roars. On the dirt tracks that
> lead to isolated outstations, the Northern Territory government
> stretches car-count meters to monitor 'public access' on and
> around Aboriginal lands. (Povinelli 1993a: 169)

In *Labor's Lot: The power, history and culture of Aboriginal action*,
anthropologist Elizabeth Povinelli describes her work among the
people of Belyuen; hunter-gatherers who, as the crow flies, live across
the harbour from Darwin, leading the culturally distinct sorts of
lives our mud trek was designed to clarify. Povinelli's main concern
was to return meaning and agency to the actions of Belyuen people,
overturning tedious arguments about their cultural inauthenticity after
so many years of exposure to and interaction with settler Australians.
In the process, Povinelli makes a point of critical importance to this
book: the engagement between Aboriginal people and the market
state also operates in reverse. Settler Australian understandings of self,
knowledge, property and nation are also impacted upon and shaped by
Aboriginality (see also Merlan 1998).

In exploring what it means to be a government official, a
bureaucrat, technocrat, a public servant tasked with worrying about
and for Aboriginal people in the Northern Territory, this work picks
up where Povinelli's groundbreaking analyses leave off. Rather than
treating the state as having some kind of anonymous authority, bar the
odd political figurehead or charismatic chief executive, in this work
personhood is returned to technocrats in order to ask the questions:
how do government officers in the helping services shape themselves in
relation to those they set out to help? How do they become both agent
of government and community advocate? What are the contradictions
and how are these resolved? What happens when people like me – white,
middle-class, tertiary-educated professionals – join the progressive
cause of helping unwell Indigenous people in their struggle for equity?

Switching the focus onto the helpers in this way makes this a rare
and necessary study. While the interdependency of Aboriginal and

non-Aboriginal knowledge systems highlighted by Povinelli is a critical insight, it has not really changed the way such non-Aboriginal others as government officials tend to be characterised. If government folk – or rather, what business and management theorist Henry Mintzberg calls 'bureau-professionals'[1] – are represented at all in Australia's postcolonial literature, it is as abstracted architects of policy and legislative change, or as silhouetted figures making unwelcome visits to Aboriginal communities. Held responsible for damaging, thwarting and otherwise interfering in the lives of Aboriginal people, bureau-professionals are not seen as forming themselves through their embattled relationships with those whose lives they are busy amending. In other words, a sense of bureaucratic self is not relevant to the analysis. Even in Povinelli's highly attuned work, officials appear as the 'hostile government' who are the sparring partners for the Aboriginal residents of the small coastal community of Belyuen, so close to the Shoal Bay mangroves trekked by public health newcomers in their annual rounds of orientational mudcrabbing (see Figure 1.1). Whites are either invisible or to blame, a moral imperative which interferes with analysis, explaining the lopsidedness of anthropological representations of cultural life in what are otherwise clearly intercultural settings.

The routine one-sidedness of descriptions of the state and matters of policy is easy enough to demonstrate. Let's compare the hunter-gatherers of Belyuen with the public servant interlopers at Shoal Bay; one to the west, the other to the east of Darwin. Just as 'Dreamings surge' from underneath aluminium motor-powered dinghies, or Japanese Toyotas transport hunter-gatherers so that they can rub sweat into country, so dot-pointed expectations of cross-cultural pedagogy and new management concepts of teamwork, diversity management and mutual respect undergird our trek through sand and silt in search of mudcrabs. Both excursions into the technological domain of the other – Aborigines' use of motorised vehicles, bureaucrats' use of dilly bags – are entanglements social scientists would feel compelled to explain.

But ahead of time, we would know to think that Aboriginal deployments of modern technologies signal the tenacity and resilience of Indigenous culture, just as we would know to deride the spectacle of pink and reddening bureaucrats knee-deep in mud and cultural complexity. Our ineptitude and lack of grace in a clearly foreign environment, our determination to enjoy the procedure and be educated by it, our inability to see the forms out at sea as potent signs of a sentient environment, our polite refusal to admit to our sweaty discomfort or yield to our suppressed desire to quickly return to air-conditioning, could all be used to illustrate contrasting forms of embodied cultural knowledge.

The attempt here is to breathe life back into the invisible ranks of mid-level and senior bureaucrats who otherwise operate anonymously in the backstage of government activity. This book tries to honour the sincere commitment that bureau-professionals in northern Australia bring to their work. It seeks to understand the claims that *being the state* makes on all of us. And it asks that we replace the suspicion with which we have learnt to view bureaucrats who work in 'development' with a sense of open-mindedness and empathy, even occasional admiration at the forms of creativity and ingenuity embedded in apparently mindless bureaucratic rituals.

Assuming a classical approach

The sense of dissonance readers may encounter on this last point suggests a key problem with analysing the state and its functionaries. It is habitual not only to scorn bureaucratic forms but also to maintain a stance that suggests 'we' are not part of the state – a self-satisfying myth about which there will be more to say. But indulging in all of that would be against the aim of this book, which is to approach the bureaucracy *anthropologically*; by acknowledging that it is a cultural system.

It should go without saying that bureau-professionals are people too. Being flesh and blood means being cultural animals, for this is how the world works. The way bureau-professionals embody and inhabit their world, the meanings they attribute to things, the emotional texture of their daily experiences, all matter in terms of how they engage with each other and with their others. More than acknowledging humanness, though, an anthropological approach should go one step further. As cultural processes are neither rational nor irrational – or rather, they are almost always both – moral judgments form part of the cultural domain to be analysed, not presupposed. But when it comes to bureaucracies, the basic ground rules of anthropological analysis disappear within a shared institutional epistemology. We fail to be enchanted by the actions of the bureau-professionals, who are the 'natives' within bureaucracies.

We forget to see any cultural mystery or magic in it and elevate ourselves as judges of the probity of their efforts instead.

Understood anthropologically, then, the inhabited world of the social service bureaucracy is a complex socio-cultural domain with its own passions and inanities, pains and pleasures, complicities and truths, mysticism and magic. Yet in giving life to bureaucrats, this work turns out to be both harsher and more empathetic than standard one-sided accounts. More empathetic, in that the bureaucracy is not theorised as something alien to life itself; and harsher, in that the persistent and self-serving infiltrations of well-meaning state interveners into the most intimate parts of Aboriginal life are systematically shown to be about one essential interest: self-perpetuation. Institutional actors look for and create intervention points which seem always to require their expert helping presence.

The challenge of this book is not only to hold all these interrelated processes in view – the bureau-professionals' perpetual recreation of a sense of urgent and unmet need and how this invites us to suggest interventions – but to be awed by the creativity and technical virtuosity that is required for such a circular cultural order to be sustained. But here's the point: siding with good Aborigines over bad (white) state employees is not our way in.

An anthropology of bureaucratised race relations in northern Australia aims at understanding the overall effects of development logic, yes. It suggests the inanity and shortcomings of some of these logics and naturally it shows the frequent gaps between rhetoric and effect. But it is neither a prescription for how to improve Aboriginal health, nor a treatise on how to make government a more inclusive or more effective enterprise. Nor should it be. As an anthropological intervention, it is a study of how bureau-professionals conceive of their own practices; how institutional routines are enacted and reproduced; and the socio-cultural contexts within which all this is played out. It brings the techniques of classical anthropology to bear on the study of a real-life institutional setting, which just so happens to be about policy, about government and about race relations in a postcolonial context. It attempts an agnostic (or openly declared biased) inquiry into the behind-the-scene realities of bureaucratic formulation and action, using techniques of insider – or what we might cheekily dub 'native' – ethnography.[2] In so doing it represents a fundamental critique of Australian anthropological studies of governance, policy and race, which tend somewhat lazily to assume that the state is an anonymous entity – and a negative and destructive entity at that. Thus this work operates simultaneously as an extended ethnographic study of governance in the flesh which refuses to substitute moral condemnation or defence for detailed anthropological analysis, *and* as a critique of anthropology.[3]

The setting

With luck, the characteristics of the setting at hand will help readers avoid the easy assumptions of superiority that tend to permeate studies of the state and the equally oppressive demand that any work on Indigenous health has to help fix 'the problem'. Territory Health Services (THS), the NT Government's principal health agency, is not a crudely tyrannical, mindlessly administrative or openly racist governmental environment, nor are its actors oblivious to or naïve about the contradictions embedded within their task. Rather, the health professionals featured here feel painfully the heartache of wanting to improve the health of Aboriginal people, still regarded as the most poorly of all fourth world peoples (Lea 2005; see also Kowal 2006). They work themselves into the ground to travel the road, to get a project funded, to consult, to attend meetings, to lobby and argue, to protest against unfairness and to rectify past wrongs. They genuinely lament the injustices in what they see as the poor health and abject poverty of their clients. In their words, they are there for the singular purpose of 'making a difference', of 'turning things around'. They are not there to perpetuate inequality for the governmental budgetary return this might generate, but to remedy inequality's effects.

Theirs is a noble, beleaguered and oft-times thankless task. For the people whose focus is Aboriginal health, whether as policy officers, cross-cultural trainers, medical staff or public health professionals, Aboriginal people are sick, and getting sicker, despite considerable effort and the investment of vast amounts of time and money. Nationally, Aborigines have the lowest life expectancy of any defined group in Australia, dying 20 years earlier than their non-Aboriginal counterparts. They are burdened by long-term chronic diseases, and across all age groups they suffer from most diseases at a greater rate and with more complications than anyone else. Many health professionals hold themselves personally accountable for the state's perceived failure to confer good health upon Aboriginal people. They feel under-resourced or not enabled to do all that is demanded of them and periodically feel that what they are doing is ultimately futile, going nowhere, the same as what's been attempted before. They will lapse into despair that there are no defensible grounds for further intrusion into Aboriginal lives and that anyway, community dysfunction is too complex and deeply embedded to overturn without an impossible return to pre-invasion circumstances.

Reflecting on their practices through theories of postcoloniality and (echoing anthropologists) a melancholic sense of the utter penetration of a polluting western culture into Aboriginal life-worlds, health professionals periodically leave themselves few spaces from which to drum up the compulsory utopianism that is essential to their work. Still, they will rally out of the inertia and pessimism and propose that, with greater strategic determination and strength of mind, things *really can* get better. Their challenge in life is cut out for them: make the Indigenous population as healthy as the 'mainstream'. How? through well-planned, collaborative, comprehensive interventions and partnerships which target every aspect of existence, for every aspect matters to improved health. The solutions, if hard to execute, are at hand, if only...

This switch between despondency and 'can do' merits closer investigation. For all that I will ask that we sympathise with the bureau-professionals' sincere desire to change the ongoing tragedy of lives lost too soon, the deeply circular and narcissistic quality of bureaucratic logic has to be brought back into view. Viewed through our harsher lens, there seems to be no way interveners can imagine betterment that does not include some form of (their) further involvement. The same apocalyptic verdicts decrying the sheer impossibility of it all are redeployed in the ongoing task of creating new points of insertion for professional activity. In THS, futility and optimism operate as a hologram; ultimately they are one and the same thing. Depending on the angle at which it is held, the hologram shows sheer crisis out there, impossible and endless work to be done, but then – wait for it – a twist, a rallying through deft re-angling will shine new light on the same image and magically transform problems into challenges that can be acted upon by the helping professional. The compulsion to act flourishes at the very point where the ability to act seems annihilated.

Take the appeal of statistics. Strung together in the proper sequence, Aboriginal health statistics tell a tale of ongoing and tragic decline, which in a strictly rationalist universe might be used to *indict* current practices. After all, if the results continue to be so bad, what does that say about the overall interventionary apparatus? Instead, accounts of failure are used to augment and extend standardised operations. Statistical decline is not evidence of a need to reverse dominant assumptions about the need for intervention *per se* but are used to preface every new case made for continuing, 'strengthening' or expanding existing approaches. The current national intervention is a case in point. New money chases old prescriptions. The repeat identification of failure is thus conscripted to the task of institutional reinvention and extension.

It recalls the model of prison reform discourse Michel Foucault describes as ultimately and from its very beginnings reinforcing the carceral society, with critiques being ever assimilated to regenerative ends:

> It should be noted that this monotonous critique of the prison always takes one of two directions: either that the prison was insufficiently corrective ... or that in attempting to be corrective it lost its power as punishment ... The answer to these criticisms was invariably the same: the reintroduction of the invariable principles of penitentiary technique. For a century and a half the prison had always been offered as its own remedy: the reactivation of the penitentiary techniques as the only means of overcoming their perpetual failure; the realization of the corrective project as the only method of overcoming the impossibility of implementing it. (Foucault 1977: 265, 268)

There is no way out of this remedial circularity, for it is fundamental to our social being. With each new attempt to make government logic better, with each new correction and critique of policy and its shortcomings, we are spiralled to a new point in an old story of compulsory intervention, propelled by the need to deal with the leftover problems of past improvement efforts and by the need to uphold the state. The compulsiveness of this urge to intervene and amend in turn eclipses something so obvious it is rarely commented upon: the 'we' in the narrative are not planning to go away, but have a vampiric dependence on those we want to help.

Vampire government

Admittedly, THS is but one of a multitude of organisations and individuals concerned with shaping Aboriginal lives for 'the better'. There are many, many more organisations and authorities involved in the governance of the health and welfare of Aboriginal people now than ever before: they exist in every conceivable concentric sphere – local, regional, national and international (see also Friedman 1998). They include not only government bodies, but also a wide range of non-profit community and social services; some are Aboriginal-controlled, some are not, but most are funded by the government to 'independently' deliver governmental objectives.

But THS represents an organisational space where the topic of Aboriginal health is given a particular urgency, keenly felt by those involved, with Aboriginal ill-health being constructed by many differently positioned protagonists as a political and moral scandal that governments cannot ignore. THS is in fact unique among Australian state government health agencies (though similar to those in parts of Canada and New Zealand) in that it has Aboriginal health at the forefront of its core activities. Elsewhere in Australia, Indigenous issues are peripheral to the core service models of administrations (appearing as part of the litany of add-ons which merit special – if only occasional – consideration alongside people from non-English speaking backgrounds, adolescents, the homeless, people with disabilities).

In the Northern Territory, Aboriginal affairs are a major administrative focus even for generic service bureaucracies concerned with the 'mainstream': the fiscal impact alone makes Aboriginal pathology the subject of intense government concern. Health professionals will tell you that while Indigenous people form approximately 30 per cent of the population, expenditure on Aboriginal morbidity and mortality accounts for 70 per cent of the health care budget.[4] Yet most of these funds are spent on acute care (coping with the already afflicted), even though it is strongly felt that calamity might be nipped in the bud or avoided completely if greater emphasis were placed on health promotion and illness prevention.

The way in which Aboriginal ill-health forms a powerful and contradictory metaphorical complex is explored at greater length throughout this ethnography. But let us take this opportunity to glimpse an instance here and now of the way narratives of woe obscure other presences and absences, of how administrators move themselves from the scene and conceal their own dependencies, leaving these in the shadows, while we all pour our attention into the seemingly undeniable problems faced by Aboriginal people.

It goes something like this. At the same time that the burden of Aboriginal health care and the immense resources thus consumed are lamented, the NT Government receives a disproportionate share of national revenue in order to maintain most of its services, predominantly on the basis of the cost burden of supporting Aboriginal people. That is, the parlous state of Aboriginal people, and the role of the nation in bearing responsibility for that sorry state, forms a key part of arguments for extra funding beyond what would ordinarily be distributed under strict per capita allocations. Despite constituting only 1 per cent of the total Australian population, the Northern Territory receives nearly 5 per cent of the total sum of federal revenue, with the level of economically defined 'disability' carried by the population employed as a basis for justifying the extra subsidisation required by the NT Government to provide 'average' levels of service to all (CGC 2001). We are not talking exclusively about supplementary funding here either – a massive 80 per cent of total NT Government revenue comes by way of federal injection, and while this support includes provision of services to the non-Indigenous population, it does indicate the high level of dependency the Northern Territory has on federal revenue, and, in a roundabout way, on the continuing service dependency of Aboriginal people (see also Altman 2005, Taylor 2004).

This sort of instance of an unacknowledged dependency on those we would prefer to call dependent is not a deliberate conspiracy, but part of what I call the magic of intervention. The effects of this magic depend in turn on intricate and repeated enactments of hand-wringing concern where the anxieties of bureaucrats form the unnoticed background to a foregrounded Aboriginal burden. Despite the leavening in of community participation under the rubrics of remedial anti-racism, human rights and social justice, with each new problem to be solved bureau-professionals inevitably fall back on answers conceptualised in terms of their own agency. The idea that Aboriginal people *need our help* is a foundational assumption. Everything else works backwards from there to create an inarguable rationale for further interventions in the bureaucrats' own image.

But there is no conspiracy here, no master controller dictating that the world of need and interventionary logic should be arranged so as to create a perpetual feedback system. The state, as Foucauldian scholar Colin Gordon puts it, 'has no essence' (Gordon 1991: 4). It does not have a conscience, misanthropic or otherwise; there is no singular architect, no authorial centre for the institutional ability to engender self-replicating practices. It is a dynamic that exceeds individual actors. As for the actual people inside a place like the health department – well, far from wanting morbidity to continue for the sake of creating additional insertion points for themselves, or a job for life, they genuinely desire urgent change. Aboriginal people are unacceptably sick; they are, in the words of one remote area doctor, 'dying like flies',[5] and in desperate need of remedy, funding and assistance. The sincerity of this compulsion to act on the shame of Aboriginal ill-health should not be negated or devalued, for all the institutional self-interest involved. Understanding how these effects are created and inhabited is the subject of this book.

The magic of intervention

When you are a helping bureau-professional, the compulsion *to do something* to fix the problems of target populations – those deemed as suffering from unequal and preventable conditions – exceeds all other impulses. Interveners perceive the world around them as always calling for more and more of their time and energy, as there are endless problems to be fixed. One cannot be content with things as they are, for passivity (or 'maintenance of the status quo') cannot be entertained. In national emergency language, it constitutes neglect, the unacceptable position of someone who agrees children should be unsafe in their own homes. 'They' *need* our greater commitment. The idea that life might be lived differently with value and meaning or that 'need' might be conceived of differently from the way in which we calculate it through our interventionary lens, becomes impossible to imagine. So new-old pathways are repeatedly reimagined: if this is not the answer, then maybe that is. Such forms of analysis become part of everyday consciousness; that is, they are interiorised. They become an indissoluble part of one's apprehension of the world, the emphatic forms of worry that license the 'we must' that prefaces 'do something'. Political or ideological positions (left or right, liberal or neo-liberal) are beside the point.

The irresistibility and credibility of interventionary thinking depends on a complete and utterly sensual absorption of its myriad forms, to the point where the intervener is fully magnetised within the force field of the humanist question: *what is to be done?* It is this inhabitation, above all other things, that defines what it means *to be* the state, and by this definition, already it is clear that most of us – employed as government functionaries or not – *think like and with* the state (see Scott 1998).

Whatever happens is unswervingly interpreted in light of the need suggested for remedy, but – and this is partly what makes it a magical sort of phenomenon – the perceptual acts involved in modifying the world into interventionary categories go unnoticed by the people doing the modifying. A bureaucratised mode of perception takes hold of intervenors so overwhelmingly, so compellingly, that the (state-derived) judgments we are projecting onto the world are literally seen as belonging to the world itself, *and not* to the perceptual acts of the bureaucratically encultured self. This taken-for-grantedness is so thorough that Aboriginal health and the need for it to be remedied by the state are seen simply as pre-existing conditions or states of being, and it becomes impossible to see how what is deemed 'need' has been constructed, or to see the human role in its creation.

Admittedly, 'magic' is not a word usually associated with the supposedly rational world of bureaucracy or public service, and it is almost never used to explain the circularity of remedial policy (but see Hansen & Stepputat 2001: 14–16 and Taussig 1997). At most, myths and magic may be referenced to explore such contemporary oddities as the role of 'new age' religions or care-of-self technologies such as yoga in the corporate workplace (Meyer & Pels 2003). Another tack might be to look at the nostalgic overlay onto Aboriginal people of a deeply mystical, animistic relation to the world, as sign of the longing of the secular professional for magical-mythical belonging.[6] But magical belief defined in institutional terms is a bit more difficult to pin down: disbelief, cynicism and a secular rationality lie at its heart. Understanding how otherwise highly educated, well-instructed and scientistically imbued western-industrial-complex subjects accept the ruse that they are not pre-framing the world about them, but simply reacting to a world whose problems are spontaneously present – and further, that the way to fix things is to have the right kind of artefacts in place (policies, programs, laws, accountability frameworks and regulations) – requires that we understand the magic of intervention.

By 'magic of intervention' I mean the faith, and all that sustains it, in the power of institutionally produced logic to fix predefined problems of the Other through acts of institutional expansion, at the same time denying the existence of any such expansionary desire. Like magical acts, interventionary logic depends precisely on its ability to displace the human actions that are necessarily involved in its perpetuation. It all seems so natural, self-evident and logical. Problems pre-exist the institutional gaze – they are not created by it – and can be fixed by strategies and mandates, which themselves seem naturally or organically generated, rather than institutionally generated responses to institutionally conceptualised needs. This is more subtle than self-deception, for the intricate process of participating in the world of policy creation while simultaneously effacing one's own agency in upholding the production process occurs (almost) unthinkingly. It is an encultured way of being. Meanwhile, policies and strategies (artefacts) come to be seen as exerting a power of their own – outside human agency – to amend the world.

The collectively maintained illusions of interventionary magic are not restricted to bureaucratic natives. External critics of policy are part of the curious complicity required to vivify policy magic too. They contribute by analysing the symbols and artefacts that bureau-professionals produce, seeing these as products of an anonymous entity called 'the state'. When, in their analyses of the state, critics focus on semiotics, instantaneously we are subject to a sleight of hand, a disappearance. Our eye is taken away from the human actions in the behind the scenes of bureaucracies, the 'invisible daily work going on behind closed doors' (Buur 2001: 158) and towards the *products* of bureaucratic work. Now this selective vision might be partly explained on the grounds of accessibility: since not everyone gets to experience the inner sanctums of policy and decision-making in order to bear witness to its living, breathing aspects, reading intentions off the face of public declarations may be the only analytical strategy at hand. But regardless of the reason, each time critics focus on the object and not the human labour of production, policy and the state assume a life and logic, an autonomy and agency of their own, independent of the actors who produced them. So while academics and journalists alike might contest what bureaucrats emit, pronouncing that the bureaucracy is failing to deliver on its promises or is delivering on the wrong priorities or is operating under false assumptions (to name only the most familiar critiques), such evaluative commentaries paradoxically support bureaucrats in their endeavour to assert the essentiality and anonymous rationality of their products and deeds. Thus placed under the spell of bureaucratic disappearance, external analysts cede a greater coherence, logic and integrity to the products of bureaucratic activity than a focus on the (oft-times surreal) conditions of production would permit.[7]

Policy animism

With bureaucrats giving disembodied self-descriptions of how the policies they produce came into being, and analysts not caring for the dramas going on behind the scenes, policy artefacts are endowed with an affective dimension that is denied to their formulators. Policies act, they have political effects: they transform and transfigure, they are well or ill regarded, they use words strategically and intentionally to regulate and circumscribe the options of others. We might give this faith in disembodied analyses of governmentality – in which the objects have become subjects and the subjects have become objects – an anthropological name: policy animism!

Truth is, a significant volume of seriously elaborate, intensely personal work pours into creating and sustaining such impersonal and de-authored institutional products. Sustaining the idea that Aboriginal people demand (as in ask for and as in require) reforming no matter what – as if this idea just happens without any elicitation or predetermination of what gets to count as need, without any authoring of who gets named as being at risk and without any coaxing of a dovetail fit between what can be delivered and what can be requested – requires ongoing finetuning. If we were to take an 'anthropologist from Mars' perspective in our study of bureaucracy, we should be gobsmacked at the creative scale of its magical forms.

But what does it mean to combine terms like 'magical' and 'bureaucratic'? In this book, the language and analogies offered by theories of magic give expression to the forms of bureaucracy that lie outside the language of political science and management studies, audit and evaluation, logic and rationality. 'Magic' helps explain the excitements and passions that commentators often miss when they go straight to the referential meanings of bureaucratic texts, scanning these for signs of evil state hegemony or honourable intent. It also provides a way into understanding how, once we start to take the agents behind-the-scenes more seriously as *cultural subjects*, bureau-professionals *sacralise* their artefacts and attribute to them a great power to amend the world. It is hard not to be swept up in this faith, in the magical properties of interventionary tools: being western intellectual subjects, we are trained to see our ordained products as secular, rational actions and our organisational intentions as prosaic, logical and evidence-based. We are trapped by a rationalistic epistemology and the associated expectations of logic and fairness which we cede to state instrumentalities, because of the assumptive habits of our own cultural world. Yet while the world of policy, public health or other, might define itself by its formal exclusion of irrationality and enchantment, it is a human domain, and that should rest the argument: organic magical-mythical ways of thinking really ought to be expected.

Policy artefacts are thus not simply statements of logical intent. They are also fetish objects or magical relics that travel through time and space, often referring to each other and just as often ghost-written, that are attributed great expressive power and controlling capacities; a power acquired through ritualistic production efforts, including the careful addition of special words and consecration by anointed reviewers. Uncovering the what, the how and the why of bureaucratic animation, understood behind the scenes, is precisely what this book is about.

In the next chapter, we will consider the arcane world of policy formulation in some depth, as it is only by giving a biography of policy artefacts that we can start to release the stranglehold that the surface logic of policy has on our analysis. Well-worded strategies and well-formulated plans become talismans against an ever-present threat of intervention failure or worse, an unintentional slur against a sensitive audience (interestingly enough in a study of bureaucratic magic, often known as 'stakeholders'). Suffice it to say, the factual quality of health policies will not be our main concern.

THE PASSION IN POLICY

On 16 March 1999, after a whirlwind period of intense bureaucratic activity, the NT Cabinet convened to decide the management fate of all five of the public hospitals in the Territory. Awaiting the Cabinet decision, senior THS bureaucrats hovered in their offices, vibrantly tense, like so many stockbrokers fixated on the cue that will tumble the index. Waiting, concentrating, hardly daring to go out, poised for the first signs of decision to break. Their work – last-minute drafting and collating, corridor dashings, urgent meetings and frenetic into-the-small-hours-of-the-night work – teeters on the brink. Already, at the second stage of the tendering process, rumour has it that the Sisters of Mercy, a Catholic order with an extensive hospital management profile in the southern states, is the favoured applicant on the shortlist of companies to be invited to proceed beyond 'expressions of interest' to the 'best and final offers' phase of the bidding process.

It is almost a foregone conclusion. The nuns will lend credibility to what has otherwise been a highly controversial attempt to outsource the management of the entire public hospital network in one hit. It all computes. Still, schooled in anticipating the unanticipatable, the bureaucrats sit tight, confident that their predictive work of previous months will hold true – the hospital management *will* be outsourced – but equally aware that theirs is a world of incremental adjustments, where nothing is certain until it is retrospective, at which point the unintended can be realigned into an original intentionality. So they anticipate, and they wait.

The next day, 17 March 1999, the official announcements are finally made. With front page headlines of 'Govt scraps plan to privatise hospitals' (English 1998), the Chief Minister of the NT Government, Dennis Burke, and his Cabinet unexpectedly decide *against* proceeding with their bold outsourcing plan. With this surprise announcement, 18 months of bureaucratic distraction slides into oblivion. And yet, as the small world of Territory Health reverts to normal, as opacity smoothly returns with the daily media exposure of previous months suddenly removed, as policy formulators shift gears back to a less breakneck speed, and as near and far stories explaining 'what really happened' spin into circulation, steps towards the pseudo-corporatisation of the public health sector continue stealthily apace.

A play in three parts

Sub-plot one: The rise and demise of a policy event

In 1998 and 1999, the NT Government considered outsourcing the management of all five of its public hospitals, as an abridged form of privatisation. In the end, it didn't happen.

There is one key anomalous aspect of this policy moment that is relevant to this tale. Normally, the detail and wording of policy agendas are worked up by scribes within government departments, but over time it became clear here that the bureaucrats were not really in control of the privatisation agenda. Instead the language and logic were being driven by a controversial private consortium, Hospitals Development International (HDI), who bypassed the administration to work directly with the Minister for Health. These invisible fracture lines subsequently deepened into a schism between senior managers in the health bureaucracy and the political office of the Minister for Health, reaching crisis point towards the end of 1998, when the momentous event – outsourcing the management of all the hospitals – ground to a halt overnight.

Sub-plot two: Surfing

At the time of my entry to the scene as ethnographer-bureaucrat in the middle of 1998, senior health managers and policy officers had only just begun to hear whispers that the Minister was considering the outsourcing idea. In these early stages, it was simply another idea from the Minister's office – it had to be fielded, but as just one among the plethora of tasks that make up a busy manager's average day. Meanwhile, THS bureaucrats had their eyes on another ballgame. Altogether separate from the Minister's plan, they had been developing what they felt would be a momentous policy shift of their own, a new strategic direction called 'Strategy 21'. Strategy 21 was a relished artefact, months in the making, which senior officials were expecting the Minister to ceremoniously debut in his keynote address to the NT Parliament in November 1998.[1]

We begin our story here in this embryonic stage, at a point when the Minister didn't know much about Strategy 21 and his bureaucrats knew very little about the hospital plot. The Minister's failure to see the emotions embedded in Strategy 21, and the bureaucrats' parallel failure to anticipate the Minister's heartfelt attachment to the outsourcing initiative, form the human conflict at the heart of this chapter.

Sub-plot three: The passion in the language

While the attempt to privatise the Territory's entire network of public hospitals in one hit is an interesting story in its own right, the area of interest to us here is the way in which policy surges sweep people into intense yet curiously repetitive forms of involvement. This historical moment expresses an essential but often overlooked characteristic of institutional work: producing boring and predictable policy is at once very formulaic and full of flurry and improvisation. This combination of in-the-moment intensity and conventionalised thinking helps explain how predigested forms of analysis and doctrinaire commentary keep on being re-offered with a flourish – and with genuine hope and enthusiasm – as if they are new and original. It is not because people are stupid or the work is routine; in fact it is quite the opposite. There is a hidden passion embedded in normative texts which is almost impossible to detect if we rely on the words alone. Deep within the backrooms of policy, there is no well-oiled machine. Rather, the seductive and exhaustive task of policy-making can often involve surfing the capricious, all-consuming and seemingly momentous issues of the day. But for all their energetic effort, smart and sassy policy practitioners continue to bring forth products that have a familiar look and sound, and that indeed reinstate familiar logics (see also Ferguson 1990: 55–73). This is the paradox of policy.

The Minister's part

On a hot day in December 1998, during Darwin's infamously sticky build-up to the monsoon season, the Minister for Health, Family and Community Services rose to stand in the chambers of the NT Parliament to outline the government's vision for the future of the Territory's hospital services. 'Madam Speaker,' he began:

> This government is committed to delivery of ongoing improvement in the health status and wellbeing of all Territorians. As we pursue this aim, three key questions are constantly with us: What is it that government should fund but not do?; what should it both fund and do?; and what should it not be in the business of at all? ...
>
> Two weeks ago, Cabinet endorsed a plan to test the market and seek expressions of interest from the private sector for the management of public hospital services. The private operator option is conceptually very simple. It operates as a 2-stage process.
>
> Step 1 sees us calling upon a cross-section of hospital providers to enter into an arrangement with government to manage and develop publicly funded health services under strict contract conditions. This is just the same as getting an obligation-free quote, only in this case we are asking experienced private sector operators, who between them provide close to one-third of all hospital episodes of care in Australia, to submit their assessment of what could be done in the Northern Territory to improve hospital facilities, provide more services, upgrade our medical equipment and provide free public hospital services. This is not privatisation, which involves the selling-off of government assets and no further responsibility on the part of government.
>
> If we move beyond this first stage, the Northern Territory government will still retain overall responsibility for public hospital care. We are not selling off our hospitals. We will know if the private sector is interested and able to meet our full expectations by March next year, when expressions of interest have been fully costed and assessed. Then, in step 2, if the options put to government present a convincing enough case, the public sector will be buying hospital services for the public, just as it currently does, this time using a private rather than a public sector

management arrangement. The vision is for a systematic upgrading, redevelopment and refurbishment of all our hospital facilities. (Part 1 – Debates – Tuesday 1 December 1998 Eighth Assembly First Session 01/12/98 – Parliamentary Record No: 13)

After a mandatory acknowledgement of the 'dedicated services of many health workers and support staff' – whom he credits with 'the huge improvements in the general health status of Territorians that we have witnessed for over the past 20 years' – the tempo quickens. Scrolling down, there is a swift accumulation of problems:

> Firstly, there are the unacceptably high levels of sickness and early death within Aboriginal groups and the extraordinary and upwardly spiralling costs of end-stage renal failure, injuries and respiratory and heart disease, which are well known to all of us here. Put simply, Aboriginal Territorians have drastically poorer health across virtually all causes of disease. Life expectancy at birth for indigenous men in the Northern Territory is 57 years compared to 77 years for other male Territorians. For indigenous women it is 61 years compared to 83 years for other women.
>
> Aboriginal health disadvantage is further reflected in Territory Health Services' gross health service expenditure. Well over half of our total spending is on a quarter of the population, yet there are no incentives in the current system to produce preventative health outcomes beyond the use of more resources and nothing to force practitioners across all fields to tie their activity to underlying causes.

Later pages witness the dramatic entrance of a rescue plot: the introduction of competitive enterprise into the outmoded and welfare-dependent hospital sector – the only real option left standing after a rapid-fire elimination of rhetorically posed counter-arguments. With simple dignity, the Health Minister urges the government to consider itself morally bound to explore private sector interest in public hospital management, as an act of wise stewardship of public monies and electorally entrusted responsibility to the Territory taxpayer: 'If we can get more out of the system and return it to people in terms of improved services, facilities and outcomes then our ethical mandate is clear.'

Where only a few short months before great ceremony had accompanied the remodelling of the entranceway to the Royal Darwin Hospital (RDH) – an architectural makeover designed, it was whispered, to sweep from sight the unseemly clusters of blackfellas escaping the high-rise air-conditioning for a smoke and the hailed greetings of countrymen by the front doors (Coulehan 1995, Sansom 1980: Ch. 8) – now the same refurbishment was derided: 'Historically, our reluctance to be realistic about the true management issues facing the health and community services arena has seen us flirting with what are, in fact, relatively minor issues: hospital waiting lists, décor and the like.'

The Royal Darwin Hospital is now admitted to the realm of the disputable: it is eight storeys too high, an ugly brick tower block rising from the mangrove swamps of a tropical cyclone-prone city that is closer to the equator than to any other capital city in the developed world, and geologically famous for attracting to its ironstone ridges the second highest lightning strike rate in the world.

No longer applauding the hospital's recent renovations, the Minister reminds listeners that the original hospital design – the blueprint of which was bequeathed to Darwinites by ignorant Commonwealth bureaucrats – is an exact duplicate of the Woden Valley Hospital in the cold national capital of Canberra. This in turn is an exact replica of a Canadian hospital from snow-bound Alberta. Now we learn of the abundant problems of ventilation, drainage, fire and flood protection, vermin sealing, water-proofing, electrical safeguarding and temperature control. Air-conditioning alone is said to cost $10,000 per day, an expense made more astonishing by the singularly useless presence of snow shields barring the water-condensed, trickling glass windows which RDH inmates must peer between to glimpse the tropical mangroves basking in the lukewarm mud flats on the horizon beyond.

'No one can tell me I don't owe it to our staff and patients to try and get them something better. But try putting all five hospitals in the public sector capital works program and see how fast we get our new hospitals,' the Minister persuasively declares.[2]

Finally, the Minister reassures the imaginary worriers in his audience, repeatedly castigated in the speech for any anticipated obduracy – 'people whose allegiance to the status quo is set in concrete', 'those whose ideology will not permit them to ever entertain new ideas' – that under private management arrangements, there will no nursing or allied health redundancies, no loss of union conditions; and no discrimination against uninsured patients. This alchemy is explained in some detail. Shareholder profit will be generated by:

» creating a luxury niche for privately insured fee-paying patients to obtain boutique services (cosmetic and other forms of non-elective surgery);

» integrating general practice and other 'ambulatory' (outside hospital) services into the hospital complex, thereby reducing the number of 'coughs and colds and little holes'[3] appearing in the Accident and Emergency Department (the principal effect being to shift costs back onto the Commonwealth-subsidised Medicare system); and

» flattening administrative hierarchies.

Only an unenlightened, recalcitrant listener would hear this reasoning as code for eliminating middle manager administrative positions. And of course, the hospitals would continue to provide free acute care services to the uninsured under the strict terms of the Medicare Agreement.

The public would barely know the difference: the successful private operator would, as owner-builder, receive a fee to make the hospital network more attractive and contemporary in the name of profitability, an arrangement which would operate just like any other form of contractual bill-paying in its invisibility to clients. Patients would continue to use the public health system oblivious to these backroom management changes; the only change would be that the facilities would be nicer and there would be more options available for the privately insured. The changes would be phased in over time, to build in an element of sensible caution ('we'll test the market first before proceeding') and to allow the magnitude of administrative recalibrations to be iteratively absorbed, less painfully, more judiciously, learning all the while from the mistakes of other jurisdictions. His argument was perfectly irresistible, irrefutable – but none of it happened.

Working words

The Minister's Statement contained within it links to other such works (many, many other such works), and it involved me directly. As ethnographer-bureaucrat, I wrote it. Or rather, to be more precise, I was responsible for orchestrating its collation from multiple inputs, catching the words of others to spin into an acceptable format (see also Riles 1998).

Having commenced the formal fieldwork for this ethnography in early 1998, by posing as a new remote area worker, I then spent time with public health professionals as they travelled in and out of remote Aboriginal communities to advocate healthier living practices. My original intention had been to conclude ethnographic fieldwork amidst policy officers in the central office of THS, working from the periphery back to the centre, so to speak. But as luck would have it, the opportunity for policy participation came smack in the middle of my remote area work, with an invitation to ghost write a Ministerial Statement on future directions in health for the November sittings of Parliament.

My field notes recall the nervousness I felt when in August 1998 I met with the Chief Executive Officer of THS to receive my writing brief. I could feel myself gushing, talking too much, laughing too loudly at my own jokes, being too quick to fill silences. The CEO knew I had been travelling around doing fieldwork with the public health officers (shadowing Environmental Health Officers as they inspected remote area latrines, as it turned out), but, he now asked, how much did I know about Strategy 21, the new strategic vision being developed for THS?

Pushing documents starkly marked 'DRAFT' and 'CONFIDENTIAL' across the glass table for later reading, the CEO told me the Minister had been impressed by the work THS had done formulating their new corporate strategy, Strategy 21, and wanted to showcase it in his next major address to parliament. 'This is big,' he added conspiratorially. 'There's even consideration of outsourcing parts of the hospital [RDH].'

Pad out and pencil clicked in anticipation, I asked what the tone and key themes of the statement would be and listed his advice as he spoke, feeling a tremulous excitement, like a gambler breathing the scent of the race track – here we go again, helter-skelter, fear and adrenaline, the nervous tingle of being back in the pack and 'in the policy know' after time away playing at ethnography in remote area communities. And I would be able to treat it as fieldwork too.

Joining the densely layered webs of management intrigue and conjecture, there was no problem for the ethnographer interested in gathering stories – it was simply a case of swimming in a narrational flood tide and co-performing on the run. Privileged insiders buttonholed each other in corridors and doorways, taking and making phone calls, trawling emails, newsletters and other conduits of corporate announcements, tuning into parliamentary broadcasts and working their personal networks for snatches of the most recent information. Rumours soon circulated that the plan, far from being about a small piece of outsourcing at RDH, was in fact about management of the entire hospital network. The sheer audacity of the Minister's proposal to outsource management of the entire public network (as opposed to picking off one hospital at a time, the stealthier practice adopted by Australian states) naturally attracted the most intense interest.

It was considered by some to be part of an ambitious game plan by the Health Minister, conventionally not the most powerful of Cabinet jobs, to stage a coup for the Chief Minister's position,[4] and I was told to 'expect a Cabinet reshuffle'. Another manager predicted that, since this would be 'Burke's swan-song [as Health Minister], he'll want to hit them hard' with the Ministerial Statement I was charged with preparing. Others claimed the Minister had been seduced by a particular consultancy consortium, Hospitals Development International, on a trip to Djakarta, Indonesia, where he'd ostensibly gone to explore health export opportunities – consultants from HDI were in fact subsequently hired, at over $5000 per day, to advise the Minister on how to get the privatisation proposal through. These same consultants, it was further rumoured, shared a Vietnam War background with Colonel Dennis Burke, the former Commanding Officer of the 2nd Cavalry Regiment.

As I talked to managers to help form a picture of the desired Ministerial Statement in my mind's eye, it was clear that very few believed the officially promulgated story, which was that the outsourcing was all about financial responsibility. 'It's interesting to me,' said one, 'that the people who promote outsourcing always have some sort of vested interest or are using a model which is inappropriate – i.e. the American model. The only country in the western world with a shit public health system is the country that has the most outsourcing, so you have to ask ...'

From Frank, the hospital manager with closest responsibility for constructing the cost imperatives for outsourcing, the man who supplied data on just how out-of-control acute care costs would get unless the privatisation solution were pursued:

Frank: Well, quite off the record, I would caution very, very strongly against outsourcing. Best way of blowing your budget, a financial disaster.

Tess: It is interesting that you say that. I ...

Frank: That's, hey that's OK, I mean if that's what they want to do, I'll go do it ... but I am not yet aware of an example of outsourcing of health care that's worked anywhere so I think it is a very brave and noble venture! One I might say I will be quite happy to take part [in], but I will be putting on my full metal jacket in the process and getting contractual exemption from any responsibility for things that are undoable or unachievable, and there'll be a lot of them.

If I counted up all the cost-saving initiatives at all the conferences I've been to, health ought to be paying us instead of us paying for health 'cause everyone saves the whole culture of health five times over, it would appear. A bit of reality checking probably needs to go on but you've got to be careful talking reality checks with [the Minister] – it's not really (laughing), it's not that popular. (shakes head) Reality.

And yet, however spurious the government's claims of anticipated private sector beneficence were deemed to be, the possibility of withdrawing from the unfolding drama was not a thought to be thought. Quite the opposite: voicing ironic opinions about the unfolding events seemed almost mandatory. Managers would move from harsh critique to compliance and back again, telling me the tone I should strike, the managerial emphases, the good staff initiatives that should be highlighted in the announcement to build credibility ... and then how preposterous it all was, in the same breath. Body postures likewise belied conformity. People would lean forward conspiratorially to make a wry comment, or stretch their legs and fold arms behind heads pleasurably as they spoke about the project's highly rejectable premises – but there were no slumped shoulders, not even the slightest resistance to my requests for constructive inputs in crafting persuasive words for the Minister's public marketing of the concept. As one manager put it to me:

I make no bones about it Tess. I see this [Ministerial Statement] as an opportunity to lock the Department in to think this way:

'Here's what the Minister said, it's what we have to do.' I mean, the public sector is not passive in this process. When you come and talk to me about what he [the Minister] might say, it's a key mechanism for us getting stuff in, and then getting it to come back out to our staff as gospel.

Tough conformity

What should we make of the apparent discrepancy between what policy people have to say in their seemingly revelatory moments of irreverence and candour and their more prosaic suggestions for what to use or leave out of a broader public script on the same policy issue? In some analyses, such disjunctions would be used as evidence of what is seen as the complicit and hidden politics of policy work. For example, organisation ethnographer Gideon Kunda, following sociologist Erving Goffman (1961), draws a distinction between the 'managerially sanctioned and enforced view of employees' and the various 'cognitive and emotional distancing' techniques (irony and humour; self-conscious parody; speech qualifiers and disclaimers etc) deployed by members of the engineering firm he studied (Kunda 1992: 160). For Kunda, such distancing techniques kick in when employees empower themselves to explicitly critique prevailing corporate ideologies. Irreverence and ironic attacks of various kinds are moments of personal autonomy struggling for emergence out of the tough conformity demanded of managers as the price of their inclusion in the senior echelons of the company:

> By choice they [managers] have entered into a contract that is more than economic, one that must contend with overt external claims on self-definition ... Although it is not immediately apparent, the price of power is submission: not necessarily to demands concerning one's behaviour, as is typical of lower status work, but to prescriptions regarding one's thoughts and feelings, supposedly the most cherished belongings of autonomous beings. (Kunda 1992: 214–15)

It is a clear binary: corporate talk is ideological, and ironic talk is an authentic expression of the individual struggling to occasionally gain distance from the otherwise total compliance demanded by the institution. Critical commentary reveals the personality that remains resistant to the hegemonic order.

Now, while forms of satire can indeed be serious, as anthropologist Allen Feldman's work on the use of songs and jokes within the prison regimes of Northern Ireland clearly demonstrates (Feldman 1991), the automatic attribution of greater authenticity to cynical language should itself be regarded with some scepticism, for it overlooks the role that critical sentiments also play in *sustaining* institutional actions. Critical comments can be seen not so much as jeopardising moments exposing suppressed deeper truths, but rather as part of the work. 'Ironically', it was by analysing what drove my own and others' intense commitment to the creation of forms which in another breath we could just as easily ridicule that I began to appreciate the constitutive dimension of irony among health professionals – and its own ironic provocation of scholarly distrust.

For social scientists who insist on neat lines separating the virtuous from the untrustworthy, ironic asides and bureaucratic shape-shifting are compelling proofs either of the suppressed individual trapped in the corporate machine, as with Kunda, or of the pretended, treacherous nature of bureaucratic ethics. Ironic banter and ambiguous politics are simply bad faith. We should be ashamed of ourselves really, especially me, an ethnographer writing hyper-bureaucratic speeches and admitting enjoying it, not feeling oppressed and degraded. Why even try to account for the pleasure of wry, critical and cynical banter or the delight of 'stress-induced camaraderie' (Cullen & Howe 1991: 20), when faced with the cocked eyebrow of academic suspicion?

Viewed another way, the power of insider cynicism lies in its style as much as its substance. Ironic commentary gives form to the performance of involvement. It makes visible the otherwise unobservable activity of scanning, monitoring and discerning that occurs as organisational events take shape. The wry commentary marks an artful sass that marks the speaker as one who is quickly knowledgeable, not naïve, and readily able to give intelligent comment. Being 'in the know', 'taking the pulse', and signalling one's knowingness through a confident ability to cast ironic and deprecating asides, exhibits the shrewdness expected of a 'good operator' (see also Munro 1999). It is a badge of one's insider authority, augmented by other curiously exhilarating symbols of insiderness: less fettered access to the Minister's office and senior executive staff; ridiculously short time frames for assignment turnaround; together with '"frenetic working displays"', privileged transport and communications, receptions and numerous other expressions of deference' (Mosse 2005: 26).

In the flux of incalculable and pressing issues that come at senior policy officers and managers riding the turbulence of major policy shifts, bureaucrats also engage in a pragmatic attempt to anticipate the outcomes that may yet unfold – failures and unexpected turns of event included. For what experienced bureaucrats know above all else is that policy events are always subject to future revisions, compromises and the need to accommodate new circumstances. In gauging what response to fashion to a new event, how to perform, what posture to adopt, and importantly, how seriously, if at all, to take any of it, wry or moderating comments are thus as much part of the procedure as assenting or optimistic ones. Such comments are neither sincere nor disingenuous – or rather, they are both at once and more besides. As American organisational analyst Robert Jackall observes in his ethnographic work on corporate managers of manufacturing corporations:

> The premium on alertness to expediency demands ... an ability and a readiness to doublethink one's way through the contradictory irrationalities of everyday problems. But standing at the middle of events grappling with exigencies, especially in a hierarchical milieu that requires authorities to display sincere conviction in their actions, seems to foster at least a kind of half belief ... in one's efforts to do what has to be done. (Jackall 1988: 188)

Adeptness in all modalities is critical to the proprietary orientation to issues of the moment that managers must manifest in order to display their policy dexterity, their 'flexibility'.[5] Bureaucrats call it having 'ownership', and believe that it is the vital ingredient without which enthusiasm for the essentially repetitive ritual flurry of policy participation cannot be mustered.

To give these observations more clarity, let's examine the hospital outsourcing case study in the same fragmentary way practitioners (cynically and joyfully) experienced it as it came together mid-flight.

Strategy 21: The spirit in dull prose

Upon re-entering the managerial layers of THS to prepare the Ministerial Statement, my original brief was not to write about the hospitals in

Strategy 21 – Directions 2005

STRATEGIC INTENT

To create and enhance a Territory-wide network of services which delivers continuing improvement in the health and well being of all Territorians

Strategic directions X **Core Business Focus** = **Stretch Goal Areas**

Building on and sharpening our core directions	New emphases in Territory Health Services' role	Achieving five practical and challenging goals
» Public Health » Primary Level Health » Acute and Specialist Care » Community Services » Organisational Support	» Policy Leader in Health for Territorians » Funder/Purchaser of Government Approved Health Services » A Core Northern Territory Provider of Non Commercial Health Services » A Catalyst for Total Health Solutions Achieved Intersectorally	» Strengthen Community Capacity » Develop a Robust Health and Community Services Sector in the Northern Territory » Significantly Increase Aboriginal Involvement in the Health and Community Service Workforce » Be a Major Contributor to the Northern Territory's Economic and Social Development » Enhance our Organisational Capability

FURTHER INFORMATION

Territory Health Services GPO Box 40596, Casurina NT 0811 Telephone: (08) 8999 2964 Facsimile (08) 8999 2600

Figure 2.1 Strategy 21 Front Page

any specific way but rather to prepare an uplifting 'progress report' on the achievements of the health portfolio in general. In updating the previous year's Ministerial Statement, I was to build narrative excitement around a series of corporate planning sessions that had already filtered the words of some 600 employees, together with other agency and non-government organisation inputs, into a small number of feeder documents. Key among these was a document demanding particular attention: Strategy 21.

At first it was difficult to see why Strategy 21 deserved such foregrounding. Coming, as I had, straight from the far field of dusty work with health's own fieldworkers, I was a stranger to its production history – *and this made all the difference.* To out-of-place eyes, Strategy 21 has the dull appearance of yet another government document, a variation on a well-established standard. An astounding 18 months in the making, it was essentially a 5-page corporate strategy miniaturising the ambitions of THS into a 'Core Business Focus' and 'Stretch Goal Areas'. In a series of dot points, it used catchy managerialisms (such as 'stretch goals' 'strengthening community capacity', 'intersectoral collaboration', 'leadership and innovation' and 'more gain') to create a tale of evolutionary advance (see Figure 2.1).

Strategy 21's recognisability went beyond layout and phraseology to theme and intent. It distilled a wider 'new public management' theme of transforming THS from an 'institutionalist' to a 'residualist' welfare organisation (Titmuss 1974): that is, one which avowedly privileges market mechanisms and prefers state sponsorship of privately provided services (with 'private' here including government-funded community sector organisations) to comprehensive public sector service provision and delivery. One of a series of attempts mediated through a range of tactics – performance management, contract employment, and the withdrawal of government from direct service provision into a more distant regulatory role – Strategy 21 simultaneously activated a corporatisation agenda and promoted a competitive enterprise culture within THS. It asked THS staff to embrace the language of outsourcing, to view time as a commercial property, to see themselves as business managers separately responsible for controlling production, purchase and supply, with associated promises of a more transparent return on investments of government capital.

In order to understand these now familiar injunctions as somehow representing radical innovations, it is worth remembering that conventionally, much health activity (like the activity of other social service agencies) is economically opaque. Health's expense claims cannot be straightforwardly tracked to direct financial returns on investment or clear social benefit outputs, and the pursuit of administratively rational ends is made suspect by health's emotive claims to responsibility for birth, life and death. In the absence of guiding business principles, new management theory argues, waste, mismanagement, duplication of effort, non-accountability and inefficiency reign. The idea expressed in Strategy 21, in as few words as possible, was that separating health's funding, purchasing and provider functions from each other would force THS actors to clearly identify and distinguish situations in which they:

1   were funding non-public sector organisations to deliver services on their behalf, or 'purchasing' goods and services which the agency could not otherwise deliver (through contracts and consultancies), from

2   those occasions where they still held primary responsibility for direct service delivery itself.

But in THS there was to be a unique local twist. The THS professional employees directly responsible for service delivery – as, say, professional nutritionists, infant health nurses or social workers – would in turn become responsible for establishing pseudo-markets for their services by negotiating the 'purchase' of their work, either by other parts of THS or by such community organisations as Aboriginal Health Boards, who were to be given government money to become proxy 'purchasers'. These organisations were promised the discretion to 'buy' what they wanted, from whomever they wanted, without being restricted to purchasing from THS, through the introduction of simulated competition in the place of state service provider monopoly. In reality, however, there are few competitors for government service provision in most parts of the Northern Territory, and much of the money non-government organisations (NGOs) have to spend is government-derived and tied to restrictive performance agreements (see also Fisher 1997). But the idea could be *made to seem liberatory*, and that was my rhetorical brief.

As it was initially conveyed to me, my task was to weave a compelling script around the abridged mercantilist logics contained within Strategy 21, to reintroduce narrative detail and homely anecdotes in order to reinvigorate the ongoing corporatisation agenda. This story was about health as an enterprise, both as an organisational ethos and as the biographical life project individual health 'consumers' are urged to self-manage. Tellingly, the concluding subscript for Strategy 21 was a metonymic device that cleverly captured the bureaucratic desire to compel precisely these identifications: 'Health is (y)our business.' (In PowerPoint presentations, the (y) flashed in and out of visibility, from 'your' to 'our', highlighting the semantic exchangeability even more powerfully.)

For those who had been personally involved in its collective production, Strategy 21 had a profundity not readily discernible in its nicely balanced sentences. For one thing, for the subtext of Strategy 21 to be executed, people's work functions would need to be redefined, new administrative structures created and former work teams broken to create new ones. The organisation itself would need restructuring to reflect new accountabilities, governance arrangements and legal frameworks. Needless to say, the speculation surrounding these impending changes fuelled a tense atmosphere of liminality that found its symbol in the five otherwise boring pages. And yet, even its interlinking with impending structural change fails to fully explain the emotion vested in Strategy 21. For one of the people involved in the formulation of Strategy 21, 'it was one of the best things' she'd ever done:

> I got so much out of it, Tess. For me it was one of the best
> exercises I've done with THS – and I mean I love what I do, I
> just really enjoy working for THS, but I found that to be one of
> the key things ... I got so much out of it ... for me personally ...
> because I just learnt so much.

Though it took me a while, eventually I understood that the striking intensity of emotion surrounding both Strategy 21 and its sister product, the speech I was coordinating, was not comprehensible through reference to textual content alone. Rather, its emotional force arose out of the interactions and exchanges that both ushered this policy text into being and followed its emergence. The 5-page artefact was a fetish object, but such an object does not concentrate any magic without first being sacralised through ritual activity. As anthropologist David Mosse so astutely observes, 'policy texts are scoreboards of relations of influence in an organisation': the negotiations around what is in and what is out are socio-political processes of high significance in their own right.

18 months x 600 people = 5 pages

Crucially, Strategy 21 emerged out of a very labour-intensive process conducted through a consultation pyramid. A highly regarded management consultant specifically recruited for the purpose had intensively trained six health service staff in the requisite interviewing techniques. Each of them had in turn trained a further 20 people, making a team of 120 trained interviewers. The interviewers then conducted focus groups, with 7 or 8 THS employees at a time, about their concerns about THS and its future directions. The material thus placed onto butcher's paper and into notebooks was categorised and summarised back up the pyramid. Finally the THS senior executives, the master facilitator and the original six interviewers met in a 2-day 'lock-up' – that is, at a site of complete physical removal from the everyday workplace – to consider the feedback from their interview team.

The drafting exercise for formulating key government documents is usually exhaustive, though not always to this extent. Ordinarily there are daily deadline pressures for junior writers, whose task it is to produce drafts, thus enabling variously positioned powerbrokers further up the line to read and respond; these drafts must be continually rewritten to exacting standards until there is collective agreement that there is a good script (see Davis-Floyd 1998, Riles 1998: 381). Internal critiques are an organic part of the institutional ritual of performing policy texts. As a genre type, Strategy 21 successfully followed the formula. It had the right kinds of words, perfectly balanced in new but recognisable ways. As anthropologist Annelise Riles notes of documents produced for the United Nations'-sponsored Fourth World Conference on Women (the 'Beijing Conference'), certain words recognisably fit with each other, creating a congruence or balance that is immediately recognised and accepted by experienced policy practitioners. Language acquires 'a shape, a rhythm, a feel, not simply a meaning' (Riles 1998: 386).

The writing instructions for policy documents are often to produce aural and visceral as well as specific content effects. With the Minister's speech, for instance, I was asked to write the Statement in a way that was 'crunchy, punchy, not navel gazing or touchy-feely', and words were suggested on the basis of their aesthetic fit. One manager promoted the terms 'funder, purchaser, provider' to describe how outsourcing would work, saying: 'I think this is [sic], ah, flavourish sorts of words, you know, that – it's sort of business language as well, you know?' Another prompted helpfully: 'These are nice words for you ... "Cybersmart GPs". I thought you could work that in. Stylish, business words.'

Recollecting the tussles over how to word the sentiment that THS should only provide programs where the non-government and private industry sectors couldn't, eventually captured in Strategy 21 with the phrase 'THS will be the lead provider of non commercial services', one senior executive easily revisited the intensity of the debate:

Executive: The Department will still remain the lead provider of 'non commercial health services' but that is exactly … I mean we argued for a long time [but] nobody came up with a better word than 'commercial' and I couldn't either. I mean I couldn't spend a lot of time [resisting it], but I don't like that. Nobody liked it, to be quite honest.

Tess: What does it mean?

Executive: Well, what'll be left to government is those services which can't be outsourced easily (laughs), and the phrase that was attached to that was 'non commercial'. A thing like child protection. Just some stuff that's so statutory and embedded in government that you couldn't possibly – you can't contract out investigation of child protection cases, you've got to do it yourself in government … But I don't think that the word 'non commercial' – I don't know, I don't know if you're going to be able to come up with a better phrase. I must say I meant to go home and do a thesaurus on it but lots of people objected to it. A lot of us said, 'No, don't like that word', so he [the facilitator] said, 'Well what do you want to put down instead?' (laugh) I said 'X.X.'

Importantly, the manager 'couldn't spend a lot of time' holding out for particular wording. Within bureaucratic settings, the insider calibrates her display of intelligent contribution within the constraints of situational acceptability. To overstay opposition, to 'die in a ditch' as policy people would say, risks the irritation and even disdain of others. The struggle is one of being artful (noticeably contributing; being 'constructive'; sounding thoughtful) without tipping the balance of group judgment against one's display. Of course the chair or facilitator also has on hand a number of techniques for rescinding unwanted objections, from an over-audible sigh to prim redirections: 'I think that takes the discussion off subject. Can we return to the point made by Peter a moment ago?'[6]

Equally, the co-performance of amiability and collegiality that professionally facilitated workshops are choreographed to foster demands that members know exactly when to put a halt to their own insistence. Especially in lock-up situations, bound within a windowless committee room, assent may be sculpted out of exhaustion, when nobody wants to fight for key words any more and it no longer matters whether it is 'community control' or 'community capacity' that is being described, just that the document is produced to form (see also Schwartzman & Berman 1994). The key is to find words that are ambitious and action-sounding but sufficiently vague to allow room for manoeuvre, for a 'multiplication of the criteria for success and the accommodation of shifting policy agendas; [for distributing] agency by allowing various actors to isolate and claim credit for desirable change' (Mosse 2005: 36).

The absorbing and frustrating process of threshing out final words for documents such as Strategy 21 is also fed by the apprehension that these well-chosen words are not the last word, but rather constitute 'conditionally definitive discourse'. Socio-linguist Donald Brenneis defines this as a forceful style of *deceptively* conclusive talk which assumes and anticipates a subsequent editorial audience: in this case, the Minister and his Cabinet colleagues – and for these, an anticipated public, mediated by journalistic reaction (Brenneis 1994: 30, 1999). Here, at 'the intersection of text and talk' (Brenneis 1994: 30), institutional words must work hard, first as statements that declare the competence of their formulators at the time of their co-performed emergence; and then, if accepted for inclusion, as words which must additionally survive later sets of judgment by successfully performing in new settings (see Brown 1986, Gronn 1983, Myers & Brenneis 1984).

Thus, collectively working with words is hard work, and the chosen words must themselves be hardworking. Not only that, but all this hard work goes into producing documents that (paradoxically) only prove the heavy work they are performing when they achieve the ubiquitous appearance and sound of any other. Innocuousness and banality are hard-won and rare qualities. How can this be?

Banality – the grandest achievement

It is not so much that institutional words are considered to have no meaning and are therefore readily exchangeable (*pace* Riles 1998), but rather that only a limited number of words can in and of themselves operate to simultaneously promise action and foreclose imagined future dissent. This is what wording wrestles are so often about. The wording for public and collectively scribed documents must confidently prefigure actions while avoiding unintended insult. More, it must sound as if absolutely *vital* government action is being catalysed *by* these very words, that these words are already statements of action. The words must additionally meet and appease (or deliberately and strategically irritate) multiple political interests.

Only a small number of polysemous or 'multi-meaning' words – the word 'commitment', say – can handle such a burden. To take a small example, the alliterative duet 'community control', which features in so many public health broadcasts, braids together calls from Aboriginal advocates for greater autonomy in running Aboriginal health services with a government desire to in fact have less responsibility for (difficult and often futile) arenas of direct service delivery. A manager describes this antonymic quality graphically:

> In terms of buy-in, we can sell Aboriginal health boards to the Aboriginal groups as about community control; and we can sell it to government as outsourcing and increasing the dollars into the Northern Territory ... I mean, what's the difference between community control and outsourcing? Community control is a softly, softly term where we have a contractual relationship with other people delivering services: same, same.

Who could dare contest the virtue of Aboriginal people being in charge of running their own health centres and of being more responsible for managing their own conditions?

The detailed work of circumventing (imagined) future squabbles through careful wording goes a long way towards explaining what critics invariably see as policy's vacuous language. For example, in the ministerial speech I eventually put together, the anticipation of staff protest over the proposed new management regime saw the inclusion of disclaimers noting that the reforms did not negate 'the dedicated services of many health workers and support staff' and further, that 'the public hospital system and staff have served Territorians well under some trying conditions. Our staff are good. They've put in hard for this community. But ...'

A different aspect of the same attempt to deflect known potential slights through careful wording is the necessity to ensure that all key regional centres in the THS network are mentioned at least once in any main script. Submitting an early draft of the Ministerial Statement for review, I was quickly advised to work in examples of 'good work' from other regions, lest people consider the document too Darwin-centric. I really should have known better. Accusations clustered around concepts of regional marginality are an automated reflex of dispersed organisations everywhere, and THS is no exception. Sensitivity to the insults encoded in phrases such as the 'Berrimah Line', a term used to describe an imaginary boundary between an outer suburb of Darwin and all other places in the Northern Territory, is one of the first lessons of bureaucratic work in the north. Central office anticipation feeds off regional office sensitivity which in turn feeds off every slip-up from Darwin, regularly confirming the need for everyone's eternal vigilance. Such auto-policing soon becomes second nature. To omit consideration of everyone south of the 'Berrimah Line' would be to concede an easy point to those regionally placed bureaucrats who are alert to the slightest infraction from Central Office; this was especially to be avoided in a text that was, after all, meant to be the result of an intensive regional consultation process.[7] And so it goes.

Surfing the serendipitous

Gathering ideas for the Health Minister's Statement, conducting yet more internal consultations, I too joined in the chorus of criticisms of 'the system', because to enter into and sustain the presumptions and conventions of bureaucratic transactions is to enter into the space of cynicism and critique. On the inside, far from being revelatory, ironical banter operates as a kind of testing, our cynical commentary anticipating the kinds of dissent both our abstract and our known audience might make. Not even cunningly, just routinely and mundanely, we sound each other out and solicit snippets of information in professional camaraderie and mild-mannered brinksmanship:

Manager: The only country in the western world with a shit public health system, America, is the country that has the most outsourcing, so you have to ask …

Tess: Oh yes! You know, the other thing I've been doing,

> just for my own sanity, is looking at the IT literature
> where they've done a lot of outsourcing and issued
> their research, and you know, for every successful case
> study there's another 20 of absolute disasters! And
> it's the success cases that obviously I need to try and
> draw stuff out of for the speech but yeah, anyway
> (wry expression) ... But do you realise that right now,
> this week, the Minister and Plummer [the CEO] are
> doing their interstate tour with the HDI consultants?
> Probably having outsourcing and privatisation pissed
> in their ear at every second. It's like the Emperor's
> clothing round here!

Manager: Absolutely! Ha! So, yeah, the issue becomes: how do you outsource something and maintain control of that, in the way that we are talking about? If I were running an outsourced organisation as a private hospital, then honestly, I wouldn't care less about the public need any more than I absolutely have to – or that it is contractually stipulated that I must. And it is impossible to contractually stipulate things like social justice. If you're the manager of Joe Bloggs Proprietary Limited, you have a legal and a moral obligation to look after your shareholders before anything else. It is not a question of right or wrong, it is a question of fiduciary duty. How do you do that [care for public patients] in an industry [private hospitals] where what you're selling is a luxury?

Tess: Yeah, that's right! OK. So forget that. If you could have your way [with how the Statement is written], how would things go?

In trying to understand the arduousness and, simultaneously, the tactical delicacy of this interactive work, it is important to abandon notions that bureaucrats are propelled by motives of logic or efficacy alone. Policy documents are talked and written into existence by sensate beings who are living the moment and interacting with its discursive twists and turns at a bodily level. Knowing how to perform with finesse, how to enact the intricate steps and elusive rules for administrative comportment (via demeanour, dress, and verbal demonstrations of tactical expertise) can be a source of intense excitement and pleasure. 'I'll play the dumb blonde now,' a fellow policy officer once whispered to me during a tense negotiation moment in a predominantly male meeting. Without need for further discussion, she worked to head off a new excursion into the familiar grooves of a well staked-out interdepartmental battle ground with a disarmingly silly query calculated to arouse their paternalistic sympathy, while I continued on a more aggressive tack.

After a particularly intensive bout of strategising, bureaucrats can be found in corridors, cafés and wine bars excitedly swapping details about who said what to whom, which words were accepted, what had to be fought over, and they will hint at the feelings that were racing through their bodies as the next moves were deciphered. The virtuosity of each person's tactical performances within these administrative dramas is scrutinised in post mortem 'debriefings', as bureaucrats subject themselves and whomever they were strategising with or competing against to close analysis.

There is exhaustion and elation, and even what one might describe as moments of policy ecstasy, when a project 'comes together', when a crisis is averted, or a deadline met with a draft that is indisputable and well regarded. Managers talk of 'thriving on the pressure' of being 'really under the pump', of being 'turned on' by the hectic pace, seduced by the adrenaline rush of making the right policy calls at the right time, of surfing the serendipitous with flair and élan. And they know at the most intense of bodily levels when they have not performed the moment correctly or well: when they did not anticipate an event on the horizon, or the strength of community feeling a government move unexpectedly catalysed; when they weren't scanning the environment with sufficient dexterity to read its clues; or when a good document, culled and coaxed through all the right stages, is nonetheless rejected at ensuing evaluative stopping stations – at the Minister's office, or by other bureaucrats in more powerfully placed agencies (such as Treasury or the Department of the Chief/Prime Minister). When something took them by unpleasant surprise and an acutely absorbing 'crisis' had to be unexpectedly managed – questions fielded, explanations drafted, anxious meetings held NOW! at the expense of every other activity. When what was supposed to be a celebration at bringing a project to a successful closure becomes a stressful reopening, and all the hard work put into attempts to hold multiple meanings within the parenthesis of texts are shown once again to be only transitory accomplishments.

A death in paradise

Despite (or because of) its initially unimpressive appearance, Strategy 21 travelled in the bureaucracy as a text that mattered. Its implementation would entail an organisational restructure and hence the promise of future remedy through institutional metamorphosis. It had solid representative collateral as a communal attestation of staff input – 600 contributors over one and a half years made it a comprehensive miniaturisation – and its encompassing word combinations and presentational style satisfied production haggles and the aesthetic and aural requirements of a modernist business-like look and sound. It was a high-status, high-gloss artefact, and involvement in its production provided opportunity for displays of competency and sass among peers of note. Its formulation, as noted, took 18 months, a fair consultation period by the most demanding of measures; and its dramatic content, combined with its circumstances of collation, gave managers the sense of being at the helm of an important sea-change in the entire administrative apparatus. It even inspired an official reformulation of the agency's Mission Statement, from 'Our Mission: To improve the health status and well-being of all people in the Northern Territory' to its current formulation: 'To create and enhance a Territory-wide network of services which delivers continuing improvement in the health status and well being of all Territorians.'

This last, apparently minor change, illustrates the argument exquisitely. In its very banality, it conceals from casual view what is, from a bureaucrat's perspective, the heart of the matter: the organisational shift towards greater levels of outsourcing. For the policy cognoscenti who could sense the consultative and significance of these words, the Mission Statement's reformulation represented a major achievement. The very fact that the new Mission Statement glides so easily past the eyeballs, just as Strategy 21 in its entirety had initially also done for me, is, in a sense, the bureaucrat's triumph – a hard-won effect of hardworking words which seem anodyne and yet resonate with all sorts of implications. Now, finally, we can see why people were so inordinately proud of Strategy 21, why the artefact was treated with such reverence and why it was being pressed upon me as something the Minister should 'put up in lights' in the speech I was preparing.

Yet, while ordinarily there will be significant agreement among the policy virtuosi on what words will do well when presented to the Minister's or other substantive critical eyes, and while usually the expert predictive work closely approximates what will be accepted, in this case the senior bureaucrats were miscalculating badly. The first text sent to the Minister was categorically rejected precisely because of its *over emphasis* on Strategy 21 – for by this time, Strategy 21 had been gazumped.

Recursivity

Just as ethnographic research is guided by drift as much as by plan (see Van Maanen 1979: 539), so too Strategy 21 and the hospital outsourcing project connected both through coincidence and through intention. Precisely when Strategy 21 was at its zenith, the hospital initiative was in ecliptic motion, quietly and surely moving into ascendancy as the new wave to be surfed. And yet, as recalled to me by the then Chief Executive, their co-emergence was entirely accidental:

Tess: Did the hospital project come out of Strategy 21 or not?

CEO: No (long pause). No. But what came out of Strategy 21 was the issue of – we should be a provider of core services only. At that time we weren't thinking, we weren't even imagining that the public hospital might be subjected to privatisation. But we had shifted to the idea that anything non-core should be shifted to the non-government or private sector and that we should start to explore that area, which was one of the outcomes that was articulated [in Strategy 21, which calls for 'a quantum shift to service delivery by others'].

Most of those in the inner circle of THS knew the Minister was investigating outsourcing possibilities for the hospitals but regarded this as a complementary and still embryonic development that would eventually dovetail into the far more significant story of Strategy 21 – perhaps acting as a hypothetical illustration of THS' mooted transformation from majority deliverer of health services to an organisation which contracts others to do this on government's behalf.

In the scanning and monitoring of policy's sound waves, the Minister's private consultants were initially diagnosed as 'peddlers of vapour ware' – in the Territory to make a fast quid like so many before them. Sure, they should be monitored carefully as they attended horse races and charity events, wining and dining the 300 Territorians they'd listed as important contacts to slide into loose bind with, using alcohol as the lubricating vector. But there was little concern that they would have a serious or lasting impact. Besides, the bureaucrats speculated, the government had just had its Referendum on Statehood unexpectedly and categorically rejected.[8] There was no way the Country Liberal Party would risk another showdown with the electorate over an issue as sensitive as the public hospitals. That was all just bluff and bluster. No, the public servants assumed, the main event was undoubtedly Strategy 21, a policy that would reposition THS for the next five years of organisational activity, leading health's way into the 21st century.

And so, in accordance with everyone's expert editorial opinion, the first draft of the Ministerial Statement I was tasked with preparing initially focused on Strategy 21. In response, the Health Minister angrily declared his complete lack of interest in amplifying the Department's corporate vision: 'There is no question,' he boomed, exasperated at the seeming ineptitude of the mandarins, 'I just want to talk about the hospitals. I just want to tell everybody the *truth*! That Strategy 21 stuff isn't even finished; why get me to talk about it now?' The bureaucrats had got it all horribly wrong. Back at THS policy headquarters, news that the Minister was more interested in privatising the hospitals than in any strategic promulgation of theirs produced tension. The Health Minister's sense of the truth that needed telling and the health bureaucrats' sense of it were massively out of kilter, an unusual and upsetting state for those well schooled in the arts of anticipating ministerial desires. Editorial changes are to be expected, yes, but wholesale rejection of one and a half years of corporate strategising was a slap in the face of significant magnitude.

'This is a political mistake,' one executive complained, conflating quintessentially bureaucratic concerns with those of that imaginary unity, 'the public':

> Burke has got it wrong. He should know that he is going to be disappointing the public, disappointing staff. We've been telling

> staff in all the [Strategy 21] consultation forums that everything
> will be made clear for them in the November Ministerial
> Statement – and now this!

Anxious weeks of to-ing and fro-ing followed, with the bureaucrats again attempting to second-guess the Minister, again getting it wrong, their radars well and truly scrambled. The Minister told me one thing, his Press Secretary another, the CEO and senior executive managers of THS something else again. The Statement would focus on Strategy 21; or it would focus exclusively on outsourcing hospital management; or it would mix both; or it would not go ahead at all. Strategy 21 was loathed by the Minister; it was supported; it would be implemented; it would be deferred.

Discussing this event with the senior managers involved over a year later, I probed the normalcy of such confusion at the penultimate stages of presenting material. This manager's responses were typical:

Tess:	So was it possible, thinking about those events, to anticipate how it all transpired?
Executive:	No ... There was nothing I could have predicted about that. Nothing at all, in fact, when I think about it, *despite all our work.*
Tess	Has there been anything else in your career to match it, in terms of turbulence, the world churning?
Executive:	Not quite ... I've had other heady times. They were heady, but not in the same way – they're more in control, with us managing and so on. This was kind of out-of-left-field stuff that you had to really go for a sleigh ride on, and really try to manage at the same time when suddenly there *ain't no rules.*

With all their techniques of anticipation apparently failing, senior policy actors were left feeling wretched. And yet, as is the way with swift policy realignments, in the short time between rejection and rewrite, the hospital initiative itself became on the nose!

Though the Minister went ahead with the speech at the scheduled time in the November Sittings, it had already lost its edge as a launch of a major initiative – the idea of outsourcing the hospital's management had been leaked to the media well before the Minister's official announcement. In the heated arguments for and against seeking private sector involvement that ensued, hospital staff groups and allied unions threatened strike action on a daily basis, and residents were letter-bombed with leaflets from the political opposition warning of the imminent 'Americanisation' of the Territory's health care system.[9] Meanwhile, the singularly poor example of private sector performance represented by Darwin Private Hospital, the only private hospital in the Northern Territory, took centre stage in media and bureaucratic debates. Close attention was paid to how, being typically understaffed and under-equipped, the private hospital had been forced to close its casualty ward, shunting its critical acute care patients back into the public system, thereby destroying in-patient expectations of any exclusive private service. As press coverage became ever more antagonistic, talkback radio and letters to the editor were also increasingly hostile to the proposal.

As they hedged their bets about the final outcome, bureaucrats began to let it be known that the cost and saving projections produced by HDI, the Minister's advising consultancy firm, did not match those of competing consultants contracted specifically for triangulation purposes. Emboldened to new wisdom by the sniff of a miscalculation, THS managers conspiratorially agreed that the Minister would have done better to woo people to the concept of outsourcing health services through the impeccable logic and considered (euphemistic) approach of Strategy 21. Instead, his decision to isolate the hospital initiative from the sounder framework of Strategy 21 had cost him the project – or so they now confidently asserted.

Retroactive alignment

We might raise a fresh eyebrow at the convenience of retrospective policy accounts telling 'what really happened', noting how rapidly the fragmentary tales have morphed into a single omniscient account. But it is not the capacity for self-deception that should amaze; it is the policy officers' sixth sense, their instinctive modulation of even their own memories to sustain the magic-myth of policy rationality. As a scepticism tonic, let us recall that the unexpected is the expected in the world of bureaucracy, where second-guessing, multiple positionings and fast switchback movements are the insurance taken out by the 'good operator' against the unknown. (Indeed, it is precisely this – the senior bureaucrat's within and withoutness, together with her narcissistic enjoyment of her own dexterity – that makes the bureau-professional so morally suspect to the outside critic.)

Naturally enough, the time between full knowledge of the Minister's serious intent to outsource all the public hospitals, and the announcement of his decision not to go ahead was more complexly inhabited. As French sociologist of science and technology networks Bruno Latour reminds us, in the beginnings of policy:

> there is no distinction between projects and objects. The two circulate from office to office in the form of paper, plans, departmental memos, speeches, scale models and occasional synopses. Here we're in the realm of signs, language, texts. (1996: 24)

In this realm of signs, language and texts, the hospital outsourcing project was still the imminent project of the moment; still subject to future-proofing through deprecating little asides. Imagine the intense work required to manifest proprietary interest right up to the last moment. The hospital project actually proceeded all the way past the 'Expressions of Interest' stage, with several companies – including religious organisations – indicating that they would be competing for the final tender. These shortlisted companies worked round the clock to prepare their best and final bid, in good faith. Imagine the intensive and serious attention the bureaucrats involved in coaxing these offers forward were still dedicating to the process. While THS bureaucrats were prophesying doom, they were nonetheless also anticipating that the project would proceed, with pre-drafted press releases in hand, complete with blank parentheses awaiting only the name of the chosen firm.

As the bureaucrats continued to busy themselves with simultaneously critiquing, subverting, and supporting behind the scenes, all the usual activities of policy surfing – assembling arguments, collating data, preparing background briefings and publicity material, securing legal advice, talking to staff groups and unions, working networks, fielding phone calls and churning through the excessive proliferation of electronic memos that surround any major event – continued into the midnight hours. And then, as they hovered in their offices awaiting a decision that seemed almost foregone, the pin was unexpectedly pulled.

In to the stunned silence that follows the cancelled outsourcing come the whispered beginnings of new policy rationales, as explanations and justifications stir into motion. Clearly, the bureaucrats decide, the Minister made a tactical error: Strategy 21 was the better vehicle for managing change. And you know, it actually suits us in THS to have the unions gloat in their assumed victory, for them to think their threats of strike action and mustering of public discord were integral to retaining public sector management of the hospitals. For really, the whole episode was designed to give the unions a little scare: while we were able to stop the Minister this time, we won't be able to change the fact that privatisation will happen in the future unless workplace reforms are agreed to ...

The show must go on

Of course the story does not end here, with policy fizzle, wearied bureaucrats and near and far stories of 'the truth', for there is no end to policy. By the time other audiences get their first taste, hearing the news on the media, the policy makers will be turning their attention to the next event, which will demand of them a unique set of repeat performances. There is a relentless circularity to policy production, with a dense and repetitive patterning visible in the form/at/ation. The timelessness, or rather the recursivity, of policy is denied and disguised by its carefully selected, passionately instrumental language, which, as the following chapters reveal, asserts a continual avant-gardism – an attempted expiation and disavowal of links with past attempts to educate and influence in similar directions. And, in order for the words and calculations to sound fresh, they must be energised by actors playing their parts with renewed interest in the here and now drama of the performance.

Policy virtuosity – or, to use THS terms, being 'a good operator' – is not permanently conceded on the basis of a single (no matter how singular) performance; it is tended and reaffirmed (or not, a fall from grace being all too easy) on an ongoing basis.[10] I used the example of the hospital drama partly because privatisation is axiomatically a 'bad thing' for liberal social critics (the 'we' who are obliged to detest profit-driven commercial logics interfering with social service provision); and because it represents a classic event for anthropological analysis. The inherent theatricality of a major new initiative appeals as a discretely analysable event, and yet it is simply one moment in an ongoing process. The endless repetition of the performance requirements of policy work is better characterised as *dynamic inertia*, for once these performance demands are over, new ones will arise, calling for fresh (re)enactments.

Borrowing from Fabian's theories of performance, we might see written policies as the visible tip of an ongoing series of rehearsals. They are moments in the elaborate ritual of statecraft, which nonetheless contain within their repetition of required and expected forms elements of spontaneous improvisation, impromptu strategising and juggling of competing interests (Fabian 1990: 11–20). At the same time, each surge has the potential to affect everyday conduct. 'New' logics do emerge, as in the case of Strategy 21, where commercialised audit language replaced the previous style of presenting the moral worthiness of fully government-run health services.

While sensitivity to the perilous nature of the hospital initiative and the outsourcing implications contained within Strategy 21 may well have given a particular intensity to their lived enactments, the anticipatory operations, the poised readiness to adopt different postures and to pursue divergent unfoldings, the intensity of debate created by the search for encompassing yet active words and the simulation of stakeholder consensus out of divergent interests, are all utterly characteristic of policies in their pre-legislative, per/formative moments of occurrence. The creation of a sense of crisis and need for change operates both as argumentative tactic, justifying new interventions into practice, and as self-inspiration at a site where the repetition of novelty propels the action. The manager who says 'the ultimate frustration is doing the same thing year after year expecting a result' is expressing more than momentary and clichéd disillusionment. Rather, the exasperation captures the essential functionality of policy and program activity: embedded within the high-speed momentum of new formulations is a tremendous sameness; both in the repetitiveness of the actions themselves and in the worried ambitions propelling the doing.[11]

Yet if we accept that policy resolution is never in fact achieved, how do we explain what is in it for practitioners, who, as their commentary reveals, cannot be conveniently dismissed as either moronic or robotic?

To get some way towards an answer to the key question of this book, let us consider the following exploratory remarks of Donald Brenneis. Pondering his role as a panel member of a national research proposal evaluation team, Brenneis was curious to explain the rapidity with which he learnt to do bureaucratic things (such as eliminating the truly unorthodox proposals from consideration, and limiting the range of things approved to more conventional research approaches) and the intense satisfaction he derived from the exercise. Rejecting explanations which spin on unquestioning conformity, conventional self-interest or a fight for peer regard, Brenneis observes that:

> We are often seduced into acquiescence or active complicity with these normalizing practices, procedures that we may well not countenance in our own scholarly work. The rewards for such seduction certainly include status, however transitory, as well as some degree of power. The relationships between these social achievements and the experience of satisfaction, however, are linked in complex ways. The enjoyment of technique, a sense not so much of responsibility as of successfully negotiating complex exchange relationships, and the shared production of social pleasure also need to be reckoned with. (Brenneis 1994: 34)

Consider also the musings of feminist theorist Carol Cohn, who, despite her determination to expose American defence analysts as cold-blooded misogynists, found herself enthralled by the privilege and sexiness of mixing terms with men she had wanted to regard as enemies, a thrill which in part came from 'the power of entering a secret kingdom' (1987: 704). Gradually mastering a conceptual system that places insiders in the active 'position of the planner, the user, the actor' as opposed to the subject or the victim (1987: 706), Cohn became someone 'in the know', able to meet prominent political figures and 'listen to Washington gossip'. The combination of renewing a sense of one's own ability to quickly adopt and flex a powerful new skill (complete with matching new vocabulary) and exhibiting this new skill in arenas which seem so supremely able to directly affect 'the real world', is potently seductive.

What these ethnographers are alluding to is the pleasure – and defeat – that is wrung out of strategising and co-performance of a particular and professionally empowered kind. Like Cohn, I would argue that being among the policy virtuosi, the elite bureaucrats who are closest to calling the bureaucratic shots – for a funding agreement or new initiative here, for determination of 'conditionally definitive' wording there, mixing it with Ministers and expensive consultants – is seductive in its own right. With Brenneis, I would say that there is an undeniable pleasure in being well regarded, be it for technical proficiency or adroitness in the ironic yet committed talk of strategy, plotting next steps. And I would further emphasise the affective dimension of being a wielder of words which overwrite the multifarious contributions of others, yet make a virtue of widespread community and employee participation, and which presume, build on and refuse to countenance alternative ideas about the merit and necessity of change, growth, development.

As Foucault reminds us, power is productive, affectively and effectively. Within the tricky, sticky entanglements of agency and obligation, within the internal animation wrought out of being at once governed and governing, our compulsion is compelling. We are the enactors of governmentality, circumscribing the disclosures of others, hooked on the highs of seeming to be the deciders rather than the decided for, even while abutting the lived-in, externally driven and consensual limits of our own agency.

Comparing my notes from August 1998, when people were on the run, to versions gathered years after the dust of the privatisation drama had settled, it was astonishing how much orderliness people retrospectively introduced to their involvement – and how moralising these later retellings were. The clarity that comes with hindsight depends on an active and mobile fastening of pared down and recast versions of the past to the needs of the instrumentalist present. Complicating the task of analysis even further, the work of preparing for such eventual perspicacity takes place prospectively. Policy practitioners iteratively prepare themselves for later realignments in policy retellings by developing infinitely adjustable interpretations of unfolding events along the way, so that whatever the outcome, it can be accorded an original intentionality. An ironic and deconstructive disposition, so very similar to the academic's pose, is critical to this in situ preparation for the certainty of uncertainty at every stage.

Strategy 21 was reasserted as the policy of the day following the renouncement of the hospital outsourcing. And as a postscript, THS was officially divided into purchaser/funder/provider units with internal work groups commissioning work from each other via contractual agreements, introducing a new framing of the requirement to report returns for action within old forms of documented activity calculation (see Power 1997). The hospital experiment was immediately reframed as simply a 'testing of the waters', as a clever strategy of sounding the public out on the most radical option among a suite of potential changes in service management. Its withdrawal was cast as an easy compromise in the context of continuing with the overall strategy. In yet later revisions, the hospital project was disengaged from Strategy 21 altogether, isolated out as a momentary political aberration when politicians tried but *ha!* failed to outwit bureau-professionals, unions and members of the public, whose struggle to overcome the misguided Minister and his worse consultants was triumphantly won by the organised will of the good guys, providing further proof of the importance of taking part in policy talk and organising public consultations. And participants have since replaced their enthusiastic involvement of the time with a more purified rejecting of the initiative as their original and consistent posture all along.[12]

The delicate arts of such upholdings are never explicitly taught – we are never told we must adjust and continuously moderate our own thoughts, feelings and experiences to assert narrative consistency, rationality and a sense of closure for policy (re)enactments. So, just how are such creative skills acquired? And how are they acquired by people who are not involved in the contortions and compromises of policy but are slaving away out in the field – the public health radicals operating against 'the system' to remedy health inequalities?

THE SELF-REPLICATING ORGANISATION

Shortly after the Northern Territory attained self-government in 1978, when a liberatory ethic of self-determination was in the air for Aborigines and administrators alike, the NT Department of Health was officially formed, out of Commonwealth department precursors; during the period I am writing about it was Territory Health Services (THS), and now it is the NT Department of Health and Families. Today, its central administration operates out of a squat pastel apricot building, five storeys high, known as 'Health House'.

Health House (Hell House or Unhealthy House in other namings) sits midpoint along one of the four long main streets that constitute the Central Business District of Darwin, Australia's smallest capital city. The official administrative functions of supporting the Health Minister, undertaking system-wide planning, monitoring and evaluation, allocating funding, establishing standards and guidelines, and providing policy and strategy advice all take place here. It is thus the main home of the strategists, analysts, planners, forecasters and advisors featured in Chapter 2, who form the cluster collectively called 'policy'. The clusters known as 'operations' are based in regional offices in Alice Springs, Tennant Creek, Katherine, Nhulunbuy and Casuarina (the latter is an outer suburb of Darwin); each of these regional offices functions as a service base for satellite outlets in surrounding regions.

These five towns also house the five public hospitals that had been earmarked for outsourcing by the Health Minister in Chapter 2. The Katherine, Nhulunbuy and Tennant Creek hospitals function as referral centres; more advanced specialist services are provided from Royal Darwin Hospital (RDH) and, when necessary, by hospitals in the southern capital cities.[1] There are also smaller primary health care service sites in all major townships and in officially recognised Aboriginal communities. Known as clinics or community health centres, these are staffed by resident nurses and Aboriginal Health Workers. Very occasionally, they may also feature a general practitioner, but more usually, therapeutic and clinical services are provided by a range of visiting professionals who fly or drive out to communities on a weekly, fortnightly or monthly basis depending on the population size, locale, ease of access and accommodation quality.[2]

The public health professionals who are the main subjects of this ethnography also travel extensively throughout the regions, representing programs spanning alcohol and other drugs, dental health, nutrition, communicable diseases, environmental health, health promotion, medical entomology and women's cancer prevention. Each program area divides the Northern Territory into administrative geographies with imaginative names. A regional officer will speak of places within her purview as 'my communities' and, as we will see, there is considerable competition among officers about who can speak most knowingly about which community.

Being able to claim intimate acquaintance with the arduous, exhausting nature of community visits is an important badge in the committed public health professionals' troop. Their trips away are usually two to three days in duration, often only a day, seldom more than a week, with partners and children left behind. In any week in which an officer plans a community visit, at least two days are spent organising getting there and another day is spent at the end restoring office order. Typically, organising a trip involves faxing the community council with details of preferred visiting dates and an abbreviated summary of the intended purpose; numerous phone calls to secure travel allowance payments, to work out who else might be heading out on the same day and to make flight bookings or to organise vehicle use. Then there are the numerous sorties to round up the items that will either be shown (posters, books) or delivered (medical supplies or grocery items for either personal use or to take to the residential clinic staff). Finally, one needs to refamiliarise oneself with the program information and educational material that form the ostensible focus of the visit.

Long preparation delays are to be expected and forbearance is the requisite posture of a fieldworker who seeks the elusive tag: 'got what it takes'. For instance, in the midst of a delay that saw us circling a coastal community from a single-engine aircraft for close to an hour, waiting for low-level cloud to lift, one public health officer remarked to me:

> The thing people don't know is that this is totally out of our
> hands – you have to learn it's incredibly important to prepare well
> but still be able to go with the flow. Are you still interested in
> being one of us, Tess?

With the exception of health promotion and some generalist research positions, public health officers have professional qualifications specific to their program area (a degree in nutrition, environmental health or dietetics, for example). In the main, they share similar ethnic backgrounds (tertiary educated Euro-Australians) and similar political allegiances (anti-elitist liberals). Concerned both to support Aboriginal struggles for empowerment and to create a vanguard against the 'clinical method', their work falls into two main areas. The first relates to preparing, implementing and supervising projects in Aboriginal communities; the second to nurturing data collections, research projects and releasing best practice guidelines. Uniting these disparate activities is a single objective. Through the encouraging processes of self-determination – or, as it is more commonly expressed in public health discourse, community development and capacity-building – the overall aim is to improve the dire state of Aboriginal health.

Without exception, all THS public health practitioners complain that they are under-equipped for the work demanded of them. They claim they need more staff, time, resources and funding. They need debriefing and stress management strategies and therefore more professional development opportunities to cope with the huge problems associated with Aboriginal ill-health. They argue that because they are stretched so thin, they have to be more effective at coordinating their activities, but that the work of coordination is itself time-consuming and bedevilled by emotionally gruelling internecine battles. And they say that having so little time and so many communities to look after results in the 'squeaky wheel syndrome', meaning they can only attend to those issues that are complained about loudest or that attract the most media attention, leaving whole sweeps of geographic areas, fundamental issues and potential clients unaided. (That there are clear selection criteria demarcating desirable from undesirable, amenable from resistant communities is less frequently acknowledged.)

Yet clumping public health professionals together in this way obscures their own sense of difference and distance, both from each other and from other groups within THS. More usually, public health professionals see themselves as divided by multiple cleavages, which can be specified in terms of their personal education profiles, their place of origin, their specialty qualifications, their outside interests, their political attitudes, values and personalities and, most caustically, each other's level of engagement or commitment to Aboriginal health. Further, the types of activities public health officers are potentially engaged in are heuristically divided by practitioners into three competing categories: prevention, early intervention and treatment. Each of these has a long and complex tradition of definitional difference and passionate philosophical adherence. Those seen to be working at the clinical or treatment end of the public health spectrum are accused of ignoring the root (social, political and historical) causes of ill-health in favour of bandaiding technical solutions; and those at the prevention end are condemned as loose-thinking 'bleeding hearts' who, in the words of one unbeliever, 'are more in need of blackfellas than blackfellas are in need of them'.[3]

Officially, THS places a high priority on public health approaches such as education, prevention and early intervention, always listing them in corporate plans as key areas for whole-of-agency attention. Yet each year, public health practitioners reliably claim that their program monies have been clawed back to bail out the acute care budget deficits inevitably created by the high-expense hospitals. Conversely, THS managers insist that public health practitioners are not cautious enough with program money, and spend too much time on workshops and activities with vague ends (such as boosting a community's self-esteem) and not enough on actions with measurable outcomes. At the same time, the very act of voicing these suspicions fuels public health workers' sense of their own radicalism. Being resisted by the trio of reactionary forces – 'management', 'economic rationalists' and the pernicious 'biomedical model' – authenticates the advocacy stance of public health.

Opportunities for enmity abound. Each district has its own local hierarchy, run by a district manager who occupies an intermediary position between Head Office and individual health workers, and has a plethora of regional roles. Together with the regional manager structurally closest to this position, the district manager faces the ongoing predicament of meshing the concerns and priorities of the senior ministerial officers and managers in Health House with the more particular and immediate demands of the local office and community. Typically, regional office staff see emanations from Health House as unsympathetic, rigid and out of touch, with little sensitivity to the nuances of local areas, always overshooting or undershooting with funding, program objectives and implementation timetables, never understanding the delicacy of liaison activities with Aboriginal people and far too impatient for returns before relationships can be properly developed.

In turn, Head Office people view regional staff complaints about being overworked and under-consulted with a short-leashed sympathy, and a sense that local officers cannot see beyond their own fine-grained concerns to the 'big picture' beyond – this is a coded reference to the range of pragmatic considerations and compromises policy formulators juggle in the process of bringing projects into being. Suspicious of the meandering involved in the sweep of activities clustered under the rubric of 'community development', they insist that public health officers adopt a project management approach, with its in-built requirements for definite conclusions, benchmarks, interim reviews, documentation, and specification of project 'deliverables' and deadlines.

Them and they

In each case, the 'they', the imagined final location of the decision-making apparatus, is always in another place. For central office personnel, the 'they' is variously positioned: an unwanted instruction may be attributed to the 'fourth floor', a reference to the Chief Executive Officer's suite on the uppermost floor of Health House; or, depending on the issue, the authorial centre of insulated and illogical decision-making may be simply 'the Minister', 'Cabinet' or 'Canberra'. For regional office staff, the originating 'they' may be any of the above and additionally, any of the regional management networks.

As anthropologist Allen Feldman notes of conspiracy rumours locating terminus sites from which the state determines who should be assassinated in Northern Ireland, these pin-pointing ascriptions – frequently parried in everyday talk – constitute 'a reaction to the actual diffuse, capillary threading of state surveillance and power through the warp of everyday life' (1997: 29). In THS, however, it is not surveillance and intrusion that are being contested; it is the implication of being 'we', not 'they', of being the state itself, inextricably embroiled in and responsible for its operations. In the convenient separation of self from state, and the refusal of agency implied by such disavowals of initiatory responsibility, the remote area health professional and central office bureaucrat alike repeat the denials of connectivity with 'the state' (variously represented as the Commonwealth, Canberra, Central Office, management or the bureaucracy). Such denials are likewise made within anthropological circles, where state power is similarly imagined as emanating from a discrete site that remains somehow other to the critical self.

Latent within the assertive passivity of 'them' and 'they' separations lies a suppressed recognition that the state *is* the self, activated through an ensemble of micro-practices which structure the very actions of the subject who prefers the political convenience of being the object. The refusal to allow that one's own mundane practices are part of the web of governmental operation is not simply a denial of imbrication. It is also a constitutive feature of organisational framing, a necessary part of learning the vocabularies and assuming the inferential classification system that distinguishes 'here' and 'us' from 'them' and 'there' within specific work sites (see Van Maanen 1978).

Indeed, doing fieldwork with brand new health professionals less than six weeks into their exposure to THS, it was hard to ignore the striking rapidity with which the registers of regional and central office distinction (dress, comportment, problem diagnosis) were absorbed. Screen-printed T-shirts with Aboriginal motifs and/or program acronyms, combined with enraged condemnation of the emblematic 'Berrimah Line' (the imaginary barricade to information exchange and initiatory involvement between Darwin proper and the outlying THS network), were swiftly adopted perceptual coordinates marking those system radicals proclaiming identification as one who lives or goes 'out bush', from those budget-obsessed bureaucrats in Head Office suspected of not really knowing or caring about Aboriginal people.

Possibly these markers cannot be taken at face value; they deceive more than they speak. But within the new recruits' accidental – or, rather, unconscious – analysis of local marks of distinction lies a mimetic uncovering of identifiers of place that are otherwise difficult to isolate. People are literally donning forms which their intuition and observation have revealed are the markers of belonging, and it is at this moment, right at the moment of wordless apprehension, that the demarcations between 'us' and 'them' are made tangible. For beneath the clothing and formulaic complaints is a form of conceptual shorthand which reveals a more systematic set of orientations – what social geographer Rob Shields calls 'the socially maintained *reputation* of a place' (1991: 14, emphasis in original).

Coordinating uncoordination

In an effort to broach the frequently lamented divide between Head Office policy staff and their regional counterparts, networking, 'professional development' or 'in-service' events such as workshops, mini-conferences, and planned joint projects are constantly in the process of either being attended or being organised. Invariably, these have coordination of activity and information sharing listed among the stated aims:

> Welcome to our first Tiwi Health Board Newsletter designed to bring everyone up to date with the activities of the Board. We aim to make sure everyone knows what we are doing and why.
> (Opening paragraph, *Tiwi for Life* Newsletter for April 1998)

Coordination is an ambition which for years has been identified as a desired state – and lack of it has been similarly offered as an explanation for continued program failure in the Aboriginal domain. Belief in its need is endlessly reinforced by 'critical' assessments from a range of consultancy, research and advocacy sources. Following examinations of the causes of ill-health, prescriptions for organisational remedy invariably include calls for greater coordination.[4]

Yet, viewed anthropologically, the proliferation of, and intense commitment to, forms of coordination (described variously as collaboration, cooperation, networking, team-building, information sharing, joint planning, industrial democracy, group work) cannot be accounted for in such barren terms. Anthropologist of development Alexander F. Robertson, commenting on the numerous formations of junior officials from different agencies into development 'teams', attempts an alternative interpretation, arguing that such institutional forms represent:

> [an] appeal for cohesion and 'inner democratisation' across
> the base of a sprawling and compartmentalised government
> hierarchy [that] may be as much a gesture of despair as a gesture
> of optimism ... a last ditch stand against bureaucratic collapse.
> 1984: 159)

But if coordination is considered less as a desperate stand against fragmentation and more as an alive social form in its own right, the sheer scale of organisational gatherings dwarfs their original coordination purpose. Continued attempts to renew linkages ironically re-create the very situation identified as a problem in the first place: mathematically speaking, more coordination creates greater dispersion and fragmentation. *Coordination* becomes a self-sustaining end in itself. Invariably 'succeeding' in their unintended consequence of pinpointing the need for more effective coordination, even as they 'fail' their avowed coordination function, micro-niches of attempted coordination act as focal points for the repeat identification of fragmentation as a problem, to the stage where exponential liaising activities contribute to an overwhelming sense of proliferating disorder, itself requiring greater coordination to solve!

Affirming the ever-present threat of wasted effort, examples of outrageously uncoordinated activity will be exchanged in multiple settings – in meetings, evaluations, in chance conversations in the shade of a tree. The refrain 'the right hand never knows what the left is doing' becomes solidified into an information-sharing economy that compels further dispersion in the name of containment and consistency. 'Everyone descends on the community and we don't even know who's going to be there,' one public health officer announced in a public health coordination meeting in the Nhulunbuy regional office, precisely as the members present were listing each East Arnhem community and what each individually had done or was planning to do in that place.

It is difficult to convey a sense of just how omnipresent the ambition towards information dissemination and exchange under the banner of coordination is within THS. It takes form in and articulates through multiple and ongoing practices at every level of interaction, posing as both outcome and approach. The organisation as a whole disseminates written information through newsletters, electronic mail, memoranda, reports, research papers, pamphlets, articles for in-house publications, media releases, conferences and research symposia; and then accounts are exchanged through countless verbal interactions in set meetings or chance encounters in corridors, tearooms and shopping centres. Add here too the peculiar intimacy of community travels taken together and opportunistic encounters in 'the field', where helping whites congregate and swap tales.

In their capacity to be viewed both as discrete phenomena – as this *particular* meeting or *that* specific newsletter – and as an enchainment of like and proliferating forms, these ever-renewing points of connection themselves assume a fractal dimension.[5] Each attempt at 'keeping everyone in the loop' resembles, even in its local (geographic, informational, configurational) specificity, the overall shape that the never-complete (infinite) system of coordinating bureaucratic forms takes on. It also contributes to what Kim Fortun, describing her own feeling of fraudulently dispersing ethnographic knowledge in her tracking of the Bhopal environmental disaster, calls 'the aleatory effect' of information deluge: 'Sources of information vary, in reliability as well as genre. Quantifications proliferate, as do references troped as unquestionable but laced with indicators of interest and institutional rationality' (1999: 213).

This sense of deluge complements the sense THS employees have of the density of their own agency networks and the terrible complication they imagine this must present for outsiders, particularly for Aboriginal communities – a problem which further corroborates the need for more coordination. Lest the message is not osmotically absorbed through the information deluge, newcomers to THS are handed an anonymously authored chart like the following (Figure 3.1).

This image itself creates a sense of bombardment, yet looking at it, I heard people comment, 'That's not all' – they could easily expand the infinite connections behind and within each box, as each organisation

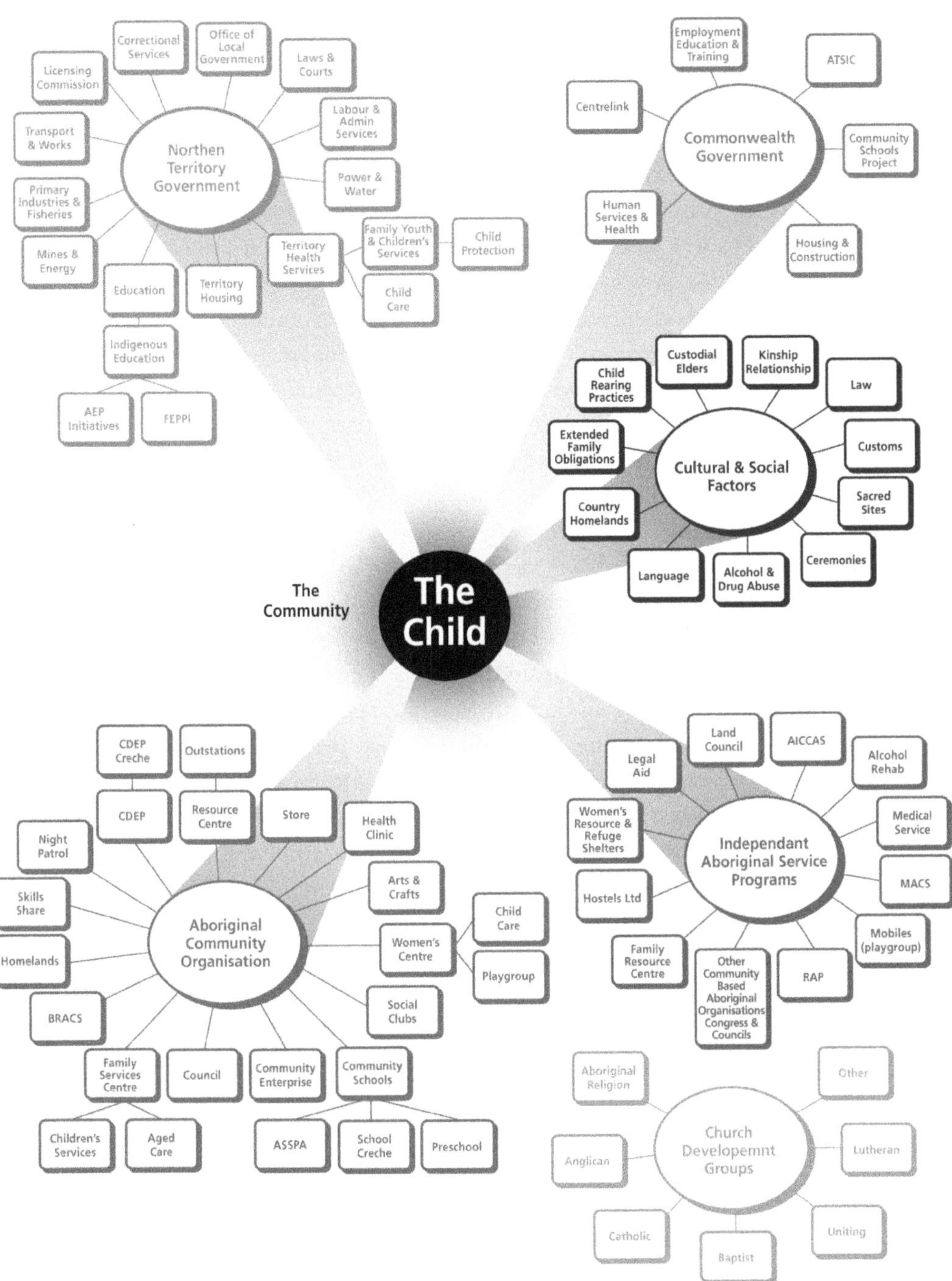

Figure 3.1 Factors affecting remote Aboriginal communities

had its own avalanche of players and programs. But then the diagram would be lost in multiple and tangled strands.

This problem of representational scale – how to make the weight of institutional proliferation visible (Strathern 1991: xiv–xv) – is itself used to prompt further analysis of the fractured and incomplete nature of bureaucratic work and of the overwhelming number of players to be considered and known. As new life is thus breathed into the incantation of the need for better coordination, the taxonomies of complexity are turned back on themselves, simultaneously perpetuating both a sense of impossibility (we can't be all things to all people) and the potential for improvement (our services need to be coordinated in the interests of efficiency and effectiveness).

The identification of fragmentation as a problem and coordination as a solution is almost perfectly infinite: almost – but not completely – self-replicating. A run of organisational restructures, plus mobile personnel (to the point where two years in any one position is seen as 'long enough'),[6] adds another dimension to coordination. Such macro and micro transformations constitute the renewable energy source of what are better called coordinations. In their concern to rapidly gain perspective on the layers they are newly enmeshed within and expected to strategically navigate, individuals who are new to tasks, topics, geographic areas or titles will alternately attend coordination events and manufacture their own. A fierce addiction to internal consultation processes, where nothing new can be contemplated without first 'workshopping' the issue with new and old powerbrokers, adds fuel to the exponential dynamic.

Whenever the density of institutional intrusion is identified as a problem, the solution is a matter of coordinating more, organising better, dovetailing approaches within and between agencies and players, thereby opening new fields of endeavour to more intense planning and integration effort. And of course coordination and collaboration, like consultation, are authoritative concepts in and of themselves, operating as unarguable tropes that can be safely deployed in summative policy-writing as words capturing the allure of deeds (action), and fixability (solution), with the added attribute of being generically inoffensive. That is to say, a call for *less coordination* is as unthinkable as calling for less community involvement.[7]

Yet it is the treacherous politics of coordination that goes a long way towards explaining how public health orthodoxies are reproduced among people who are otherwise independent thinkers. There is no conspiracy at the centre. In Mosse's words, 'policy models do not generate practices, they are sustained *by* them' (2005: 182, emphasis in original).

Navigating the network

As the Northern Territory's capital, Darwin also serves as the administrative and networking base for a large range of authorities and industries, each with its own bureaucracy and layers of coordination and information flow. Many of these organisations receive substantial grants from THS, which extends the reach of service availability beyond the organisation's limits while broadening responsibility for rationing through multiple intermediaries (see Preston, Chua & Neu 1997). While these linked extensions are not represented on corporate charts as part of the organisation, it is expected that staff will form alliances and collaborative networks with the many others who might have an interest in or an overlapping responsibility with their work, necessitating ongoing and daily 'liaison' activities.

For all middle-ranking officers and higher, such work takes place in formal committees, task groups and official working parties, membership of which reflects one's standing and authority. Liaison activities are usually face-to-face, in expressly purposeful but formally agenda-less meetings.[8] It needs noting here that while there are titled, salaried and ranked grades and different classificatory streams (professional, administrative, technical, medical, executive, executive contract, and so forth) within the health bureaucracy, the politics of rank, repute and renown within each classification is more permeable, transient and less sequential than the nominal hierarchy implies.

One means of placing an iodine trace on the unofficial reporting lines and the invisible matrices of status and authority they reflect is to capture their operation in the spaces of the brokenly said and tacitly decided. People continually sound each other out as part of the work of their frequent encounters, to glean other officer characteristics and fealties. Let me illustrate by quick example.

During a discussion commissioned to analyse budget figures, a completely separate and minor new project was hatched in an aside to the routine finance talk, together with a preliminary assessment of who might qualify to lead the project if it eventuated. 'What about Eliza? Could she manage that?' asked one manager of the other about a more junior project officer known to them both. Quickly assessing the meaning and intent of the snuffled grimace and modest shoulder shrug of the responder, the inquiring manager seamlessly echoed the wordless rejection: 'No? Yeah, no, I agree, she's a good marketer, but not one to lead strategy.' And so, in the continual trade of exchanges estimating people's capacities and situation-specific worthiness, Eliza's fitness was at once assembled and disassembled without need for reference to 'objective' criteria or further investigation.

The official status of these prompt-response floats of speculation and innuendo is interactively negotiated. It could be that an idea or decision needs to be documented 'for the record', in which case it will be taken to an authorising body for a recorded, technically official response that can be subsequently represented as the outcome of a more 'transparent' procedure. Formal rank and representative function matter in these authorising spaces most of all, for of course bureaucratic work cannot proceed without the sanction of those who are literally entitled to 'sign off'. But members of the organisation must also apprehend *unstated* webs of authority and influence if they are to successfully navigate their own systems.

Within each and every project there is a core and a marginal stakeholder community. With the exception of people in the hierarchical positions documented in organisational charts, these alternative matrices index ephemeral locations as people travel the structure and as projects change. And just as the relative fitness of individuals can be (re)arranged through casual diagnosis, so too are the attributes of representatives from other organisations. Even the status of entire geographic areas and categories of people may be reassessed in casual exchange. The Education Department is a 'real old boys club, straight out of Moresby'; the Aboriginal settlement of Numbulwar on the Arnhem coast 'is really turning things around with the new community health nurse there, she's working really well with the elders, they have some strong leaders there'; the young lads in Wadeye, a community southwest of Darwin which distils the essence of dysfunction in bureaucratic talk, 'need our help – they're bored, they use Don Dale as a new rite of passage'.[9]

Weaving tangled webs

To appreciate the complexity of the THS organisational structure as it is enacted every day in official and unofficial information retrieval, consultation and reporting circuits, consider the following brief case study, drawn from the dispersed array of activities assembled under the program title 'Environmental Health'.

In 1994, the former Commonwealth-funded Aboriginal and Torres Strait Islander Commission (ATSIC) established the Health Infrastructure Priority Projects (HIPP) scheme. HIPP specifically targeted large-scale housing and infrastructure requirements (such as roads, water and power supplies, effluent disposal systems) considered to be too large for any lone community to finance. The scheme also aimed to be a complete environmental health intervention: it intended to improve Aboriginal health by attending to living conditions and ensuring less overcrowding; by developing more appropriately designed and durable housing; by arranging for safe water and sewage disposal; and by organising reliable power supplies. Importantly, the program also incorporated the training of Aboriginal people in correct infrastructure maintenance techniques to ensure ongoing sustainability of the installations. Finally, the scheme had an avowed coordination function: from the outset, the program was to be resourced through shared funding and servicing arrangements between state governments, the Commonwealth and other industry partners.

NT Government officials had successfully appealed to this coordination ambition when, in 1996, they organised a cross-agency submission for funding – itself a triumph of coordination and hasty meetings. In their submission, policy officers argued the Territory's case for the lion's share of the available national funding (see THS 1995), claiming a backlog of $1 billion of the estimated $4 billion required to solve the problem nation-wide. To justify this, officers relied on the classification of Aboriginal spaces as arenas of dire ill-health, a situation they attributed to the vast unmet demand for housing and amenities. This, they argued, would require urgent national funding to remedy.

The submission was further able to depend on the known biases of its southern administrative readership. Well acquainted with imagining Aboriginal domains as 'the space of alterity itself' (Stewart 1996: 67), southerners most often imagine Aboriginal communities in the frontier north as deeply distressed and historically ravaged, replete with makeshift corrugated iron humpies, beds of moth-eaten blankets piled in the dirt, shared with half-alive worm-infested dogs. Or southerners might imagine tumble-down two-room huts, built badly in mission and welfare times, and despised by contemporary advocates because of their evocation of a paternalistic yesteryear when the people weren't consulted about housing design or sympathetically given skills in how to maintain the new facilities (see Heppel 1979). Playing to this, it was easy for NT officials to justify their need for the lion's share. Given the small size of the NT Government's administrative network – and its (purportedly) consequent 'agility' – they were also able to claim superior capacity *to coordinate.*

Fast forward now to the point where the money has been 'won'. ATSIC decided to allocate over half the available national bucket ($48 million from $80.43 million) to the Northern Territory, and contracted engineering and architectural firms as project managers (with a preference of course for Aboriginal organisations) to install housing and infrastructure in remote area communities. As part of its coordination promise in its original submission, the NT Government had promised that it would evaluate the impact of the infrastructure investments on people's health (ATSIC 1995: 153).

As THS was the lead agency responsible for health, it established a steering committee to follow through on this coordination promise. Nearly 18 months into the life of the committee, however, the issue of how to conduct the promised evaluation had become a standing agenda item, and attending members were increasingly impatient with the circular skirmishes and indecision provoked by debate over the evaluation design and focus. Delays were also caused by the irregularity of formal committee meetings, as the participation of certain people was deemed essential – their frequent cancellations were thus both a reason for rescheduling and a way of signalling their precedence as high-status, terribly pressed officers (see Schwartzman 1989). The mounting tensions between committee members started to become explicit, and there was increasing pressure to 'produce a result' after so much 'fucking around'. At the same time, the project officer originally assigned to coordinate the evaluation effort became increasingly regarded as inadequate to the task; however, other potential candidates for the job were quickly dismissed as shorthanded and overworked.

Given the relentless pursuit of closure that bureaucratic operations are typified as seeking, the scene was set for an enthusiastic researcher from THS' Alice Springs office to propose a way forward.

Switch to Central Australia: After a period of months during which she ferreted out as much information as she could about the national and local intricacies of the HIPP scheme, and held intensive negotiation and coordination meetings with her regional office counterparts to garner their support for what was really a non-assigned piece of work dreamt up in Darwin, Gwen Mark, an epidemiologist with no prior involvement in HIPP activities, but inspired by its aims, put together a comprehensive evaluation proposal. She had worked long hours into many nights piecing the proposal together – balancing the wording inputs of contributors from both the THS regional office and NGOs in Central Australia to finally produce a generically acceptable text. In the context of the steering committee's evaluation impasse, Gwen's proposal was a breakthrough.

Moreover, much of the negotiation work for its implementation was already complete. Gwen had already approached two recently renovated communities earmarked[10] for the evaluation proper and received favourable preliminary responses. Candidates from the Alice Springs project team nominated to actually conduct the evaluation had not only indicated their availability to take on the extra work but had also been vetted and found suitable by the appropriate players during quick reputation exchanges. A regional committee had even been established, with representatives from the other NT Government agencies based in Alice Springs. As Gwen described it, the committee would 'coordinate agency input and ensure [that] the proposed new database does not duplicate any existing information sets'.

As if this wasn't already supreme effort enough, as icing on the cake, Gwen had discovered a mechanism for salvaging the evaluation funds set aside by the Darwin steering committee: arranging their transfer to an incorporated body. This would ensure that annual budget claw-backs of unspent monies – a real threat in this project after so much planning delay – did not now impose an impossible timeframe on the proposed evaluation.[11] Thus, all key elements had been accounted for, and the evaluation proposal only needed official endorsement by the steering committee, the next evaluative transit point for Gwen's near-final text, to let the project commence at last.

But unexpectedly, a complaint was received by one of two THS executive representatives on the steering committee. A senior ATSIC manager (remember, ATSIC was in Canberra) wanted to know why someone unknown to ATSIC, some junior woman from THS, purportedly from Alice Springs, had contacted the National Audit Office in Canberra 'demanding' the terms of reference for a project the Office of Audit was not even undertaking, namely, an audit of HIPP. ATSIC were, it transpired, undertaking a routine internal administrative review of their program, a review that was of no concern to either the National Audit Office or to THS, but somehow in Gwen's networking, she had garbled the connections and her quest to coordinate evaluation efforts had gone off on a confused tangent. Worse yet, the engineering company ATSIC had commissioned to oversee all their projects was also complaining: they said a woman called 'Gwen' has been asking for data they were not sure she – unvouched for, unknown and a bit too strident and pushy for their liking – should have. 'By whose authority is she seeking information?' they asked. 'And what do you [THS senior officers] want them [ATSIC's consultants] to say to her?'

In the flurry of sorting through the chain of small misunderstandings, Gwen's previously admired pro-activity was now 'out of line', her intelligent pursuit of background information a breach of delicate protocols. In that breach, she had unintentionally executed an ever-so-slight impugning of the management acumen of the two executive managers on the THS steering committee, who felt co-implicated by her lack of finesse. So, when an advance copy of Gwen's hard-worked near-final draft of the evaluation proposal was faxed through from Alice Springs for pre-assessment and review – a standard vetting practice designed to remove surprises from formal steering committee considerations – three of the more senior committee members, including the chair, met to informally discuss how 'to rein Gwen back into line'.

Switch to Darwin: During this smaller, more task-focused, gathering of decision-makers, Gwen's draft proposal was pedantically analysed, line by line. A section detailing how 'any change in community perceptions of quality of life' would be quantitatively measured was isolated for special attack. Like her, it 'went too far'. It was intrusive, the select group said. It didn't respect Aboriginal people's privacy; it 'assume[d] "quality of life" [wa]s a shared cultural concept'. Finally, they concurred that it would be 'far too risky' to permit the fraught activity of what amounted to 'psychological testing', so dangerously akin to the 'head measuring' colonial researchers used to inflict on Aboriginal people, to proceed in the hands of a yes, well-intentioned, but let's face it, essentially inexpert regional officer.

While the rest of the proposal was deemed roughly acceptable, the judges agreed that the problematic section on quality of life should be refused funding and then removed. Moreover, the wording of her draft could not be endorsed: as sign of their disapproval, the group insisted on painstaking re-editing and re-submittal. Finally, in order to ensure that 'the politics are better managed in future', it was decided that someone from Health House would be put on Gwen's proposed project team 'to keep an eye on things'. Gwen would also be instructed to invite a member of the Alice Springs ATSIC regional office to participate (a friend of one of the three), 'to ensure good information flow'.

Historical containment

As this brief description of project politics suggests, there is an inherent instability to both reputation and alliances; and sticky aspects to coordination that enmesh as much as they transmit information. Before the evaluation even got going, Gwen's project team was recombined, precipitated by a mishandling so subtle Gwen may never know what sin she committed. She is now judged well-meaning and bright, but undependably naïve. She 'needs to be managed' – a typical description of any over-enthusiastic regional project officer – in this case one who has elicited negative attention from other organisations (formal offence) and who does not know that the National Audit Office should not be approached by a relatively junior regional officer (informal offence). That is, she failed to accurately apprehend and uphold the tacit reputational order.

As it is recorded in the minutes and presented to the full steering committee (who are ignorant both of the complaints and of the subsequent mini-meeting and are thus still enthusiastic supporters of that keen officer in Alice who seemed so on the ball), the clipping of the proposal was framed as necessary for different reasons entirely. The component on quality of life was removed 'for the moment', because first, it was more complex than the other proposed evaluation tasks, and second, decisions on the overall plan were required urgently. As the Chair framed it for committee members, the basis for deferring the 'quality of life' measurement:

> ... at the moment is that we need to make a decision very quickly, at least on the bulk of the proposed study, which is relatively uncomplicated – though people may have comments that they want to make on it – so [let's] get on with that. It is rather less complex than the quality of life area which will probably involve a bit more discussion with more agencies at a higher level. It doesn't mean it's been dropped, it means it's been taken off this particular proposal for the purpose of this particular meeting. (Meeting transcript, 21 April 1998)

Tellingly, the aesthetic of right and wrong regarding Aboriginal people, so potently wielded in the pre-committee dissection of Gwen's faxed proposal, disappeared from view in the steering committee meeting proper, camouflaged under a rubric of strategic priority (quick decisions on the bulk) and the need for more senior inter-agency liaison. This reframing both preserves a sense of mutuality with regard to producing joint practical actions within the committee – they can discuss all aspects of the proposal, except just this one part, and even this pause is ever so temporary – and endows the action with an organisational logic that can be recorded in the minutes (Gumperz & Cook-Gumperz 1982: 146, 150).

For of course, as we have seen, minutes, like every other form of official documentation, are collectively agreed scripts which come to be so agreed by a proper engineering of a specific collectivity in which agreement itself makes and breaks alliances. Such documents must achieve a coalition character and anticipate the possibility of future scrutiny while smoothing over and writing out the more discordant performances that actually occur in meetings. Banality, we will recall, is a hard-worked and essential requirement of institutional texts.

Despite the implication wrought by its very absence, the Chair has further determined to disallow an explicit use of prescriptions about what is right or not for Aboriginal people – while it was so successfully flourished within the powerful 'mini-meeting', it could spiral into a new contest here. Without saying anything, for there is much tacit social knowledge pulsing through such ordered occasions, the Chair knows that a discussion on the politics of Aboriginal sensitivities would open space for competitive displays of intimate and superior knowledge about the Other and diminutive tests of loyalty within the steering committee. In other words, it would create opportunities for rupture that only much more talk work could close, as opposed to the neat elision offered by the more procedural argument the Chair in fact puts for the committee's formal consideration (see Boden 1994). Trading on a different rationale in the committee meeting proper thus ensures that a clean rebuke of Gwen takes place in the defensible guise of a quick decision to proceed; a progression which cannot be easily contested in the context of months of procrastination and indecision. But in its covertness, the invocation of cultural (in)appropriateness reveals the intensity of its import as a transactional tool for bureaucratic decision-making, authorising some actions and denying legitimacy to others. Indeed, as we will see, the intricacies of asserting authority in relation to knowing specific Aboriginal people and speaking about their generic needs and desires, forms the lifeblood of reputation damage and sustenance within public health webs of opinion formation and classification.

Conclusion

The work of creating the look of rational progress is not done only by policy formulators, PR folk or 'management'. Rather, it is a voluntary technique of perpetuation, unconsciously learnt through experiencing little checks and stonewalls and forming networks of affiliation. Such forms of patrimonial bureaucracy show up in a range of institutional settings.

As it transpired, in both of the communities eventually evaluated for the health impact of infrastructure improvements, non-Aboriginal expatriate residents were found to monopolise the most functional and least crowded houses. But the story about poor Gwen Marks, ubiquitous and real, also shows the uses of history in the everyday of the said and the unsayable. Though the players do not admit to what they are doing in claiming to purge Gwen's research proposal of its assumed traumatic, if unstated and unintended, resemblance to the head-counting and brain-measuring practices of our colonial forebears, we do not need much in the way of historical detail about such practices for their efficacy as indictment to work.

Lived out daily, these historical and cultural abstractions are the raw material for the tacit little acts of semiotic damage that people in THS enact on each other's work, while executing reputation maintenance and disassembly. In this instance, the factoid historical references to such inarguably denounceable acts as head-measuring lend their weight to the need to appear industrious and ethically concerned as Gwen's administrative slap is plotted. At every step, the reasonableness of proceedings is executed perfectly.

PART II

ABSORBING and DELIVERING

LEARNING THE ARTS OF HELPING

This chapter is driven by the beguilingly simple question underlying this whole book. How does one learn to do and say bureaucratic things? As it seems so simple, the question lends itself to a deceptively easy answer. Adopting the orthodoxies of social scientific judgment, it's all simply a matter of complicity. Ingratiating bureaucrats readily adopt the stances required of them if they are to be regarded as competent or worthy in the eyes of important superiors (see Jackall 1988, Kunda 1992, Munro 1999). They will act and speak in organisationally acceptable ways. They will knowingly contrive acceptable arguments or affect displays of loyalty to issues of the moment, performing as expected while evincing ironic distance, exactly fitting the complicit disposition. Equally, bureau-speak can be glossed as 'jargon', and viewed as constituting its own world of circumscribed disclosure, comprehensible to an inner sanctum alone. In such closed spaces of self-fulfilling and self-generating organisational forms and language codes, the argument so easily goes, bureaucrats simply do whatever it takes to achieve the *effect* of indispensability (Apthorpe 1985: 91–93).[1]

Given the ethnographic material presented thus far, it is a difficult conclusion to contradict. Rather than rejecting conformity as an explanation, then, this chapter takes the puzzle of conformity and institutional socialisation as its core questions. As well, it grapples with the need to account for the tremendous speed with which the performative aspects of public health interaction are both imbibed and reproduced, to the point where newcomers are able to mimic bodily dispositions and clothing styles, and cite key words, stories and anti/institutionalisms within a few short weeks of their starting in the organisation. While such identity markers are clearly organisationally produced, they are not included in the formal content of induction materials, nor are they open to the explicit control of managers – much to their regret. It is as if a public health sensorium is developed in spite of, whilst clearly also informed by, formal processes of bureaucratic knowledge transfer. 'Conformity' might not be of participants' choice, but it is certainly of their making ...

Three unique devices are key to this speedy transmission: first, the fact that public health is a talking profession, attuned to endless bouts of professional reflexivity and introspection; second, the ubiquity of workshops as a device for group discussion, together with the interpellating effect of such 'neutral' technologies as whiteboards and butcher's paper; and third, the surprising role played by anthropological knowledge in creating the tension-filled and adversarial yet terribly polite circumstances in which institutional knowledges are auto-policed and reproduced.

Device 1: The work of talk in talk of work

The first clue for understanding institutional socialisation lies in the fact that public health is both an intensely earnest and an intensely verbalising profession, where people like to 'think through' things in groups. A number of accounts of the talk work that takes place in workplace gatherings focus on their constituting function,[2] but this book also shows that acquiring an eye for the look of a thing, an ear for its sound, is informed by but *transcends* the specific content of spoken words. People come to comprehend the operating rules of professional public health deportment beyond the explicit instructions they may receive in formal induction programs and guidelines, beyond the words (see Wikan 1994), without disregarding the effect of specific and explicit instructions on how to act and be. (This is of course what happens in any similar group, reminding us once again that the bureaucracy is peopled.)

The realm of understandings that exceed explicit rules is also the preoccupation of anthropologist Michael Taussig (1999), who is concerned to evoke the 'more' in social life that defies codification but is no less intimately understood for being mute. We might understand this 'more' as the realm of the tacit and intuited, as life lived outside the ambit of words or reflection, either because it is so automatic and habitual that it has passed into non-reflection, or because it is what people intimately and intricately learn without ever articulating directly (what linguistic anthropologists term, awkwardly, 'silential relations' (Becker 1996: 143)). As socio-linguists John Gumperz and Jenny Cook-Gumperz put it:

> The very constraints under which individuals communicate favor
> the emergence of strategies governing what is to be put into
> words, how it is to be made salient, and what can be left unsaid.
> Over time, these strategies tend to become conventionalised
> and to become part of the standards by which effectiveness is
> judged. *Such conventions can only be learned through face-to-face
> interaction.* (1982: 162, emphasis added)

Device 2: The forcefulness of workshops

Workshops are a powerful form of bureaucratic immersion enabling just the type of tacitly rule-bound face-to-face interactions that allow participants to quickly and smoothly imbibe the conventions of public health.[3] Once associated with the fixing of machines, now a new form of mechanical practices are implicit in participation in a 'workshop'. At any given moment in the THS network, any number of workshops will be taking place, and each will exert forceful claims on how people narrate, write, comport and analyse. Workshops are potent because of the democratic and inclusive ways in which they police and silence. They are by nature and design intensely participatory and emotionally draining. Participants *must* participate – but workshops' deliberately structured and oppressively friendly *inclusivity* makes them almost impossible to disrupt with aberrant remarks or recalcitrant behaviour. More, because they are designed to appear as sites where people can disclose freely, the ways in which participants constrain, shape and censor each other is almost analytically invisible. It is, frankly, hard to bring to the surface the leaden weight of orthodoxy in situations which seem fractured by – and in fact ostensibly encourage – fierce debate, questioning, emotive reflexivity, non-hierarchical discussion and heated participation.

Device 3: Anthropology as censuring device

The third dynamic propelling quick learning relates to the describing of Aboriginal problems, almost always a feature of THS exchanges. Here, traces of anthropological knowledges inflect THS talk work, presenting first as conventions of fact and solution and second as the basis for subtly competitive displays of intimate knowledge about the Other. Beyond their general drenching in Australia's foundational racial codes, anthropological 'truths' are also deployed as a managerial device, assisting new fieldworkers to interpret their early field experiences and direct their enthusiasms and initial perceptions in certain ways. With anthropologised knowledges as authorising capital, newcomers are helped to adopt the particularities of 'how we view things around here'. Correctness about Aboriginal issues, backed by the authenticity of one's own ethnographic experiences – the 'being there' factor – is a powerful instrument for establishing a reputation as an expert within THS.

Professionals thus join anthropological theorists in conscripting ethnographic experience into professional social capital, making an interpersonal resource out of classifications of cultural alterity, at the same time as their ethnographic persona becomes a role to be managed through correct rules of engagement. Now, for anthropologists, the most outstanding initial feature of how their wisdom circulates in the helping professions is how fixed and definitive their more contextual, provisional and disputed knowledges have become. So where, for example, an anthropologist such as Basil Sansom might make a complex and provisional argument about how Aboriginal people use words as currency,[4] this nuanced argument is then presented as a codified cultural fact in THS, transformed into a more stark identity difference and definitive rule to act by: Aboriginal people do not like to be asked direct questions, so be advised to approach issues gingerly, in a roundabout fashion.[5]

But it is not only that anthropologisms become didactic instruments of institutional socialisation. In THS, 'learning the ropes' also means learning to handle and deploy the subtle and imaginative ways in which colleagues diagnose, treat and police each other's ethnographic slippages and inadequacies, within a seemingly supportive and yet, it transpires, highly coercive framework of industrial democracy and professional collegiality.

A small example will illustrate this transformation of ethnography into a precondition of bureaucratic practice and a phenomenon thereof, showing all three of our learning devices in play.

Learning the arts of bureau-anthropologic display

In a large conference room in Nhulunbuy, 640 kilometres from Darwin, all the East Arnhem Regional Office representatives of public health have gathered for a fortnightly coordination meeting. Like so many such gatherings before and after, the meeting is at once a routine, practical matter – health professionals need to coordinate their travel activities to reduce overlap and unnecessary expense – and a powerful mix of subtle and blunt techniques of bureaucratic absorption. In this part of the meeting, the Chair, in structural terms an equal peer to those assembled, is calling out the names of regional communities from Milingimbi to Umbakumba one by one, eliciting group advice on the general 'tone' of the community and commentary on visits, either planned or just transpired.

After two hours of recounting, we are finally down to the last community, Nhulunbuy itself, the main service centre for the East Arnhem region. Xavier, a relative newcomer to the Territory, and respectfully silent to this point, shyly mentions a community development committee he has been working on, but struggles to remember the name of an Aboriginal man who seems to be a particularly noteworthy committee member: 'not Gatjil but someone other'. A team member helpfully prompts with 'Merrilin?' but Xavier shakes his head, and, clarifying, adds, 'No, it was a man, not a woman.' The others look at each other, lean back in their chairs and guffaw. Releasing Xavier from his bewilderment, we are told Merrilin *is* a man, not a woman! Xavier, blushing, waves his hand dismissively in the air. 'Oh, whatever,' he says. Not willing to let the cultural faux pas slip by so easily, the pedantic Chair stills the laughter in the room, splaying the outward palm of his hand to the assembly, elbow on the table, building a second of silence before saying in a deepened, laughter-halting tone: 'There is some important history for you to know about him. Last year, his son was caught drinking and driving and was told off. He [the son] went home and shot himself.'

His neck turning from pink to white to red with the ignominy of being found so comprehensively ignorant, Xavier dropped his eyes to the table, crushed. 'Oh,' he quietly demurred, in the now sombre room.

It is in such slender moments of humiliation that newcomers like Xavier learn, through the powerful tutelage of shaming, both the appropriate disposition of the novice and the kinds of grammar required to signal true familiarity with and competency to talk about Aboriginal people – how, in other words, to demonstrate that you are someone in the know, the right kind of white. A cascade of limits on how and what can be said buffets down on Xavier's bowed head as he learns an excruciating lesson in the poetics of knowing.

Yet, just as importantly for learning, what unites Xavier to the group at his point of acutely felt excision, as he sits immersed in what he later told me was an exquisite if momentary agony of heightened self-consciousness – the sounds of the room as the meeting resumed echoing as hollow noises, far away and barely registered – what bonds him to the others is being positioned to speak about absent Aborigines. Beyond the time-slowing, heightened sensory impact of his minor public shaming, in other words, the meeting re-establishes an absolute distance between those who can know and those who are known (Fabian 1983, cf. Said 1985). More, it shows that to be 'in the know', one has to have command of key pieces of information, or ethnographic capital. Knowing what confers authority, and what is irrelevant to that task, are ciphers that Xavier will quickly absorb; his speed of learning accelerated by the acute professional fear of being shown to be ignorant, with any failure to absorb the lessons a signification of his inadequacies as someone who has 'what it takes' to deal with Aboriginal people.

As this small case study illustrates, upholding the existing order of things in public health is simultaneously an explicit and an elusive process. It is not maintained, as crude theories of state power might have it, through acts of institutional brainwashing and indoctrination, but through seemingly provisional and emergent co-constructions such as these, where work narratives, facts, gossip, humour and mortification are constitutive elements of the assembly. Such talk work, and the texts devised out of such talk work, precede, shape and are reaffirmed by the embodied interactions health professionals have in more remote locations, when they hit 'the field' and visit communities. Co-performed and interactive, bureau-professional forms of anthropology play a key role in THS shaping processes, not only as a form of expertise in figuring the native's point of view and how best to comport oneself in relation to that knowledge (on which more below), but as a critical element in the politics of silencing and display, of slighting and showing.

Merrilin, maybe the committee man, maybe not, father of a dead son anyway, a son made suicidal from being told off, by whom we never get to know, for such a wee adolescent thing, drink driving. What do our panel members make of these fragments? For the beginnings of an answer, let's turn to the official THS induction process, where newcomers are immersed in the formal and informal logics of both the organisation and the problem of representing one's knowledge about Aborigines in a concentrated adult education forum.

We're here to learn

As a result of a hard-won policy pushed by advocates tired of seeing new staff arriving in communities with no sense of what they should do or of how they should do it, all newcomers to THS who plan to work in a regional office or in a community development capacity are required to undertake the THS Remote Area Orientation Course. In the program outline, drip-fed to us by a facilitator so frightened of any speed-reading that he strategically shielded the full text with a piece of paper, the orientation course aims to develop:

» Team working
» Two-way learning and cultural awareness
» Cross-cultural partnerships ('A key if we are going to work effectively out in the bush,' the facilitator takes a moment to stress)
» Primary health care
» Reflections on experiences ('It is critical during the next two weeks that people share ideas and swap stories so we can learn from one another')
» A realistic view ('Right now the picture of Aboriginal health is not great, so we are trying to be as realistic as possible about

what we can achieve and about what our limitations are').

Day 1, and Bob Spicer and Julie Nelson, our pastoral guides for the next fortnight, watch over their latest batch of neophytes as we settle at one of four evenly spaced out hexagonal tables. Colourful posters featuring Aboriginal subjects at play and work adorn the walls, proclaiming 'Reconciliation', 'Bush Tucker' and 'Land is Life', but their transfixed animation is unable to boost the drab effect of the streaky pastel green linoleum floor and ancient beige walls that still mark this room as a former hospital dormitory.

We are assembled for a formal introduction to THS and its expectations of our remote area health work with Aboriginal people: me, somewhat fraudulently as ethnographer; others because as doctors, nurses, nutritionists and communicable disease specialists, they have real work to do. On each table, navy and black whiteboard markers jostle alongside a roll of blank white stickers. These fragile structures sit on top of information folders, headed 'Let's work together to fill the gaps', water-marked underneath with a honeycomb design and a bumble bee: a mnemonic, we will learn, for the holistic, coordinated approach we must adopt if we're to remove the discrepancy between the health status of non-Indigenous and that of Indigenous Australians.

Despite our novice status, our trainee impulses have us cueing off each other to write our names in large print on the stickers, decorating our chests with the self-identification; small habitual acts we carry out without being told to as we await the instructor's first words. As our murmurs and movements still, an expectant silence marks the session's beginning: 'I think you all know that my name is Bob Spicer. Can we spend a moment now just introducing who we are – starting from this table?'[6]

House rules are specified – or rather, in the first of a series of inveiglings which commit members to the labour of participation (Goffman 1971), house rules are co-formulated. 'Give each other room to move and space to make comments,' Bob's co-presenter Julie begins, sweeping her eyes over the audience. 'Is that OK, is that reasonable?' (nods and murmured uh-huhs). 'If anyone here has mobile phones or beepers, can you explain for others how you are going to manage them?' Katrina, a doctor at my table, the one who will later in the course avow her love of unripe cheeky plums on our way to hunt for mudcrabs (Chapter 1), says she will take herself outside and answer any calls out of hearing.

'Be punctual' (pause). 'Anything else, anybody? Does that sound reasonable?' (no disagreement).

'The last thing is the evaluation sheets. We will be handing these out each day and it is really important that you fill them in honestly. We know everyone groans about evaluation, but we regard this program as unfinished. We are always working on it to improve it and make it of real use for people, so we really need your feedback, OK? We will be giving you a summary at the end of the two weeks of what you reckon, OK?'

And so it went, some small rituals to begin our institutional ritual[7] of the penultimate anthropological ritual, the initiation ceremony: not so much a triumph of disorder to remould initiates into new forms of being (Turner 1982: 42–48) as an immersion in gentle tedium, where rules will be honoured in the breach. There are latecomers every day, certain presenters will not show, key questions are not answered, and at every table there is at least one dominating speaker silencing others. Not that any of this will be reported in our daily evaluation sheets, for the type of honesty required of us concerns only 'constructive' summaries of what we learnt and which session worked best. Already there is much that we know about what not to show and what merits a note in these supposedly unfettered accounts of our learning.

By Day 5, we've endured a long first week of the THS Remote Area Orientation boot-camp. We have toured the hospital, including the Cowdy Ward for mental health patients, and we've hunted for mudcrabs and mangrove worms, walked long in the hot sun and eaten gritty damper at Shoal Bay. We have received visits from a bewildering number of THS program representatives, all of whom have given us listings of the multiple phone numbers and position titles in their respective work areas, and urged the criticality of networking and coordination to the effectiveness of our function. The once empty pockets in our handy introductory kits now bulge with essential contacts and program descriptions, admitting us to the staggering interdependencies, the enchainment of like and proliferating institutional forms we are urged to work within and against, creating virtual communication lines to supplement official information flows. It will be our own fault if we keep ourselves in the dark:

There is always capacity for moving things through the

organisation – you just have to know what they are and how to
do it. The other reason why it is good to know the structure, to
have structure in the first place, is to have clear direction and lines
of responsibilities. Everybody has a right to information about
who they are in the system and who they report to. People have
a right to be managed. But the structures do not eliminate the
peer support and communication lines between people. **Use them**
... There should be some mechanism for you to find out what is
going on – if you ever find yourself operating in a void, complain
loudly and do something about it. There's no excuse for being a
mushroom. (Visiting Senior Manager to the Orientation)

Representatives from Health House, 30 minutes' drive and a world
of abstract managerial principles away, have taken us through the
Corporate Plan and its five key strategic directions, stressing health's
business realities. Government's dominance of service provision – soon
to be represented as an anachronistic mode of organisation for THS in
Strategy 21 – here still innocently marks this place as unique. Unlike
other jurisdictions, which have extensive private and not-for-profit
corporations defraying the direct cost to government of health service
provision, in THS, the managers tell us, we are spread more thinly:

> When people come to the Territory, they bring with them an idea
> that health is the summation of individual episodes of care and
> that your job is to provide excellent quality within your discrete
> realm of expertise. It is a reasonable point of view when you are
> well resourced and have good infrastructure and other service
> groups and private providers [are] around to support you. But a
> different scenario exists up here. Services are spread more thinly
> and clients are more needy and it requires stepping back and
> trying to organise services for clients in a more systematic way.
> You either directly service clients or provide services to those that
> do. Everyone falls into one or another category – no ifs, buts or
> maybes. Either way your job is to do the best you can. (Senior
> Manager, Orientation)

We have been urged to strive continuously to seek ways of doing more
with less; to see Aboriginal people as our clients who deserve a quality
customer service; and to simultaneously view ourselves as the most
important resources the organisation has. Promoting 'creative energy and
productivity in our workplace' is critical, managers assure us, because:

> Without being trite, the asset THS has is in people's heads. To
> revive some Marxist terminology, the means of production is in
> people's brains, not their hands – so we never know if they're on
> strike or not!

Now, on the afternoon of Day 5, reiterating the orientation's motif
theme on the heroic qualities required for work in Aboriginal health,
Bob Spicer is keen that we comprehend and thereby exercise greater
control over our personal limitations, 'because you don't really know
what's going on in [Aboriginal] communities and your desire to get
something rolling isn't enough in itself. You have to deal with your lack
of power.'

Approaching the electronic whiteboard, Bob asks that we 'look now
at why we would want to do this work, what draws us to it. What are the
"Good Things" and what are the "Challenges"?' The session generates
a lot of discussion among people now familiar with each other and the
rhythm of our workshop interactions. As people speak, Bob captures
their observations in bullet points on the whiteboard. Responding to
the initial call for Good Things, one participant suggests:

> Hopping onto the plane and leaving Darwin behind always gives
> me a good feeling – it's just the total opposite to the eastern part
> of Australia, you're not fighting the traffic, the timeframes are so
> much more relaxed, you go through magnificent landscapes.

Bob captions on the whiteboard:

»   leaving town

Then onto the negatives:

> The split from service delivery makes research difficult and the
> antipathies between different THS service providers – well, it just
> makes me tired.

Bob writes:

»   fatigue

> I feel frustrated being seen as a service deliverer, as a doctor first,
> there only to see sick people. All I see are people with pus, with
> sores. As a visitor I cannot spend time with people working on
> more chronic issues.

<table>
<tr><td>

Good things

- » enjoy challenge
- » big learning experience
- » learning about Aboriginal culture
- » nine-to-five routine
- » the people
- » leaving town
- » autonomy

</td><td>

Challenges

- » fatigue
- » lack of continuity
- » lack of coordination
- » inability to work up programs
- » workload
- » lack of power
- » not feeling valued
- » isolation
- » lack of opportunity for relationship development
- » lack of time
- » lack of debriefing opportunities
- » need to network

</td></tr>
</table>

Figure 4.1 Good things and challenges

Bob writes:

> » inability to work up programs

> And the trauma for the families is unreal. I take it out on my kids. I found it really, really hard … I would come back from field trips when I first started and I was so frustrated and depressed at the levels of sickness and feeling powerless to deal with it, depressed that I was not affecting anything. And I would take it out on my kids; abuse them for being so privileged. I really coped very badly. I couldn't talk to my husband for at least the first hour after I got back. I would have to take myself out of the house, go for a walk, go to the gym, something … It was so hard.

Another member chimes in:

> I would agree with that. It took me at least a day to get over bush trips here – and I have never had that experience in any of the places I have worked – not even Africa.

Bob writes:

»   lack of debriefing opportunities

and then takes the opportunity to elaborate the point:

> You can't lay it on your family – the amount of illness and death
> – you come home, you're tired from going out bush, and your
> partner can't bear your load. But the Department is not going to
> solve it for you: you have to. So what are some strategies?

A participant obliges with a handy hint for making an organisational
burden a private coping task:

> On a personal level, at Umbakumba, we forged really strong
> relationships among the teachers and other [white] residents. And
> now I think that is important too.

Bob writes:

»   need to network

The point about dot points

While the condensations clearly missed the richness of what people
were enunciating, nobody much minded, for in a sense the workshop
was the debriefing session, admissions of failure tumbling one after the
other, outranking by far the humble good things. The doctor's powerful
articulation of powerlessness – so traumatised by her own failure she
comes home to abuse her children for their good fortune – was not
erased or eased but *affirmed* through the process of synthesis. Even
when with a deft semantic manipulation of the ambiguities in 'makes
me tired', the deletions shifted blame away from the structure of work
and internecine divisions to a private and idiosyncratic state of 'fatigue',
it was of no particular consternation.

The speaking and sharing seemed powerful enough to lessen the
importance of the actual wording, firmly cementing the situational
collectivity through a sense of shared adversity and small joys. There
was a neat ceremonial economy to the process, and a minor pleasure to
be had from projecting the right response, receiving affirmation from
others on offering up concepts that fit, that matched the request for
revelation with just the right degree of rectitude. Here are experiences
worth attending to, the whiteboard seemed to declare. Perhaps others

are able to speak to their spouse upon return from community work, but we can all feel there is no one to talk to – other than those of us who are in the same boat. In the familiar self-help genre of the support group and after a week of mixed activities together, in and out of hours, we are united and heroic. We also feel, subtly and without personal bruising, that it is up to us to foster the right attitude, not the organisation. It is a relaxed conformity.

Even so, there is a pressure and a code being enacted here: not to admit to some form of hardship is to deny membership of the fraternity, but a full confession of inability to cope would invite excision.

Hold onto that thought – but also be in no doubt. Remote area work can be extremely stressful and demanding, involving frequent and exhausting travel, tense liaison with particularly placed Aboriginal and resident whites in communities, and ongoing battles over emphasis and approach with fellow bureaucrats in THS and other agencies. Public health remains the poor relation of clinical work and its practitioners cannot always summon the enthusiasm to cheerfully do more with less. Funding is never secure, and the pilot projects which demand such intense organisational savvy, verve and personal commitment to initiate are ever vulnerable to non-renewal. But, complex though it may already appear to be, an explanation which describes only the therapeutic effect of bemoaning circumstances in the soft encounter of the group ignores, because it cannot account for, the extraordinary investment in workshopping as a process that public health practitioners will commit to even while complaining bitterly of their time-wasting irrelevance.[8] It also leaves aside the self-work the work of talk calls upon its formulators to do and the intricate work involved in learning the narrative strategies which make an experience tellable in the first place.

Suffering for beliefs

Conversation analyst Harvey Sacks described the differential access to what he called 'entitlement experiences', being the anthropologically familiar difference between being the person who was there (witnessing, encountering, feeling) and who therefore now has first-person storytelling 'rights', and the person who gains vicarious access to another person's experience through their narration of it:

> The idea is that in encountering an event, and encountering it as
> a witness or someone who in part suffered by it, one is entitled to
> an experience, whereas the sheer fact of having access to things
> in the world, for example, getting a story from another, is quite a
> different thing. (Sacks 1984: 424–25)

'Entitlement experiences' are to be distinguished from the circulation of snatches of information that may become part of the general stock of knowledge not only in their different distributional qualities ('It is extremely difficult to spread joy. It is extremely easy to spread information' [Sacks 1984: 426]), but in the type of perceptual constraints embedded within their uptake and narratability. It's not as if, Sacks argues, once a person has had an experience worth telling (in chancing to see the tailings of a gruesome car accident on their way home, he instances), they can do with it what they will: 'No. You have to form it up as the thing that it ordinarily is, and then mesh your experience with that' (1984: 426–27). That is, many unsaid interpretations and ways of feeling and responding to the experience are casually renounced in the condition of both encountering and telling, and these in turn mark the teller and the receiver as both ordinary (reasonable, appropriate) and in proportion.

It would not be right to claim to have been destroyed to the point of madness by having witnessed a car accident involving complete strangers and no injuries, let's say – for it was, after all, just another accident, an everyday sort of calamity. Nor would it be right for the person un-entitled to the visual experience, likewise a stranger to the victims and helpers, to claim great impact from *just hearing the story* second-hand from the original passer-by, the 'just' reminding us of the depths of constraint imbuing the having of experiences. (This could be played with endlessly. It might, for instance, be appropriate to tell the unusual tale of someone else who witnessed a wreck that had nothing to do with them and was driven to insanity as a result, but it would not do to be driven mad by the anecdote itself!) In other words, the narrative forms through which people learn to have and to relate their experiences are thoroughly social.

More than just disabusing us of the notion that the subject can ever really be the author of her own narrations, Sacks' sketch of the bindings on perception and recall highlights the active social role of agents in making experience intelligible and recognisable in the first instance.

Being ordinary, being reasonable, is itself a phenomenon that requires investments of self and co-performed work to shape and maintain.

Let's push Sacks' insights a bit further than perhaps he intended in our attempt to explain the speed with which public health grammars are adopted in THS. Recall, for a moment, some of the characteristic attributes of public health professionals. Besides being well educated, they are used to having the worth of their inputs called into question by many protagonists, from their managers through to those they want to help. Theirs is an agonistic, quarrelsome kind of work. They are also adept in deploying the psychologised modalities of collaboration and confessional self-help as methods for coping with their abused positions. They share the widespread view that verbalising painful or difficult events is an important step to personal recovery, that re-storying stops one from internalising troubles and progressively being affected by that suppression.

This builds on the (equally common) humanist assumption that felt experiences, most especially negative ones, are fully self-presenting, standing as unmediated explanations of themselves, as authentic accounts which are somehow free of artifice and ideology, and that expressing these in a supportive group context is its own form of therapy. Thus, the emotional forcefulness of many public health workshop encounters helps give them a guileless appearance, as if what emerges is not already thoroughly imbued with institutional and cultural values.[9] But the secret of this magic is that these are the confessions that intimate workshops *are designed to draw out*. At the same time, and this is critical, the process preserves and constructs the very ordinary (expected, orthodox) extraordinariness of the public health persona.[10]

Extraordinary: unlike the enemy 'them' and 'they' who seem indifferent or hostile to Aboriginal suffering, these are people volunteering to operate in the near war zone of disease-ridden Aboriginal communities with their 'busted-arse clinics that may as well be khaki tents with a red cross painted on' (District Medical Officer). It is now the zone of a declared national emergency intervention, no less. Loneliness, disillusionment, physical and emotional strain, even management vilification, could well result. But these formulations are themselves posed in recognisable registers: that is, they are ordinary; they seem not unreasonable in the circumstances. It is here, I want to argue, here within the selection of hardships to relate (in the well-proportioned anecdote and the emotions attested, in the sympathetic reception and confirming responses of others), that the complex regulation of the 'romance of raw experience' is accomplished. It is here that the genesis of institutional self-perpetuation and its obscuring from itself can be located. The trick is to recognise the heavy-handed stamp of the ordinary in constructions of the extraordinary public health professional. And further, to see that these constraints arise out of the close inspection and recuperation of failure within such free-flowing processes as confessions in a workshop, which, it comes to pass, is an equally regimented organisational form.

Not unreasonable in the circumstances. And what circumstances are these? Bob Spicer tells us our work is something to be survived: 'It's hot country out there and you will need skills in how to hang in.' Others testify to its thanklessness, its professional isolation, the continual need for optimism in the face of so little explicit progress, the need for longevity yet the impossibility of ever having enough time to build relationships, the fear of using the wrong processes or committing a wrong approach, and the ever-present danger of doing too much *for*, rather than *with* Aboriginal people, thus exacerbating the dependency that is at the core of the failure to achieve true health and self-determination.

On the final day, an occupational health specialist has even taken us through martial arts exercises in self-defence, how to break a stranglehold and such, lest we are assaulted in our roles as isolated health personnel:[11]

'What other sorts of things might affect you out in the scrub?'

'Stress.'

'Ross River Fever.'

'Yes. Actually this reminds me of another incident, in East Arnhem Land. I'd been out meeting with people all day and the nurse invited me to lunch, but to get to her quarters we had to go through spear grass. Now this stuff was shoulder high and every part of my exposed skin was smothered in mozzies. It would have been a simple thing to keep that place safer. Anybody got any ideas of any others?

'Scabies, nits.'

'Yes, yes, these are all compensable claims. Caravans are tinder boxes too. You can get these work safety issues addressed. Come to us in Occ. Health and Safety. Don't complain about it among yourselves – do something about it! And remember, aggression concerns everyone. The Department will support any staff who choose to evacuate in fear of their life.'

Leaving aside the puzzling question of whose aggression we are managing (another unsaid: the lurking threat of Aboriginal delinquency), these are amazing stories, a smorgasbord of hazards to whet the sense of extraordinary public health endeavour. Feeling frustrated and unable to talk to one's non-comprehending kith and kin is certainly reasonable in the circumstances. As is wanting to do something about it.

Ah, and there is Bob Spicer, encouraging as always, urging us to view our problems in terms of their opportunities:

Bob: When I first started [remote area public health work] I was visiting 15 communities and I couldn't develop relationships with people on a once-every-three-months basis. I couldn't do what I knew needed to be done and I think, rather than thrash ourselves for the failure, it is important to know what our limitations are and work from there. Stress is a *big* issue – they stick us out there, and it's the last we see of them – I don't think that happens in THS so much any more but stress is still a big issue for us to manage. So what can we do?

Dennis: Develop relationships with people.

Amanda: That takes time.

Bob: Is there any substitute for time?

Amanda: I don't think so.

Bob: That's right. That's right. My feeling is there is no substitute for time. So we should be more relaxed about that, and know that in 12 months' time, we'll know a bit more and be a bit more effective.

Jan: I take photos of myself doing things in different situations and of my family and show that to

> community people and tell stories about them [the photos] and then answer questions so people can see Jan having a life somewhere and what that might be about, you know? People love the photos, too, and it really helps, I think.

Dennis: So we need to recognise what we can and can't achieve.

Jan: In a lot of the places you spend time with people who can be very negative about their jobs but not change themselves. My strategy is to avoid those people and think positively for myself. It is important to do things for yourself too, to look after yourself.

Amanda: I feel uncomfortable about talking about developing relationships with other people in order to get done what I need to get done. It took time for me to get past my own cynicism about that, the sort of exploitativeness of it.

The self-ministering administrator

Teaching people to occupy themselves with themselves, tending to their own negativity and learning to verbalise or disclose the efforts involved, Foucault tells us, is essential to the task of become permanently self-administrating subjects without much need of force or overt coercion (Foucault 1982: 208–10, 1988: 45; cf. Burchell 1993). Health professionals confess, Foucault might say, in order to restore their distress into a productive self-discipline; they expose their fractures the better to recuperate them. Thus even blaming the organisation (it will not help you, it dumps you out there, it's up to us) upholds the instrumental logic.

In the reductionist process of dot-pointing, it now appears, there is much being achieved in terms of learning how to do and say bureaucratic things. But what of the people we are wanting to help, the people for whom all this self-directed effort is being harnessed? What else are we specifically told to think and say about them, and just as importantly, what remains unsaid but just as effectively relayed?

Bearing in mind

No self-respecting orientation program in a government agency which proclaims Aboriginal issues as part of its core business could fail to specifically cover 'working cross-culturally'. In THS, the Aboriginal Cultural Awareness Program operates independently of the orientation course. It is hierarchically staged, ranging from a one-day 'taster' that is compulsory for all employees, whatever their rank, through to a supervised four-day bush camp in an Aboriginal community for the smaller handful of employees who will be residing in communities. A specially modified program, led by Aboriginal facilitators, is included in the remote area orientation course, not as short as one day but not the full residential course either. Having repeatedly established how fraught community work is, in the second week of public health boot-camp, we now have two days to learn lessons on 'culture', the truisms about difference and cultural peculiarity which anthropology has made complex and yet prescriptive enough to become rules about self and other.

There are many things we are told we need to 'just bear in mind'. In a series of ambiguous descriptions which seem to take us to surfaces alone, we've learnt (with just about exactly this much detail) that country is important; that land is sacred; and there are secret men's and women's ceremonies that consume Aboriginal people's attention at the expense of other priorities. We've learnt that 'professional loitering' is an official term used to describe a studied casualness both in bodily movement and concern for time that government health professionals should affect when working in Territory communities. We're to avoid looking Aboriginal people directly in the eye, but we should remove our sunglasses to ensure that our own orbs are not obscured from a reciprocal black gaze. Women are to keep their knees covered with long hemlines, and select non-transparent apparel – but never trousers, lest this draw too much attention to sexual parts.

Bear in mind that Aboriginal people will say yes just to please you, and do not ask direct questions. That it is best not to consult with the people on pay day, as their concern for cash will outstrip any other. That kinship is of overriding importance and incorporates everyone, including health professionals, who may be 'adopted into the system and given a skin name so that you can be fitted in', incurring vague and unspecifiable yet ever possible and emergent reciprocal obligations. Bear in mind that Aborigines don't turn up for health treatments with early symptoms because they have a higher tolerance for pain; that even their babies manifest illness differently (see Chapter 5). That they will supplement the illness diagnoses of western science (which explain the how), with concepts of spirits and sorcery (which explain the why). And that the Aboriginal understanding of health is that 'life equals death equals life'.[12]

As descriptions of Aboriginality piled one on top of the other, there were sufficient variations on the common wisdoms for the cross-cultural sessions to assume a deeply thoughtful feel. Take, for example, the following spontaneous workshop discussion, as fellow orientees discussed the semantic implications of the meaning of the Alma Ata Declaration of 1978 (WHO 1978), a seminal document for public healthers:

Trish: When they [WHO] say it [primary health care] is based on 'practical, scientifically sound practice' I hope they don't mean just that – because there are alternative ways of doing things that are valid within the [Aboriginal] culture. It doesn't have to be western science.

Simon: For me, 'scientifically sound' (quotation marks aerially signified) means it is observable and shown to work, is believed to work, within a setting, that it has efficacy.

Trish: Can I comment? I've found in working with Aboriginal people that their ability to fit in our views is very good. At Batchelor College, I talk about germ theory and my students talk about being sung. And being sung explains why some people get germs and others do not. So both world views are incorporated.

Simon: It is critical that we undo the classic definition of science and accommodate different worldviews.

Dave: (Dave is a late arrival) We haven't used the word 'holistic', but in Africa, I would deal with malaria with my white medicine but people wanted to know who sent the mosquito. The traditional healers would sort that out, and combined, the person got better.

Contemplating the conflict and then the possibility of harmony between professionals' own (now deemed sterile) scientific world view and the more deeply spiritual and profound Indigenous analysis which explains the 'why me? why now?', we forget momentarily that 'we' do already have available a set of explanations which attributes the 'why me?' to the susceptibility born of Aboriginal poverty, colonialism and disease-causing contemporary lifestyles. No matter. The associations and distinctions continue apace. A lecturer from Batchelor Institute of Indigenous Tertiary Education concluded her presentation on the workplace training needs of Aboriginal Health Workers with what she clearly intended as a provocation:

> The knowledge and power is deemed to belong to the non-Aboriginal professionals who are meant to teach the others. We should say to AHWs, 'And what do you think? What do you think is happening?' Make your respect obvious – and Aboriginal Health Workers will be more productive, more interested and more involved.

A concerned fellow participant queries, having just learnt the importance of not directly questioning Aborigines: 'But isn't asking "What do you think?" a bit confrontational?'

'There are different ways of doing it,' the lecturer vaguely reassured.[13]

Manufacturing consensus

It's time to return to our interest in how health professionals learn what to say, what not to say and when best to say things – to the fashioning of a bureaucratic self – by paying attention to the special power exerted by workshop procedures as social forces in and of themselves. Now we can build upon the linguistic patterning inherent within the turn-taking of workshop exchanges, to see how these extract consensus in ways more powerful than any overt indoctrination could ever hope to.

We've noted how a particular stress is placed within public health on maintaining principles of stakeholder involvement and collaborative practices within all aspects of one's work. The obligation to maintain open, committed and participatory forums for analysing issues of all kinds and for many purposes (for example, a text that needs to be prepared, a training program that needs to be developed, a public consultation to assess the needs of a given target group) is invariably enacted through a workshop process. This is of no small consequence.

Take, for instance, the guidelines available within public health literature for the discursive techniques and procedural strategies most likely to help people freely participate in consultative workshops. Here we find explicit how-to instructions designed to help facilitators solicit uninhibited critique on a sensitive topic when people might otherwise be circumspect (note that it is already assumed the forum will be a workshop):

> The group leader puts on the wall a large sheet of butcher's paper and divides it into 4 columns. In the left hand column he/she writes down 5 or 6 items which are aspects about the programme that the group wants to comment on. These should be agreed on before proceeding ... The next column is headed up 'positive comments' or 'good things'. The third column is headed up 'negative comments' or 'bad things' and the last column is titled 'recommendations' or 'suggestions'. The reason for this framework comes from the experience that people are more likely to feel comfortable about giving negative feedback if they are given the chance to turn this criticism into a recommendation or something constructive. (Hawe, Degeling & Hall 1991: 64)

Where these authors claim that honest criticism is liberated by clearing space for useful negativity in the fourth column, it could be argued the compelling qualities of workshop participation stem from a more complex combination of forces. There is a straitjacketing of open-endedness, a compulsion exerted by the empty column, a dictatorship within the consensus achieved out of 'uninhibited' workshop talk, an unbearable pressure for agreement exacted by the polite force of the gathering itself. This force goes beyond what is said to the scene of the relating and back again.

To begin with, far from being passive, there is the micro-power of the columns themselves in predirecting the analytic style, type and look of the in-filling required. Imagine a set of labelled but empty columns on a whiteboard. In the setting of the *workshop*, the seemingly neutral medium of the whiteboard transforms into an aesthetic object which 'exercises a demand on the one who performs or observes it; [and] through this demand, it reveals a desire-to-be that somehow warrants its being' (Dufrenne 1987: 6). The accusatory emptiness of the columns silently exhorts inscription: a collective mutiny would be afoot were the room to remain silent in their presence.

The first notation sets the scene for every other; its style exemplifies the pattern to be followed. Then there is the heaviness of the facilitator's pauses within heavily time-monitored sessions, aimed at obtaining a covenant, a collective agreement, before movement to the next point can be made. The person who wants to disrupt the whiteboarding process (by, say, refusing to fill in a column, or suggesting responses which are stylistically at odds with the other suggestions) will either sense her solitude and be subdued, or will find that her disruption stalls proceedings only momentarily. Dissent is quickly and subtly colonised.[14]

And so we abide, we 'conform', one might say, to the point of resenting interruptions. During an orientation workshop session probing the issues surrounding the affordability and universality of primary health care, for instance, one participant scorned the rose-tinted listing of the desirable characteristics of good primary health care services that had appeared on an overhead.

'Where is primary health care being done properly in the NT?' he angrily demanded. 'I don't think I've seen all those things you've listed here anywhere! Where is it? This is a bloody joke!'

His outburst had an immediate, visceral impact on the group: where previously participants had been open-faced and full of suggestions, now everyone looked ever-so-slightly uncomfortable. As one, we dropped our eyes and stopped calling out whiteboard responses. In the tight silence that followed, one participant shuffled papers on the table and others started to fidget. Sensing that this part of the exercise had petered out, the facilitator switched tack by illuminating a new overhead, saying as she swiftly moved that we needed 'something more practical to cheer us up'. With the silence thus recovered, members participated once more, happy to have group amiability and forward momentum restored, a transition catalysed by our absolute desire to proceed to a more satisfactory finish, to do what it takes to complete the exercise and waste no more time. (And eventually the angry man joined in again too; the power of the group is not be sneezed at.)

Even 'angry' professional confrontations can have a sanitised, choreographed feel to them. Indeed, at public health events which feature Aboriginal health employees, along with ritual acknowledgments thanking traditional owners for their permission to hold this session on their country (were they ever asked? can they say no? do they care about the event?), it is almost obligatory for an indigenous advocate to berate participants about the disgraceful lack of Aboriginal representation, whether it be in terms of the lack of Indigenous people at the gathering itself, or, as a more general point, the dominating number of professional positions that are occupied by whites and paid for with 'black dollars'. It is just as expected – it is ordinary and is thus an equally constitutive element of the process – for the audience to temporarily fold in on itself, momentarily cowed in a way that displays its assent to the verdict, with the drubbing and the contrition both verifying the all-round sense that the burden being carried is indeed a thankless one. Someone will berate, another will accept the berating, saying they agree with whatever half-baked critique of white oppression was just said, and how important it is that we now work in a spirit of partnership and mutual learning.

Self-sustaining

But consent does not always bounce off dissent. Take another (non-orientation) case in point, one inhabited by experienced institutional actors for whom bureaucratic conceptualisations have become both easy to think and easy to say.

In the year 2000, two highly paid consultants from South Australia were commissioned to review the effectiveness of those Aboriginal hearing services that are jointly funded through the federal and state education and health departments. Several contextualising points can be noted here. Having talked to carefully chosen representatives in community schools and clinics, the evaluators are now 'consulting' with senior health and education policy and program managers about their preliminary findings. Close to finalising their report, they have arranged a workshop to present their draft recommendations for interim endorsement and finetuning.

The consultants feel they have already negotiated meanings with factionally divided organisational representatives across the Territory. The report's draft wording thus already contains many trade-offs and amendments. In contrast, the managers in the room, who are already familiar with the fractured history of hearing services and were sufficiently concerned to support an external evaluation, are now expecting the consultants to tell them how to fix a service delivery field well known for its internecine battles. They regard this as constituting the single major purpose of the evaluation and the main reason 'outsiders' were commissioned to do it.

It is a bitter disappointment for many, then, when, previewing their investigation of the coordination problems, the consultants proudly inform the assembled managers, with all the confidence of a profound revelation:

> There is a lack of coordination of visits to remote communities in
> many situations – most people don't know who else is involved,
> what services are available and who to contact.

In fact, they'd already formatted the diagnosis of '• lack of coordination' as a caption point for the draft executive summary, which had been photocopied for group analysis and included in the workshop papers. Yet, while the managers mutter to each other across tables about paying a high consultancy price for such an unnecessary restatement of the problems, continuing their acerbic criticisms of the consultants' patronising and money-wasting platitudes in tea breaks and post-workshop debriefs, the workshop itself is characterised by the language of policy, with high-minded statements of goodwill and marked displays of professional consensus.

Is this a cut and dried case of complicity? Or is it also the confluence of institutional structure and intersubjective effect in a neat little nutshell? The categories and procedures for doing bureaucratic things are learnt by pressures internal to the gathering itself, which also contains within it infinite opportunities for instructing all comers in the setting's operating conceptual schemas.

As part of their final report, the consultants want to present an action plan and a vision statement because, they say, they are not going to have their report join others gathering dust on the shelves. No, this is going to be action-oriented: 'Ear disease is the single most preventable health issue affecting the poor learning of Aboriginal kids in school, so we want to make this report count.'

With one consultant poised by a whiteboard, the group as a whole is asked, 'What are some of the words that would need to go in the

One last thing to learn

In the final days of our two-week orientation, we are getting into the
nuts and bolts of working with Aborigines in remote areas, no longer as
a series of injunctions about the nature of Aboriginal culture but more
and hereafter in every form of workplace encounter where entitlement
anecdotes are swapped by experienced players) by way of parables.

The venue is now very different. We have moved from the old
pital ward to the restaurant of the Genghis Khan, a seedy hotel on
of the main routes into the Darwin CBD. Dining tables are stacked
e side, while lingering traces of stale cigarette smoke course
h the tired air-conditioning system. The dusty remains of plastic
as decorations are still in sad evidence, here at the onset of
nurse, Cheryl Bailey, introduced to us as a woman of lengthy
e 'out bush', has come to talk about new clinical practice
with overheads and handouts. Embellishing her description of
consultative work involved in preparing the new guidelines,
proof of their validity as good advice, Cheryl also inserts
collections of her experiences as a neophyte nurse:

es, and we're new, and we're working in a cross-
ironment, confronting your own ethnocentricities
about the community's structure in an emergency
t the best way, but sometimes the only way.

ency epiphany, she now relates, came when she was
t onto an ambulance trolley to be evacuated out by
ed the on-duty Aboriginal Health Worker, a hefty
g nearby, for some assistance, but was ignored.
t. He remained silent. Repeating it again, he left
ing her thinking, 'Great! Now what?'
s someone else turned up and assisted. Later,
afely on the plane, the Aboriginal Health
her requests for help reappeared to explain
other, whom he could not touch. Cheryl
t I learned a very important message that
thing. You just might not know it at the

re – kinship connections that are barely
s powerfully controlling – reminding

---

vision statement?' 'It is a difficult problem we have,' they go on to stress,
'for there is a tendency to think "It's all too hard." So let's focus on the
opportunities, because there are things that can be done. And remember,
nobody can do it by themselves, we really need to act together.' And in
so saying, the remarks are designed not only to elicit remedies but also
to establish as precondition for participation the morally binding need
to appear collaborative:

'I guess I would like the word "innovative" in there,' someone
suggests, breaking the ice and setting the scene.

Hardworking banalities trip off tongues:

'Flexible'

'Community control'

'Successful'

'Acceptable to all the stakeholders'

'Equity'

'Practical – with reality checks built in'

'Collaborative – because if we don't know where everyone is
coming from, we won't work together'

'Partnerships'

'Can we have culturally aware?'

'What about culturally appropriate?'

'Respect?'

'Does "inclusivity" cover that?'

'Resources – it needs to be adequately resourced. It comes into
equity.'

'I think it is really important that we have "clearly defined roles
and responsibilities".'

'I think another good one is "awareness of remote communities".'

'The services shouldn't be one off – "sustainable".'

'What about "multi-disciplinary"?'

'Going back to "culturally aware", a new word I heard the other day was "competence"—"cultural competence". It really brings in the need for *effect*.'

Embedded within these doctrinal formulations are depths of encounter where we've learnt, time after time, to project correctly, to articulate in bulleted mode using the right kinds of worthwhile associations and remedies (Aborigines 1 Partnerships 1 Cultural awareness/appropriateness/competence). We contribute as experienced professionals, not as novices in an orientation session needing to give elaborate spiels that require further condensation by the facilitator, but as old hands, efficient at delivering the desired abstractions.

Yet while our adeptness in the summary modes of diagnosing problems of Aboriginal service provision is revealed, the highly fettered language is in fact one which refuses certain analyses. Circular and self-justifying, the alternatives to further institutional exposure for Aboriginal people are effectively narrowed down. While systematic doubt about what we are doing is mandatory, a radical questioning of our entitlement to do anything, to be there in the first place, or of the radical inability of interventionist explanation to undo or deny or escape its externality, is not sustainable. Something has to be deemed a failure before action can be called for, and the action called for is something more from us. Those other unthinkable concepts hang suspended in a wordless vacuum: they are inexplicable in terms of interventionist apperception. Improvement and greater stakeholder inclusion are always possible, as outsider critiques of our gaps and shortcomings also seem at such pains to remind us. Coordinated hearing services are necessary because the children suffer disproportionate hearing problems that negatively affect their schooling outcomes. Education is a taken for granted good because it gives Aboriginal people a greater range of choice, employability and self-esteem. Lack of coordination cries out for more coordination. More coordination requires meetings, workshops, information sharing. Information sharing must have as its preceding action consensus about what needs to be shared, a consensus in turn forged out of a coordination process such as this, with masters

of bureaucratic recital giving their inputs through consultation information sharing needs its corollary – a translation of profe intents into culturally appropriate/aware/competent formats.

It is a dutiful offering up of expected answers in the spontaneous suggestions. Participants will walk out, blaming c for what they recognise to be stale diagnoses, when all t consultants are simply playing a part in a series of institu which reproduce a shared and greater whole. How good t' may or may not have been is irrelevant, because the v like meetings, requires such attentive work from co-pa becomes action itself (see Riles 2000: 143–45, 171– 1989). Hence our collective fetishistic attribution images of action as the report and its vision statem

Because the 'action plan' the consultants w workshop consultations for the evaluation of Abc complete with its carefully worded vision sta heavy work of coordinating and collaboratin will feel as if a large chunk of the work is a the work of enunciating the further work itself an endpoint — and therein lies its form of analytical and declarative worl the ritual process. As Riles points o how effectively participating builds or, to use her words, 'the effecti effect of effectiveness' (2000: 17

And clearly, talking about through talking that speciall magical ability to 'make a d work that professionals and diagnosis in parade in techniques for recup the same.

This draws us insert a final wc now fluent in th discussions.

us again, if we needed reminding, of the mysterious inexplicability of Aboriginal people lurking beyond the dot-pointed summaries of their culture; what French phenomenologist Maurice Merleau-Ponty described as the tendency to congeal insurmountable difference into our (non) understanding of 'elementary societies' (1964: 115). In the encapsulated and yet endlessly provisional knowledge forms of THS, there is a reason for everything, even that which lies beyond our immediate reason.

It is of no small consequence that the timing of the quick lessons on self-defence comes at the very end of two weeks of immersion in eulogising summaries of Aboriginal cultural traditions and techniques for taming uncertainty with the uplifting prose of supportive networking, self-care and community development. Practising karate had not been

---

Box 4.1   Occupational health and safety orientation aims and objectives

OCCUPATIONAL HEALTH & SAFETY FOR REMOTE AREA HEALTH PROVIDERS

PRIMARY AIM OF ORIENTATION

To provide new staff to remote area health with an introduction to relevant occupational health and safety issues, protocols, strategies, and training opportunities.

KEY OBJECTIVES

To achieve the core aim the following objectives will form the basis of the session:

I   Ensure awareness of occupational health & safety issues within remote communities and mechanisms by which to address them

II   Ensure awareness of the THS Policy and Code of Practice on Safety in Remote Areas and understand its contents

III   Introduce participants to the topics of critical incident stress, the general management of stress, and the management of aggression in the remote area workplace

IV   Provide participants with strategies and protocols for the occupational and health topics outlined above.

listed on our orientation agenda. Our bulging kits contain nothing to indicate that we are going to learn what to do if (a black) someone comes at us with a knife threatening to rape, maim or rob. Or rather, it was listed, in bureaucratised terms of inoffence, with words meant to mean more than they say in the midst of their apparent innocuousness.[15] I refer in particular to point III: (Box 4.1).

'How do people get to feel threatened in their work?' we are asked, safely back in workshop mode after the physicality of practising sharp arm and kicking motions to block imaginary assaults:

> 'Well, the use of weapons makes it pretty clear – spears and guns.'

> 'Equipment left outside the clinic will be broken or left on the doorstep.'

> 'Old staff will refuse to recognise that you are there, there's no validation for new staff – it's a system of bastardisation.'

> 'Threats to disemploy you — like "You'll be out of a job, you white cunt" or "You're here to do what we say", or "We won't let your partner stay", things like that.'

From these abbreviated selections of startling threats, which demarcate the initiated from the new, we craft a cryptic list of risks ripe for transformation into pseudo-strategies. Having no authority as official policy formulations, the whiteboarding joins our role plays of being attacked as a half-hearted simulation in policy analysis. An abbreviated portrait of the brutality of Aboriginal community life was first inserted into our imaginings of Aboriginal alterity and then returned as a series of pragmatic accounts amenable to community development action:

> spears

> guns

> threats

> punch

> fuel (fire bomb)

> non-verbal passive aggression

> loud verbals

sexual aggression – from rape to annoying remarks

accidental aggression – posturing without intent

'What are we going to do about it? Let's look at why first. What are some of the reasons for aggression?' (Note how quickly we have learnt to abbreviate the symptom analysis for the purposes of whiteboarding):

'They drink.'

On the board:

» alcohol and other drugs

'Tolerance – they have low trust levels.'

On the board:

» low trust

'The fact that they don't like the work that you do.'

On the board:

» type of work

'Forms of mental illness can be manifest as aggression.'

On the board:

» mental illness

'Low self-esteem.'

On the board:

» low self-esteem

'Domestic unhappiness or violence.'

On the board:

» domestic problems

'People who are chronically or acutely stressed.'

On the board:

» low self-esteem (given a double tick)

'People who aren't well, who are in pain.'

On the board:

» ill-health

'You're white; you're the wrong culture.'

On the board:

» wrong culture

'Cultural misunderstandings – things that are perceived as rudeness.'

On the board:

» cultural misunderstandings

And cutely, from me, 'Different perceptions about what violence and its need for suppression might mean – not everyone thinks it is something to be feared or avoided – perhaps it can be joyful', drawing a redirecting affirmation from a co-participant, a mental health worker, 'Yes, it becomes a vicious cycle, doesn't it? Violence becomes an accepted and expected part of the culture.'

On the board:

» vicious cycle

'How can we break it?'

I later try to imagine what kind of response would have been given if someone had confessed to experiences of terror, fear and isolation from colleagues and residents in suburban Darwin. Would THS promise to evacuate staff then? But I already know the answer, not just because the policy of evacuating health personnel applies to remote area staff alone, with its default exclusion of the suburbs. The picture of the small, lonely clinic and the embattled health professional in the harsh outback is conceptually reliant on its counterpoint image of suburban enclaves, where security screens, police patrols, professionally landscaped gardens and neatly subdivided suburbs give the promise of well-ordered inviolability (see Lea 2006). Like nepotism in commerce, violence needs to be considered as exceptional and out there, not a routine element of western life. It must be presented as that which happens, unscheduled and uninvited, in another place, on the periphery and in situations of marginality (see Feldman 2001).

There are many things we are not saying here, when finally we are discussing an issue which seems by its very nature (violence, physical threat, suspicion and fear) to suspend the need for coded talk. But no, even now, participants carefully formulate sermonising caption points from the span of the allowed and the not said. Terror has to have both a home and a cause — and not just any old causal analysis will do. It must be treatable and even preventable, given the right collaborative diagnosis and sensitive approach. By extension, we might ignite the black man's anger and have his knife against our throats if the right protocols are not observed and the true underlying causes not properly understood and sensitively acted upon, for what is known of the other can quickly turn into a thin surface obscuring a mysterious and unpredictable, even repugnant, depth (Taussig 1999: 5).[16]

Conclusion: Dot point vicious cycle

I feel we have gone full circle in the closed loops of our own vicious cycle, from the codes for expanding contact with Aboriginal people through being sensitively engaged, through to techniques in warding off yet assimilating violence to our soft welfare logics. Neither is more right or wrong than the other; they are two extremes of the same continuum that ultimately preserves the separateness of the domain of otherness to be operated on, even as we are urged to merge and form relationships in the name of better cross-cultural practice, keeping our own normative practices safe from harsh scrutiny as we learn to self-reflect. But of course it is not a closed loop; it is fed by many insistences.

In THS, anecdotes and classifications are the stuff of everyday transaction. Swapping tales, authoritatively from an instructor's virtual pulpit in front of a whiteboard, or as the collegial constructions of a coordination meeting, in the enforced democracy of a butcher's paper or whiteboard exercise, in debriefing gossip, purposively or unintentionally according to context, reproduces the tacit knowledge one must acquire to have an eye for the look of a thing, an ear for its sound. These are self-feeding knowledge practices which consume their own representations, becoming the copies without originals Baudrillard (1988) saw as more real than the real. Public health professionals and bureaucrats more generally would call it building on what others have learned (Lea 2001, 2005).

The techniques of the workshop create a storied self who can descend into the projected abjection of Aboriginal communities and return, aided by elegant manners (Aboriginal people are that, so treat them this way then restore yourself like this) imbibed in the trade in truisms and displays of entitlement or 'being there' experiences. The continual sharing of experiences within bureau-professional practice is thus not just an airing of anxiety in order to be purged. It is also an exercise in returning self- and system-criticism to its proper administrative place, while learning the signal terms with which to declare sovereign competence over cross-cultural mystery, itself a source of intersubjective rivalry in the endless contests for credibility. Public health workshops work to bring diverse and at times warring health professionals together within a rigidly democratic cauldron which politely and solicitously fuses small antagonisms into a coalition. More, these straitjacketing interaction methods become models of the approaches to be used when participants in turn consult with their others, especially in communities, with our/their 'potential, expected, elicited, elastic group response(s)' (Robinson 1995: 326) remaining ever bound to the broad-minded constraints of the form. It is not forced, either. Try getting anything done without collecting before a whiteboard or convening a discussion group and see how far you get.

More than anything else, the orientation has confirmed that the negotiation of cultural difference is fraught indeed. A total schema for apprehending the frightening space between us and them has been signed, sealed and delivered, with rules for respectful dialogue and lessons in self-defence. Further, as Xavier's early humbling lesson clearly revealed, when professionals carry over their codified cross-cultural education into direct encounters, the permanent threat of not getting one's demonstrations right in front of one's peers and the equally permanent need to be seen as liked by Aborigines, form a relentless performance pressure. Professional gatherings of all kinds affirm the self-consciousness and fear of transgression which people carry into encounters with Aboriginal people, and the iconic abstractions they arm themselves with to help get through. Being acutely sensitised at all times to possible error, professionals must hedge towards banality – not just in their documentation, but, as I will go on to show, in their self-representation – as a direct result of their absorption of, their incorporation of, the corporation.

THE SOCIAL LIFE OF HEALTH FACTS

Whenever bureau-professionals grapple with the intransigencies of ill-health in the colonised Aboriginal populations of the Northern Territory, the question of *what has to be done* quickly comes to the fore. The urgency of the question is relentlessly reinforced through sources that, while diverse, are perhaps most remarkable for their homogeneity. In thick books and thin reports, in long lists of articles (MEDLINE-indexed), in declarations of national emergencies and in the pieties of a scientific seminar, the urgency is drilled in. Contrast and compare the following two accounts: both are almost identical in their format, their language, and their conceptualisation of both the problem and the solution – and in their simultaneous conveyance of hope and despair. All this in spite of being deeply personalised expressions of anxiety and unique experience:

> In the last year I have really begun to wonder about how I am going to cope. I am really clinging on by my fingernails and some weeks are worse than others. I am at a low ebb right now and have begun applying for other jobs. If we can get the houses functional there will be a dramatic improvement in people's health. I really believe that. Skin disease, respiratory illness, and gastro-enteritis are the lead hospitalisation items – 70 per cent can be fixed through amenities. It is not their [the managers'] kids, so they don't care; that's what I think. They have silicon chips inside their heads that blinker them. I asked [a health manager]: 'Would

you live in a house up here without a fridge, without a washing machine?' Of course not! I am tempted to leave. (Male remote area public health professional, Nhulunbuy, since departed)

It's paradise over there, just beautiful. But it staggers me, the sickness, the squalor in the middle of paradise. I go there, and get up and watch the sun rise, the sea eagles circling overhead, it is magic, heavenly. And then I go into town (grimace and long pause) … I heard that the Tiwi people have the highest attempted suicide rate in the country, at least one a week. I think it is to do with the squalor, the lack of hope, the poverty. Nobody wants to live that way. Those young men know what they're missing, they're not stupid. They can see what they're missing on the TV. It just must be so hard. But I shouldn't get so depressed. The Tiwi people are determined to turn all this around and so I'm here to follow their lead. (Female remote area public health professional, Darwin Rural, since departed)

Imagine sitting now in a darkened room, blinds drawn shut. In the hushed artificial darkness, a PowerPoint conspectus lights up, transmitting THS' epidemiological knowledge of Aboriginal disease categories:

Box 5.1   Introductory slide

Life expectancy at birth

Age-adjusted mortality

Rate of death:

      25–44 year olds

      45–64 year olds

Infant mortality rate

Stillbirth rate

Infant growth rate

The conspectus is specially designed for inducting health professionals new to the Northern Territory. The information-dense tabulations embedded within the deep blue illuminations are interspersed with sombre commentary: 'Unusually, the female Aboriginal mortality rate is far worse than the male in all age groups.' And:

> We are actually getting bigger infants, birth weight is increasing,
> but after one year of age the weights aren't sustained. In one
> community we've studied, every single baby under 12 months of
> age is evacuated out in an emergency condition at least once in the
> first year of life. Injuries aside, the high death rates in the 25–44
> year old category are from poor childhood health. Truth told,
> these remain third world conditions in a first world country.

As the next graph illuminates the room, we are told:

> Like people in many developing countries, Indigenous people
> wage an *unnoticed struggle* against disease. Low birth weight
> and failure to thrive from malnutrition and under-nutrition is
> implicated in the onset of diabetes, heart disease and cancer later
> in life. (emphasis added)

With the lights back on, a doctor in the audience asks what work is
being done to explain to Aboriginal people why these rates are as they
are: 'The data just says what happens, not why. If Aboriginal people
knew that the high rate of infant illness contributed to these high death
rates later on, they'd be interested in acting on it. In public health
generally, is anyone working on this?'

'Yes,' replies the presenter, 'yes, people are. But we really need
community-specific data so we can sit down with groups and say, "This
is what is happening for you mob here." But we are a few years off
having that ... We have new information systems being put in place
but it will still take a few years for community-level data to be easily
available. The populations are pretty fluid too, and that creates its own
problems.'

Ever true to the narrative formulations of public health, the worried
discussion moves from opening depictions of direness to hope and then
back again to overwhelming difficulty. From the depths of gravity arises
the search for the more that can be done, against the harshest of odds.
The answer, with better data and information sharing, is just around
the corner – but it will take time and be a densely problematic process.
Yet, while the research is never complete and the data have infinite
gaps, what is revealed is sufficiently alarming to warrant immediate
and deeply concerned remedial attention.

The anthropologist from Mars questions I want to explore here
are: what are health professionals assuming when they assume that

facts incite people to act? And what kind of 'sensory alterity' (Feldman 1997: 31) is imagined of Aboriginal people in schemes to repackage statistics in the name of internalisation?

The social distribution of worry

Pondering the route of travelling facts, bio-science ethnographer Joseph Dumit asks, 'Who takes up facts? Who does not? How are they produced and distributed?' (Dumit 1997: 83). Given our all-over dependence on categories of scientific knowledge for our lived sense of healthfulness, personhood and function (Haraway 1991, Martin 1994), we might gloss one answer as: it is 'we' who take up facts, it is Aboriginal people who are deemed not to do so, and it is to the epidemiologists and public health professionals in THS that we turn to remedy this inequity.

At first blush, accounting for both the large amounts of health information and the conscientious attention that is paid to how best to circulate it is relatively straightforward. For sociologist Ulrich Beck (1992), risk consciousness is the defining feature of late modernity, where the production of more and more hazards has prompted higher and higher levels of anxiety. Yet the structural conditions for reflexivity and knowledge about causes and effects is unequally distributed (see also Lash 1994). Why do 'we' know about being healthy? Because 'we' are structurally enabled to produce and consume the information; we know about the risks, and in a liberal politic, access to information equates to power to act.[1] By definition, it is a symptom of the ongoing existence of racist inequality in Australia that Aboriginal people are burdened by the premature death and illness captured in multiple enlistments of rates and figures, and it is a matter of social justice that they be truthfully informed of the outrage of their own unhealthiness.

As public health practitioners work slavishly to reduce the high levels of Indigenous morbidity and mortality, an obsessional endpoint becomes the need to share their health information and 'capacity-build', to the point where Aboriginal people are inspired and empowered to transform themselves. The underlying theory is relatively straightforward: if Aboriginal people knew exactly how sick they were, and if they knew the real causes, they would want to work on themselves with greater vigour and determination. If only Aboriginal people understood the true import of the alarming data that professionals have to hand, they would readily commit to appropriate lifestyle changes. As one health bulletin recently put it, 'How can people be expected to manage their disease if they do not understand it?' (Glover 2001: 1). The unstated corollary is this: Aboriginal people could not possibly live as they do *knowingly*.

Accordingly, health professionals are at great pains to collect accurate data about the prevalence and incidence of various categories of disease and their aetiologies, and to measure the efficacy of their interventions. But not any old kind of public health strategy or action will do. It has to be the right kind. It has to help, not harm; include, not intrude; assist, not alter.[2]

Health professionals know better than anyone that when attempts are made to enumerate the scandalous depths of Aboriginal illness and premature death – *preventable* death – the visceral reality of pain, disability, dismemberment, fluids and poisoned systems is lost. Transformed into the barren terms of epidemiological rates and population-generic representations, items that are meant to reflect embodied experiences of death and disease become meaningless to the people who are meant to be incited to act. Health professionals are thus confronted with the additional dilemma of translation. How are they to exhibit their objective and emotionless numbers, graphs and facts in terms which make sense, which are real, are made human and comprehensible for the people whose actual sickness and death they abstractly index? Without causing offence or being insensitive? In ways that do not add to the problem load of those they want to help, or that do not give more ammunition to jackbooted interveners who pay no respect to community development protocols?

A public health physician who has worked long and hard on sensitive ways of presenting information on death rates, comparing the persuasive power of pie charts versus bar graphs among various Aboriginal groups,[3] says one of his most frequently asked questions is, 'Do Aboriginal people know how unwell they are?' This, he reflects, is very difficult to answer:

> Clearly some, especially in the health field, have heard the
> statistics. Others have not. Almost all Aboriginal people
> have personally experienced the death of one or more family
> members. But even so, many seem surprised by our presentation
> of mortality information [which] began by acknowledging the

> grief of individuals and explicitly linked statistical information
> with personal stories and local issues ... The implication is that
> information can remain abstract, external and cold, or it can
> become internal and warmed by contact with emotional feelings
> and personal experiences. (Weeramanthri undated: 7)

The solution, he feels, lies in the empowering effects of well-designed and meaningfully presented information. Statistics that have been warmed, demystified, their tears returned and secret meanings rendered.

What we see played out in the many internal pedagogic sessions within THS is an infusing of a scientised knowledge among practitioners, so that they are themselves better informed about why they are there to help. It inspires practitioners to want to act. It is a small step to assume that this same data need only be retold to be internalised; 'heated up' to render its full emotional import; or appropriately translated to allow reversals in unhealthy behaviours to flow. Within the search for better professional understanding lies the assumption (understandable, and so ubiquitous as never to be seen, let alone questioned) that better quality and more accurate information will eventually become better self-understanding for the Aborigines: the better 'we' collect and analyse, the more we know, the more we are impelled to want to act, the more important it is that we helpfully demonstrate how it all looks to Aboriginal people, so that they too will feel the same compulsion.

But then again, as an anthropological representation of the native theories of factual transfer operating in this environment, such a simple one-to-one domino image of information transmission and uptake is more aspirational than actual. It straightens out what is in reality a more chaotic informatics phenomenon. It is too matter-of-fact to imagine the pathway as a recitation of serious facts, followed by their uptake by the health professionals, followed by an attempted transmission to Aboriginal people, as if it is all to do with a more-or-less simple matter of more-or-less complex translation. For translation, as the philosopher and cultural critic Walter Benjamin reminds us, is never a neutral transmitting device (Benjamin 1977).

Learning how to see, Scene 1

It is the year 2000, and Day 4 of a week-long remote area nurses' in-service training session for the East Arnhem Region in the Nhulunbuy

Hospital staff conference room. This afternoon's session is dedicated to discussing the Growth Assessment and Action program, a screening protocol targeting poor growth in Indigenous children from birth to 5 years of age. Under the program, children are measured regularly, according to a schedule; their growth is plotted against international benchmarks; checkpoints to trigger alarm are carefully specified; and any concerns are discussed with relevant kin. The growth information is then entered onto a computerised information system and aggregated reports are produced to educate the community, with the whole program hailed as an important intervention in the management and prevention of early childhood disease.

At one stage it was found that community-based nurses were religiously documenting the shorter statures and slighter weights of Aboriginal children in early childhood, but not intervening to correct them, partly because the children seemed otherwise so abundantly energetic (Ruben & Walker 1995). Now, annual clinic data must be collected and returned to epidemiologists in Health House, who then aggregate it for pedagogic use back in the communities, though it is up to the nurses to decide whether the re-presented data will indeed provide helpful community feedback. So part of today's session is learning the importance of entering data and of reviewing the central office community feedback data tableau.

Example community reports are distributed for earnest dissection and debate. The prototype 'Growth Assessment and Action Reports' exude an aesthetic of conscientious simplification, intended to facilitate cross-cultural information transfer. There is minimal text, and what there is is all in large print. Instead, simplified diagrams and vividly coloured drawings replace the dense exegesis of standard epidemiology reports.[4]

As the longest serving remote area nurse in the Arnhem region, it falls to Peg Andelwar to lead her counterparts page by page through the feedback reports. With Peg are eight nurses who've already attempted to use the previous year's material in feedback sessions with Aboriginal Health Workers – workers who are frequently treated as the standardised representatives of the (poorly literate) 'grass-roots' and thus as the litmus test (and equally often as the endpoint) for 'community' feedback.

It is getting late in the day. The nurses are cynical; they've seen it all before. 'But this is about moving from interpreting the data to doing something about it,' rallies Peg, warming to her temporary leadership role. 'The question of "Why bother?" is they're saying now that the first two years of life is really important for preventing chronic disease later on. So keep going, guys – this really is important.'

And so they keep going, combing through the revised layouts of this year's tabulated data in light of shared snippets concerning previous efforts at 'community feedback'. They describe what seemed to work and what did not in terms of creating Aboriginal interest: the merits of pie charts versus bar graphs; the use of people figures rather than numbers; of fluorescent lime-green and fire-truck red squares in a coloured grid as opposed to the more usual black and white or pastel colours. One nurse suggests that a table showing comparative statistics of the community in relation to the region, to the Northern Territory and to the rest of Australia should not be shown at all because it does not tell a positive story. Concern is expressed that the lack of good news may dispirit community members, risking further defeatism, when it is engaged agency that the material is meant to inspire.[5]

'People here get swamped in bad news all the time. We want them to feel better about themselves, not worse,' the nurse-critic cautioned. Peg wrote the comments down, for 'feeding back' to central office staff, who in turn will need to revise future community reports with this in mind (with the whole in-house process destined for future policy description as 'community consultations').

Central Office has requested that the nurses also consider ways of presenting the information to the community as a whole, rather than through clinic interactions. 'We don't have any fantastic ideas about this part. You can't post it up at the store or clinic without explanation. And you really need your Health Workers to take people through it,' notes one. 'But do you think your Health Workers really understand it?' asks another. Peg responds, transplanting the genesis of the Growth Assessment and Action initiative to an ignorance now assumed to be shared by all Aboriginal Health Workers:

> Well, it's really important that you sit down with them and talk
> them through it because they're the ones most likely to tell others.
> I think it is good for people to get an idea of how many kids
> there are and what the consequences are. They know the kids are
> skinny, but they see them running around all day and they eat at
> least one meal so [they think] what's the problem?

Absorbing and transmitting: Scene 2

'A view from the other side', Jimmy Kneeler's seminar presentation for a new batch of doctors and nurses being orientated to remote area work, was scheduled for the post-lunch seminar slot and he knew it would be a tough call. Held in Block Four, a Stalinist-sounding name housing the health professionals who work in the remote area communities surrounding Darwin, it took the best part of an hour. Kneeler had been hoping to make his presentation more interesting with a greater use of visuals, after feedback from another session indicated that he'd talked too much. He began by drawing a rough graph on the whiteboard (Figure 5.1), saying that world populations remained fairly static until quite recently.

Why the relatively sudden surge? Basically, Jimmy says, it boils down to three things: sanitation, housing, and occupational health and safety. With the agricultural revolution, people were removed from their lands and forced to move into the cities. There they lived in unsanitary overcrowded slums. Then, with the industrial revolution came not only the need for a healthy workforce but also the organisation of unions and a demand for food security:

> My point is that underlying all these reforms were issues of social equity. That is really important to bear in mind for health because

Figure 5.1   Jimmy's epidemiology

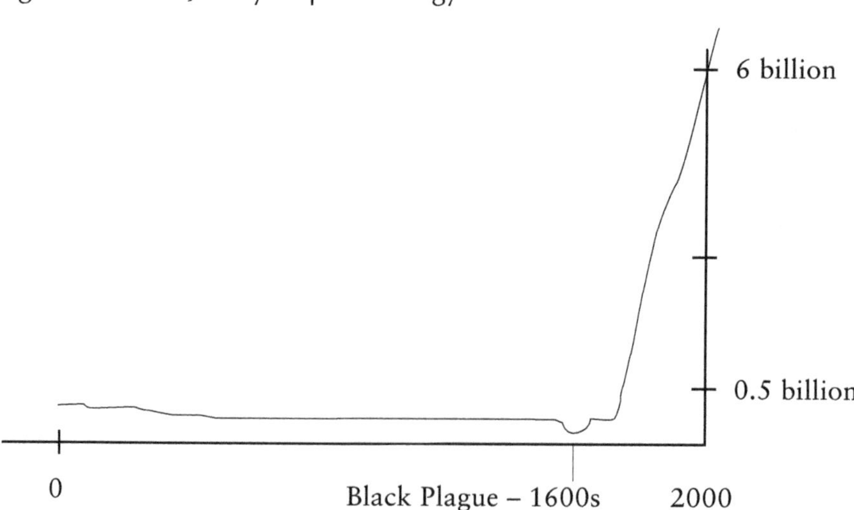

a lot of this (pointing to the graph) is not about affluence. Saudi Arabia is a very, very rich country but it still has high levels of infant mortality, quite probably because of the position of women in that country. And that is what I want to stress: it is a bigger picture than health.

He sketched another graph, to symbolise the history of TB's demise in the west:

Figure 5.2   Engineering versus antibiotics

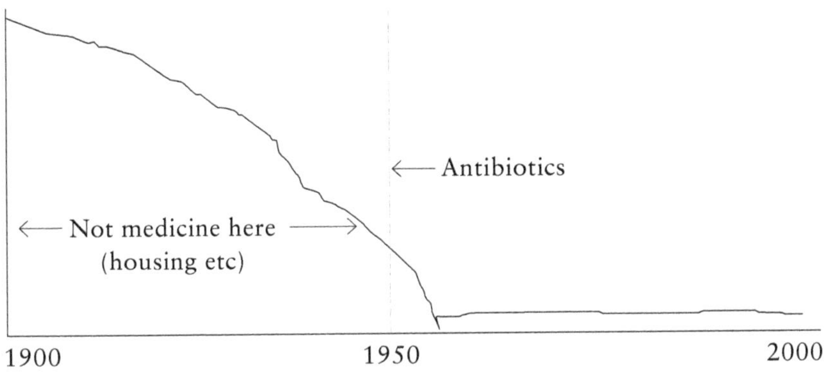

For the decline [in TB-related deaths] before antibiotics, it was the same things that happened with the increased population. So we now know that better environment leads to better health – that can be taken as a given. In the Northern Territory, Aboriginal infant mortality has come down, but if you break it up, the drop has been in the hospital domain, because we can evacuate the kids to hospital and treat them there.

A woman from the audience spoke up: 'So that's still a bandaid thing, isn't it?'

Basically yes. Those of you who are doctors and nurses, you know that basically we treat communicable diseases and we're good at sending people to hospital, fixing them and sending them home, but that in the community, environmental conditions could be way better. But it would be a mistake to think we can just copy the patterns of 18th and 19th century Europe and reproduce that in Aboriginal communities. These were changes which were based on mass colonisation, on slavery, on extracting the wealth of other lands, minerals and all that, to build up places like London. Nor is it as simple as transferring what happens in the third world to a fourth world situation. Basically Aboriginal communities have no fiscal independence to start with; there's very little employment in communities and what is there is usually government funded. I guess that's where our job in environmental health becomes a bit interesting.

Leaning back on their chairs, members of the audience slowly nod.

So what do people need to live healthy lives? There's been some good work. About ten years ago, an anthropologist, a doctor and an architect got together and decided to answer this question. They worked out that there were these nine things ...

Jimmy illuminates an overhead, showing the nine things prioritised in order of their likely impact on health improvement:

1. Washing people
2. Washing clothes/bedding
3. Removing waste
4. Improving nutrition
5. Reducing crowding
6. Separation of dogs and children
7. Controlling dust
8. Temperature control
9. Reducing trauma

And continues his narrative:

... and then they measured people's ability to do these things and found that the hardware in houses was so dysfunctional, people couldn't act on these basic things. Every three months they measured household capacity and they wrote down what they found in this book [holding up a copy of *Housing for Health*[6]], which some of you may have seen. It says basically things aren't working for three main reasons: poor design, poor construction and no repair and maintenance. They dispelled a lot of myths and showed that if you put functioning infrastructure in, people will use it. The breakdowns aren't because of people wrecking houses, misuse, vandalism, not even from overcrowding, but because the original construction is crappy, the designs are bad, and the materials aren't built for longevity. The load on houses is much greater too. The same mob did a washing machine survey in the centre [Central Australia] and found that the machines don't deal with the really high levels of calcium you get in that country and with having heavy blankets full of dust. Those machines go for four or five hours per day, but when you count the cycles, they break down at the same point machines in Alice [Springs] would – only that time comes around quicker in a community.

I guess you've all heard the one about how Aboriginal people trash the floorboards for firewood? I've heard it lots of times, but in all my years I've never seen it. It's really important to put these myths into perspective, because some of you are only going to be here for a short while and then you will go south and, given your contact with Aboriginal people, you will speak with a certain authority, and if you perpetuate the myths, then it just makes our job up here that much harder.

One of the audience members, an Aboriginal man, humphs agreement and nods vigorously at Jimmy's last remarks, folding his hands together across his paunch as he settles further into the chair.

'So how do you think that went?' I ask Jimmy afterwards.

'I talked too much again.'

The more things change

Thus far I have attempted to follow the routes of health fact exchange, to give some sense of how belief in the compulsion to intervene and the necessity of sharing information is reinforced.

Aboriginal people do not know how unwell they are: if they did know, they would surely prevent their own disorders and live differently.

But in the face of this determined finding, very little is known about Aboriginal incorporation of statistics. The prevailing assumption is that scientised facts have a considerable capacity to engender particular sorts of behaviour change, as long as the right kinds of media for transfer are provided (Lea 2005). But what exactly is this assumed edification power, and why does aiming for it fire the professional imagination so powerfully?

To better explore these questions, let's assume that Aboriginal ill-health has been statistically encountered, at least by the health professionals. In fact, let us see this statistical encounter not as an orderly transmission of facts in tutorial sessions but rather as an informational deluge, as a swamping of data which points to its own infinity and scarcity at one and the same time. For despite the layers upon already-sedimented layers of over-documented material, which allows Aboriginal institutional players to claim the (unverifiable) status of being the most over-researched people in the world, enough can never be known, and what is known is always uncertain.[7] Within the health bureaucracy, and well beyond it, facts about the poor health of Aborigines come from random and arbitrary directions – dinner party conversations, political inquiries, breakthrough reports, corridor talk, policy documents, media articles, polemical speeches, academic papers and research seminars.

Rueful or condemnatory facts about Aboriginal morbidity regularly erupt in scandalised re-recognitions of racial inequality, with the release of every 'groundbreaking' piece of health and well-being research. These regularly recurring aghast rediscoveries or 'fact-events' (Dumit 2000: 6, 2004) statistically re-prove that government efforts towards reconciliation are not working hard or fast enough, that the system is continuing to fail Aboriginal people, that there are inequalities in resourcing and funding, that injustice still reigns, or, as in case of the current national intervention, that emergency action of both distal and proximate kinds are immediately warranted.

In each case, the chaotic repetition and heterogeneous iteration and absorption of health facts has its own specific density of encounter (see Hacking 1991), but at the same time, each moment forms part of a wider patterning. It both draws on and reifies particular historical classifications (the agreed constellations of phenomena that warrant sombre measurement) and a culturally established 'trust in numbers' (Porter 1995). That is, each iteration embeds and is embedded within a deep socio-cultural underpinning that imbues statistical representations with a logic and comprehensibility they would not otherwise have, given their highly abstracted character (see also Martin 1994, Rapp 1997). This heritage enables, first, the authoring of factual research within health (and ordains the institutional resources such authoring relies upon), and second, the widespread acceptance that such cultural artefacts are transparent representations of a more serious underlying social reality they purport to explain.

The social life of health facts becomes denser still if we add a chrono-historical dimension to the laterally replicating fact-events.

Looking back, it is possible to trace the same concern that Aboriginal people do not know the detail of their own pathology and/or what to do about it from the present day right though to the very beginnings of colonial medicine in the Northern Territory. Though each historical moment reveals its own idiosyncratic specificity, in the archival work undertaken for this ethnography, the core of the formulations surrounding ill-health, social disorder and what to do about them has shifted surprisingly little. Calls for community involvement and greater awareness, more research and better coordination abound, and have done so for an extraordinarily long period.

Among other effects, this relentless framing of both the problem and solution contributes to participants' sense that despite extensive re-analysis, critique and an ever-widening sphere of interventions and pronouncement, things remain the same. Hence, even though a central origin point for the information deluge about Indigenous morbidity and mortality may be impossible to isolate (as facts and factoids emerge chaotically from random directions), at the same time it remains a *deterministic* phenomenon, with a tremendous sameness characterising the history and style of our professional worry and diagnosis for urgent remedial action.

Take, for instance, a summary report depicting Aboriginal health 30 years ago:

> The poor health of Aboriginal people is a matter for concern ... comprehensive figures are not available, but it is known that in some areas Aboriginal babies die at a rate five times greater than other infants in the Australian population ... Low incomes, poor housing conditions and lack of appropriate knowledge continue to affect the health of Aboriginal adults and children. (Australian Reference Service 1976: 11)

Or, for a moment of cross-bureaucratic replication, look closely at the pattern of Mark Smith's briefing notes for the fledgling executive of the newly independent Northern Territory Department of Education, 'on intellectual handicaps and mental retardation within Aboriginal children in communities'. As the Principal Education Advisor on Guidance and Special Education, Smith set the scene by citing extracts from another government report, the Commonwealth Department of Health's *1977/78 Annual Report*:

> The more one studies the evolution of the Northern Territory,
> the more one is struck by its short history of development ... far
> too many Aboriginals live in grinding poverty with poor or non-
> existent water supplies and dangerous sanitary conditions. It is
> small wonder that babies brought up beneath the shelter of a piece
> of corrugated iron to fend off the blazing sun of the day and the
> sometimes sub-zero temperatures of the night have a high infant
> mortality rate, that intestinal parasites abound and infection is the
> commonest cause of morbidity and mortality. (Smith 1977: facing
> page)

Completing these alarming selections from the Commonwealth's report,
Smith cites the words of a prominent NT local, Dr Charles Gurd:

> Aboriginals live in an 'Oliver Twist' world of blinding poverty
> with 19th century demographic patterns of high birth rates, high
> population growth, high mortality rates both adult and infant,
> as well as high levels of illiteracy and unemployment and a high
> incidence of morbidity largely of an infectious nature. Trachoma,
> leprosy, tuberculosis, otitis media, bronchitis, pneumonia and
> gastro-enteritis are the order of the day. (Smith 1977: facing page)

Then, after carefully acknowledging the extraordinary array of efforts
currently being undertaken by the education department, Smith raises
their inadequacy: 'What more can the Department of Education do to
face the situation?' His answer is achingly familiar:

> ... on its own it can do little more than it is doing at present ...
> It may well be that in league with other Departmental agencies,
> greater success can be achieved than is being achieved now ...
> Such interagency coordination would ultimately depend on the
> establishment of a departmental task force [which] would have
> the task of:
>
> » establishing a data base through detailed research.
> » establishing lines of interdepartmental communication.
> » recommending more appropriate courses of action to
>   departments and courses of action between departments.
>   (Smith 1977: 4, §4.1)

And so fractal coordinations and recursive definitions of the problem
are given new life, and the agency offers a solution that reproduces its

internal forms, within the unarguable frame of improving things for the disadvantaged Aborigine in the abject beyond.

Fact impacts

We can now imagine facts as travelling and transmuting between encounters with interlocutors, as travelling like particles in heated animation, simultaneously bombarding health professionals from indeterminate directions and operating according to a set of rules.[8] We can further imagine facts as able to be acted upon – fired up to create scandal, warmed to subjectively link to people's lives, or cooled down to become the object of serious epidemiological work.[9]

Now let us imagine the health professional as akin to the suspended particle, held in equilibrium by the bombardment of data on Aboriginal health, data which abstractly index alarming infinities of illness and disadvantage. It is an equilibrium created out of the sense that there is no room to move (the ill-health is so complex, and ultimately caused by unretractable colonisation itself), yet still so very much to be done. Always there is scope for better management, more research, less turnover, more commitment, more resources, more action, more coordination, more planning and review, more learning, more dialogue, more partnerships, more data and better information transfer.

While the Brownian metaphor of the suspended particle is mine, it draws attention to the analyses health bureau-professionals make of their own inundation.[10] In describing their work, health professionals complain of things heating up, of the increasingly fast tempo required of their outputs, and of the rapidly accelerating overflow of things to know, read, keep abreast of, and participate in formulating. They pine for a time when the busyness ceases and they can take stock and plan, but they also say things are so dire, so critical, that their presence is required now. They strive for new approaches yet complain that nothing changes, that things have been as they are for so long now, and are getting worse in fact, if indeed we turn to the facts. We've done/ we're doing all we can. And yet, on the horizon, around the corner, embedded within (select) program success stories and deliverable with (infinitely unachievable) perfection of data, lies the possibility of improvement … if the more that can always be done could just be achieved with redirection of effort, with more consistent funding, enhanced coordination and the design of a better approach. Or, when improvement is achieved, if it could be sustained, or if it is sustained, updated, and when it is updated, made more Aboriginal. With each problem diagnosis, new life is breathed into the proliferating need to share information and better coordinate with each other, and with the Other. On the one hand, 'We'll all be rooned', it is such a catastrophe; and on the other, let's get to it, there's still so much to be done:

> The Department always seems to be putting out statistical documents and each time they say the same sort of thing. What's the point? I read them and I think 'Ah yeah, so Aboriginal kids are fucked, they've got everything; and adults are fucked too, they've got everything as well.' I guess it's great to know, but there's never enough attention paid to how we're going to do it. (Male remote area public health professional, Darwin Rural, since departed)

If we invert the notion that it is Aboriginal disease – passive and silent – that triggers professional alarm, then perhaps it is the case that we worry ourselves sick about their sickness via other means. Health professionals embrace information sharing as a key tool for activating a motivating alarm for Aboriginal participants (and funders), because alarm has transfixed *them* via their own constant immersion in the catastrophe of ill-health. It is the avalanche of catastrophe and opportunity that animates health statistics, and which convinces health professionals that a key requirement of betterment is that Aboriginal people know how sick they are through an appropriately alarming rendition of the available statistics. One could say that health professionals' deep concern to extend and improve the lives of Indigenous people is expressed in their labour to produce and share health information.

With their worry fully embedded in the data they collect in order to shine a light on the exact dimensions of the problems to be fixed, what happens next is truly fantastic. As if it is a fetish object, data acquires quite magical, transformative properties in the professionals' imagination. In the small move from seeing data as the key to being empowered to seeing data itself as inherently powerful, information alone assumes an independent, universal and highly potent ability to change people's lives and behaviours. The health professionals' *depiction* of pathology is itself imputed a magical ability to influence that which it is, theoretically, merely a copy of. It gets to the point where information alone, stripped of its interpretive history and reasons for existence, perhaps made more pictorial for the illiterate client, comes to be seen as key to politicising individuals *en masse* and thus mobilising positive, health-affirming lifestyle change.

The heady desire to empower and enable through friendly forms of data sharing obscures more than the highly symbolic character of what are quintessentially abstract cultural forms (graphs, didactic images and pie-charts, for instance). The passion and anxiety that professionals clearly invest in their material also gets obscured. Data masquerades instead as expertly legitimated material that may need to be reconfigured to make it comprehensible, but that is otherwise an expertly elicited account of an otherwise unmediated reality. Of course health statistics do not simply speak for themselves – they require cultural familiarity and interpretive training to be comprehensible (see Helman 1991, Lea 2005, Martin 1994). But this is not why they are attributed such a potent power. On the contrary, health statistics alarm health professionals precisely because they seem to speak for themselves (as indeed they do for those of us who trawl through scientised gleanings and automatically calibrate our lifestyles to stave off decrepitude). The very possibility of proliferating statistical refinements in the name of change and cure creates a dynamic stasis which exhausts and compels its knowers towards producing, sharing and consuming more of the same. The well-designed pie-chart or fire engine red community report aimed at achieving the alchemy of Aboriginal transformation is, in short, a culturally stylised abstraction of our own governing imperfections. And as we are moved to act or feel defeated by these prompts, so shall Aboriginal people be. Our own cultural fascinations are held to fascinate others, and not for the first time.

More ordinarily, both in the workaday world of the health professional and in critiques of biomedical approaches, the virulence of facts is the focus. With anxieties about objectification processes duly aired and fought over, well-intentioned efforts are made to create ever more persuasive ways of speeding up the 'infectiousness' of health facts within the Aboriginal population. But it is not until we consider how health statistics are produced and consumed – indeed, made animate – in and through the bodies of worried whites, that the transformational power and motivational force ascribed to information can be accounted for. Health professionals are held in suspended animation both by the sheer force of the factual emissions they help generate, and by their relentless everyday battles (against system resistance to their work, under-resourcing, the wider societal hostility to Aboriginal people, or the vexations of upholding an anti-racist identity in the earnest bid to do things *with* rather than *for*). The information that has such salience for the health professional is reimagined as a mirror and reflected back to Aborigines, with the hope that not only will they 'see' and experience this factual viscerality for themselves, but they will embrace the public health effort and form mutually satisfying partnerships. The attraction of these facts about Aboriginal health as objects of knowledge, as magical artefacts, is because of their visceral relation to our own bodies, their (poorly understood) significance for our own experiencing of the world as worried intervenors.

Dismembering

Speaking of bodies, there is another curious disembodiment effect of the fetishisation of statistics: despite the constant talk about what needs to be done to reduce the burden of disease carried by the population of Aboriginal bodies, visceral imagery seldom underscores the worry. While public health is fundamentally concerned with the most intimate aspects of bodily function and daily life (eating, sleeping, cleaning, procreating, caring, rearing), it has curiously little to say about questions of embodiment. In the process of creating the scandal of Indigenous health, it seems unnecessary for the audience of interveners and sympathisers to vicariously sense what chronic disease might mean as a fully enfleshed and felt phenomenon. This is not to say that images of pathology are nowhere deployed: the current national intervention shows just how many uses images of ruin and decay can have. But isn't it odd that chronic disease, known to be eventually debilitating and life terminating, is presented as a stripped and straightened syndrome of rates and costs, and not an embodied state? In a context where 'Aboriginal' and 'at risk' have become synonyms, why doesn't it matter to learn what embodying every known risk factor from birth might actually feel like?

Perhaps even more curiously, when we consider the conscientious attention given to securing non-victim blaming explanations for why projects fail within the progressive politics of public health, the unwellness of Aboriginal participants never features as its own explanatory trope. What might easily be deployed as a sympathetic explanatory device for the seeming intransigency, poor compliance and service-resistance of Aboriginal people – namely, their apparently permanent states of depletion or chronic unwellness – is strangely not used. The disruptive condition of being made painfully aware of one's organs, internal functions and impairments as part and parcel of encroaching chronic dis/ease is rarely brought into view as part of what one must 'bear in mind' when talking to Aboriginal people about heath matters. And yet, deaths from the 'new' chronic diseases are, as medical anthropologist Nancy Scheper-Hughes (1992: 285) notes:

> prolonged, painful, and both socially and psychologically troublesome, as one must observe the slow, yet irreversible loss of the body's capacities and functions as well as the diminution of one's social roles, social network and economic resources.

Aboriginal ill-health is not just vicariously experienced as disembodied by health professionals; it is also seen to be disembodied for its carriers. Health professionals are told that Aboriginal people are often unaware of just how ill they actually are. The Aboriginal population is 'young and very sick', though the people themselves do not necessarily know it (yet), since they suffer diseases that 'are relatively asymptomatic for prolonged phases' (Wright 1996: 506). Indeed, the basic operating premise of chronic disease management, as reported in the *THS Preventable Chronic Disease Strategy*, is this:

> Chronic diseases, by definition, do not arise overnight. Instead, they *develop silently* over years until something serious happens that forces a person to attend a health centre, and interventions are required in the *silent period long before the disease itself appears*.[11] (emphases added)

Even trained health professionals may not be aware of just how sick Aboriginal people are (as when remote area nurses diligently measured and recorded childhood growth patterns yet were unable to 'see' the stunting in the otherwise live-wire, energetic little black bodies in front of their eyes). As the visual image may lack the look of disease, and fail to enact the performative dimension of unwellness,[12] the asymptomatically diseased Indigenous body cannot be trusted to tell an immediately ascertainable story. The aetiological opacity of chronic disease is further compounded, it is said, by a cultural tendency for Aboriginal people to deny or to tolerate pain until it is too late.[13]

So, given the need to create empathy in conditions of invisibility, what to make of the absence of sensory imagery in discourses of Aboriginal disease? Arguably it is an entirely logical omission. A sociological explanation would point to the immersion of health professionals in the disembodied and barely sensuous tropes of intellectualist modes and methods of accounting for the world. But that explanation won't do, for we've seen how the inadequacies of statistical artefacts do not go unrecognised within THS. Indeed, they are given their own explicit discourse of agonised analysis, and fuel ongoing attempts to enliven the exhibits.

Clinician-turned-philosopher Drew Leder (1990) identifies a different reason for the dearth of sensory imagery in efforts to compel public health attention, pointing to the enduring force of Cartesian dualism in western consciousness. Leder argues that despite its being in disrepute, the Cartesian habit of separating mind from body, sense from intellect, nonetheless makes good sense. We tend to remember our bodies in moments of sickness and distress, physical dysfunction or dismemberment, or when certain functional needs (hunger, thirst, fatigue) assert themselves. When our hands shake as performance anxiety takes hold, or when we accidentally slice a thumb, this humble digit's taken-for-granted use in our everyday life brought to a sensitive fore. Leder calls these events moments of 'dys-appearance', emphasising the fact that such physiological reawakenings are usually associated with troublesome states. According to Leder, such dys-appearances invert the alter state of the pain-free body. Pain-free, we comfortably inhabit ourselves, without having our corporeality surface as explicit grounds for doing and being.[14] Pain-free, the body disappears from casual awareness; in pain, it re- or dys-appears.

Writes Leder, the two words 'dys-appearance and disappearance have an antonymic significance':

> It is precisely because the normal and healthy body largely disappears that direct experience of the body is skewed towards times of dysfunction. These phenomenological modes are mutually implicatory, as can be seen in relation both to the body surface and the visceral depths ... Self-forgetting is thus intrinsic to body function. (Leder 1990: 86)

For Leder, this phenomenon explains perfectly the enduring significance of Cartesian dualism, for Cartesianism is a life-world epistemology, not just a mechanistic doctrine. It is precisely 'because the body is a tacit and self-concealing structure [that] the rational mind can come to seem disembodied' (1990: 86).

The lack of professional speculation about the possible disruptive effects of chronic pain and episodic illness on how Aborigines inhabit their days can likewise be explained as making good phenomenological sense. It is not just, or not only, that there is a trained tendency within health sciences towards objectification. Physical effects are also in play. In the very performance of abstract thought and formulation, as the body disappears into its own functioning and exquisite intellectualist worry, the professional transcends her own sense of physicality. In the process, any question of (own or other) corporeality is instinctively put to one side. Additionally, the cultural and economic status of the average bureau-professional confers the affluent comfort of bodily absence, even though it is the problematic organic operations of black bodies that are the subject at hand. We might say it is a sleight of mind over matter.

Moreover, within the humanist imagining that all people are not only psychological but also visceral carbon copies of ourselves, it is easy to sustain the paradoxical imagining that Aboriginal people are both riddled with disease and simultaneously living and moving through the world with the same bodily dis/dys-appearances as healthy professionals. In other words, the corporeality which is backgrounded for the intellectualising white is likewise not relevant to stories explaining either Aboriginal affliction or their apparent acquiescence in their own poor health. And so the middle-class norm of the disappearing body, in concert with mechanistic drives to express our professional concerns in scientistic and managerial modes, as opposed to somatically, directs the bureau-professional's interpretive moves. In the process, the professional's deeply encultured inhabitation of a disappeared body becomes the assumed viscerality of everyone (see Scheper-Hughes 1992: 185). This dance between unacknowledged universalisms and exaggerated ethnologisms is the defining feature of postcolonial liberal states in their helping guise.

One final and more salutary reason for the curious omission of Aboriginal corporeality from the repertoire of liberally decent vindicatory explanations for Indigenous people's apparently refractory lifestyles in the face of ongoing illness might be offered. There are two major sympathetic explanatory schemas available to public health – namely, that the burden of Aboriginal ill-health is a legacy of western colonisation, and that the pathology of Aboriginal lifestyles testifies to current government failure – and their crucial uniting feature is the tremendous scope left open for intervention. If Aboriginal people act the way they do because of what was done to them in the past, the action needed is clear: we must refuse to be like the oppressors of yesteryear. We must be more inclusive, more culturally sensitive, more willing to recognise, respect and even make use of cultural difference if we are to have any hope of 'turning things around', 'making a difference' or 'closing the gap'. And equally, if past and current projects have limited impact because of administrative failings (such as under-resourcing, lack of system coordination, too many projects underway at any one time, poor staff preparation, insufficient data, failure of political will, inadequate community consultation and involvement, or failure to transfer expertise to create sustainability), institutional solutions are at hand.

In contrast, an analysis that syllogistically suggests that a partial cause of continued Aboriginal ill-health is precisely the lethargy and hermeneutic disinterest caused by ill-health (its cause not being my concern here) is refused a place in public health discourse because it suggests no slot for bureaucratic intervention. Its endless circularity forecloses the possibility of expertly advised improvement and precludes any opportunity for government-led community self-development. It therefore simply cannot be admitted. As bureaucrats do indeed say when rejecting analyses that fail to respond to their depictions of trouble by recommending avenues for government action, 'it leaves no room to move'. For creating that room, maintaining the faith in intervention, is the single most intricate challenge facing bureaucrats and bleeding hearts.

MANUFACTURING OPTIMISM, MAINTAINING FAITH

Entering THS at any time during the 1990s, one quickly learnt the name of the Strong Women, Strong Babies, Strong Culture (SWSBSC) program. Even today, the Strong Women's project is frequently mentioned and newcomers are soon able to at least recognise the title, if not the program's precise history or content. Given the vast mass of program stories available, why is it that this tale above all others is so quickly acclaimed and transmitted? What recommends SWSBSC in particular as a good news story that should be repeated?

One explanation lies in its clear claim to that rare and elusive quality, 'real health gains' (Cross-Cultural-Consultants 1996: 4):

> Evaluation of the Strong Women, Strong Babies program for those
> communities involved in the project has shown a 43% reduction
> in the number of low birth weight infants, a 55% reduction in the
> number of premature births and a 140g increase in the mean birth
> weight (pre natal n = 226, post natal n = 137).[1]

But the program's quantifiable eligibility for the label 'successful' is only part of the story. There are other remedial interventions which could be related, others which have more striking numeric proof of their effectiveness – TB eradication, say, or sexually transmitted disease reductions – that do not circulate with anywhere near the same rapidity.

So the appeal of the Strong Women's program must lie in other, less tangible, uncountable aspects. Understanding this appeal takes us a long way into both sharing the helping white's interventionary dilemma, and understanding the convoluted work involved in holding at bay the contradictions embedded within progressivist postcolonial toil.

Let me tell the Strong Women story as it has been described to me by health professionals, as I myself have described it for others in policy writings, and as it is presented in numerous summary reports. Developed in 1993, the program was catalysed by numerous studies indicating that greater numbers of low birth weight babies are born to Aboriginal than to non-Aboriginal women (Markey et al. 1998, Sayers & Powers 1997). Such lightweight infants are more likely to die in their first year or have significant illness problems in early childhood than their heavier counterparts, with cumulative effects manifesting in such chronic and debilitating adult diseases as diabetes, hypertension, renal failure, and ischaemic and rheumatic heart disease. Low birth weight infants are also susceptible to multiple and simultaneous infections throughout their lives (d'Espaignet et al. 1998, Kruske, Ruben & Brewster 1999, Lee et al. 1994, Mathews 1996).

The SWSBSC program intends to disrupt such lifetime susceptibility by having older Aboriginal women share with younger women 'The Strong Women's Story', an affirmative narrative that uses graphic images to provide information about the nutritional status of women and their general reproductive health. The Strong Women's narrative is built around a flip-chart showing the road to good health as involving a series of rejections: don't drink too much alcohol or eat fatty foods, don't smoke *gunja*[2] and don't have unprotected sex. I recall one page showing a line drawing of such a good health road wending over a peninsula with tangents leading people to fall off cliffs called 'alcohol' and 'gambling'. Little people figures scramble up ladders from the rocks below their falls, others are lying still, *them ones finished up now*, while the steadfast remainder stay dedicated to the path, unswerving in their commitment to the health of their own and their baby's fragile bodies. The flip-chart is used as a pedagogical device to educate young girls and expectant mothers on how best to comport themselves throughout pregnancy and beyond; it is used alongside advice on the critical times for presenting to the health clinic for examinations and monitoring.

Since its inception and up to her retirement in June 1998, the public face of the SWSBSC program was Lorna Fejo.[3] A venerated Aboriginal woman, in 1992 Lorna was employed to coordinate an antenatal education program targeting Aboriginal women – and, importantly, was paid 'at a salary level usually paid to professional staff' (Fejo & Rae 1996: 2). In the first three communities targeted, Galiwinku, Wadeye and Milingimbi, the program operated on a cascade model. Respecting the cultural truism that pregnancy, birth and infant care fall into the domain of 'women's business', teams of strong women workers were meant to be nominated by the targeted communities on the basis of their cultural standing and then trained in maternal and infant nutrition and infection control. The team co-developed the 'Strong Women's Story' as the medium to promote antenatal discussions. The strong women workers in turn trained non-Aboriginal staff on the nature of those *non-western* antenatal practices that were formerly prevalent in communities. These retrieved rites were then incorporated into the program:

> [The women] focused on images of the smoking ceremony, which
> in contemporary times had fallen into disuse. The whole concept
> of ante-natal care became interwoven into a holistic and very
> powerful vision of women as nurturers of their culture represented
> by their participation in the smoking ceremony and other women's
> ceremonies. (Cross-Cultural-Consultants 1996: 18–19)

As a result of the SWSBSC interventions, younger women in the three pilot communities presented for antenatal care in community health centres more frequently and earlier in their pregnancies than before. This outcome has since been correlated with reduced incidences of recurrent infections in both the target women and their children, with increased pregnancy weight gains and increased infant birth weights. Such highly desired outcomes led to the program being implemented in other NT communities, including some in the southern desert areas. The increased birth weights also 'catapulted the program to national attention' (Kowal 2006a: 71), attracting interest from Indigenous communities in Queensland and Western Australia as a program which apparently was succeeding *because* of its recognition of the traditional nurturing and healing practices of Aboriginal women (THS 1999).

Don't let details get in the way

For those closest to the Strong Women program, naturally the program takes on a far more complex hue. Like so many public health professionals I've encountered, Jan Paddle, a nutritionist, was thrown into her first meetings with Aboriginal women armed only with a profound sense of wanting to transform the community's health and well-being – in Jan's case, Yolngu[4] people in northern East Arnhem Land – by using community development methodologies:

> When I first started, I can remember meeting one of the managers from Territory Health ... Out for a routine visit she [the manager] wanted to get a [Strong Women's] program started at Yirrkala.[5] And we were sitting at this meeting at Yirrkala when the manager said [indicating phantom Aboriginal women], 'All right, you, you and you are strong women, and Jan – you'll come out on Monday. All right, I'm going back to Darwin.' This was about the Thursday of my second week and I thought, 'Far out! I don't know what the program's about, I don't know the women, what do I do?' And I felt really discomforted going out on that Monday and walking into the Women's Resource Centre. Walking in, I didn't know what to say, I didn't know what to do. Don't know what to go on: how do I develop a program from here?
>
> It was horrible! Just a really horrible period. I just didn't know; I didn't know how to do it. And yet, *we're all meant to know* community development somehow! I was given this program to support and given the [women] – not through my own nomination – but given the women, and it wasn't even the women's nomination, it was just 'You and you, you're doing it' so the process to get me there on the Monday wasn't consultive [sic]. It wasn't through the community development model, it wasn't consultive. Every time I'd go out, the women weren't there. I couldn't understand the language, I didn't understand the people. It took about six months before we actually got it together. I'd be going out, not knowing what people were doing or key things that were happening. (Transcript, February 2000)

Three years later, the women nominated under the 'You, you and you' (Aboriginal-designed-and-led participatory process) had long since abandoned the program. So Jan 'worked with the Council and the Women's Centre to identify new ones [Strong Women workers]'. Only now she had to prove to her regional managers that the autonomous

Strong Women Workers really were working autonomously, by insisting that they keep daily diaries to record exactly how many other community women they talk to and refer to the clinic, and how many attend the clinic as a result.

At the same time, the new Aboriginal coordinator of the overall program who had replaced Lorna Fejo was worried abut the flip-charts she'd inherited from Lorna. She felt that the Strong Women Workers were reluctant to use such overly moralistic media. Instead, she had ideas of her own that she wanted to develop. She wanted to talk to the young girls about how poison transmits to the foetus through the umbilical cord and to develop a new handbook describing how much 'gut damage' (villi stunting) occurs with repeat gastrointestinal infections in young children.[6] Jan, in turn, was worried that the Strong Women Workers had not had any professional development since the program was originally conceived and that Head Office only seemed to care about the number of communities enrolled in the program. To Jan's mind, Health House was not interested in any real information about the program's ongoing impact. Nor did they appear concerned by the fact that the Strong Women were expected to repeat the same activities year in, year out, without baulking at the tedium. Worse, whenever Head Office did pay attention, they demanded bizarre quantifications, exerting forms of vertical control that made no sense in the field, such as insisting that the Strong Women Workers keep diary records of any clinic visits from expectant mothers that could be attributed to SWSBSC interventions:

> So I said, 'So how about giving them some literacy skills? How about giving them a place in the clinic to store these diaries? How about giving them a role in the clinic?' These women find it hard to even have knives in the home! It is so unrealistic! The strength of Strong Women is that it started as a grass-roots project and now with all these new expectations but no additional support the women don't know what they should be doing any more. With all the intrusions from THS, it is losing its power.

At the same time that both the new coordinator and the nutritionist complained that the 'grass-roots' Aboriginal women were not sufficiently respected, their battle was also with each other – over who consults with the community women the best. At one stage, an educational workshop for the Strong Women Workers was being planned (one of many and not particularly special), but there was intense disagreement between the two about the workshop focus and approach. Jan wanted to tackle the issue of gut damage indirectly, at what she imagined to be the women's pace, in the spaces between catch-up gossip and basket weaving with stripped pandanus leaves. They should build up to the complex issue of villi attrition slowly, by carefully introducing the intestinal system and the critical function of the minute, finger-like vascular filaments plushly matting the insides of the small intestine. Jan believed that the issues to be explained were complex and the cause and effect patterns difficult to explain. The bush women would need time to learn. But the new program coordinator didn't want a slow, indirect approach. For her, the issue was far too important: it must be tackled head-on. They should adopt a more assertive tack and set the agenda in advance. 'The women will wonder what the workshop is for if all they do is gather bush tucker, and anyway it is not Jan's program!' she simmered – and, so powerfully unsaid it hovered in the air: unlike her, Jan's not Aboriginal, so what could she know?

Meanwhile the chief paediatrician at Royal Darwin Hospital was fuming about the entire program. He felt no one was talking to Aboriginal people properly about the grave implications of the intestinal damage, the villi atrophy and microcephaly[7] he was witnessing on a scale that would be considered a national emergency if this was a refugee camp! (Is he now eating these words?) To his mind, it is because we are a first world country full of postcolonial guilt that we're content to kill people with a benign refusal to attribute blame and locate responsibility accurately. Let's face it, he says, the Strong Women program is nice and all but it really isn't getting to the heart of the issue:

> We have got to put pressure on communities to get their act
> together ... because of white man's burden, we get this, 'Oh it's
> all our fault' sort of thing so people back off from saying what
> needs to be said. I think that no longer can we accept this guilt/
> blame scenario; that's got to end. It's amazing to me. I have two
> black children; I've spent 20 years in the developing world on
> a miserable salary, so I really don't have [this silencing guilt]. I
> mean in Africa, if you have white man's burden you're dead on
> the ground 'cause they know how to play it! They're much more
> sophisticated in West Africa, they're playing white people. I just
> see this all the time around me [here], white people back off and
> don't say anything – except totally acceptable points of view. I

think that's got to end ... in the Territory we've got microcephaly in much, much higher proportions that I've ever seen before ... I mean in Africa a breastfeeding mother that hasn't got AIDS, they're healthy, they'll survive, they do fine, they get diarrhoea and they recover. It's a very different situation here and why is that? I think it's because they've got *worse* underlying gut rot, because the hygiene situation and their skin is much more diseased and there's much more infection of their gut. [Their skin and intestines] get colonised and diseased much more than in the developing world or in many developing countries. OK, it would be nice to fix that overnight, but the interventions that fix that are not readily available in a dysfunctional community. It takes time, years of time. What's concerning me is that we're really not addressing this even in the long term.

Not all successes succeed

Theorist of science and technology cultures Joseph Dumit (1997: 99–100, n.5) terms the hybrid anecdotes which circulate with the efficacy of the tabloid story and the believability of the established truth 'factoids'. In THS, health factoids circulate as authoritative accounts of success, of the grass being greener on the other side and of a good approach that worked elsewhere and could be made to work here too. Factoids do not need to be seen to be believed; iteration is all that is required. For example:

> *I know* that in 1991 when we were looking at changing the health system in Queensland, we were looking to the Territory for all the answers, and you know, at that stage *we thought*: the Territory, they've got [Aboriginal] Health Workers running clinics, they've got this, they've got that ... we can do this too! And we did it. But then I come to the Territory, I found that it's nothing like our projections and there's only very isolated pockets of talented people. And they, the [Aboriginal] Health Workers, seem to be alienated, disempowered. I think *once there were* some really good strong systems for education, training and support that are not here now and consequently we have a fairly dysfunctional Health Worker workforce. Now, I don't think we can't turn that around. I think that we can and we have started to, but *it's going to take a lot of work and effort.* (Rural Health Manager, since returned to Queensland)

The factoid story from afar that inspired belief in NT primary health care approaches dissolved up close, but hope was resurrected by referencing a past when it worked, and a future when it would again. Without the circulating 'good news', health professionals become bleak, pessimistic, mired in the mass of previous efforts. They cannot see how to keep on doing. They suffer 'burnout': a phenomenon that results from pitting one's own helpfulness against an alterity that refuses to budge in the direction of performance indicators:

> It got to the stage where if I heard one more person tell me to get 'runs on the board', if I had to organise one more trip, to badger a group of people who see me as no different to all the other bloody whitefellas that have been before me, I was going to go under. I had to stop. I was being set up to fail. Set up. I'd been doing it for too long by then. Lost my naïveté. (Remote area worker, Darwin rural, since departed)

As a factoid, then, the Strong Women, Strong Babies, Strong Culture story remains to this day the story of a program approach that 'works', that people continue to cite in happily vague awareness of its implementation trials and tribulations. Why? Because it provides a rare affirmation of the community development mantra that, encouraged to call on a sanctified past (reconstructed in terms recognisable to the public health imagination) and design something for themselves (within set program parameters), Aboriginal people can overcome their own grim present. Under SWSBSC, Aboriginal health is saved by resurrecting and paying equal wages for a faded and regionally specific custom reformulated in the direction of contemporary care plans. And in that small, liberatory program manoeuvre, the Health Department functionalises and becomes the institutional bearer of 'Aboriginal culture', no longer part of the threat that came with colonisation, but that culture's greatest institutional supporter. The story assuages health professionals' greatest fear: that attempts to transform Aboriginal health necessarily involve collateral damage to Aboriginal traditions and lifestyle, which is not even one step removed from what their destructive colonial forebears did.

The SWSBSC factoid proves that the elusive techniques of community development are the right tools for 'helping whites' to adapt, regardless of what critics such as Noel Pearson might say. This is why the story is repeated, why 140 or 79 grams of extra baby weight slam dunks the achievements of other programs. It is the holy grail of public health work. It proves that, if approached the right way, Aboriginal people really can be made healthy without enduring further damage to their culture. In other words, the *value* of it being true outranks other reportable gains and withstands known schisms in practice because it meets a need larger than the literal program itself: namely, the need for evidence of the efficacy of community development as both philosophy and method.

SWSBSC speaks of a break with the colonial past in the same moment that the authentic Aboriginal past is sympathetically retrieved from the disease-causing weight of invasion history. In the world of THS's treacherous postcolonial mind games, this is an important achievement. Retaining a progressive identity is assisted through the promulgation of 'good news' stories such as these; stories which in turn weave selected historical threads and a hint of the hopeful future into the warp and weft of an anti-racist public health agenda. Program achievements based on medical therapies, clinical interventions or improved infrastructure (better airstrips that lead to faster emergency retrievals and fewer infant deaths), for instance, do not have the same currency as stories which proffer the hope that one day, Aboriginal people will no longer need to be acted upon. They will instead be just as self-regulating as the professional classes, *cultural distinctiveness intact*. As one senior manager put it, describing the symbolism of the program:

> So much of what we do is unconsciously culturally biased. Most
> of our approaches are bound up in our own culture. Strong
> Women Strong Babies is a rare counter example. It is quite clearly
> successful because it belongs to the women, to the community,
> and not just with the Department.

History bent to optimistic projection has little need for detailed empiricism: this is the kind of story public healthers need to believe in. At any rate, no project can ever really withstand the multiple tests of truth that could be lined up to gun down its claims. A constituency of upholders is necessary for any effort to have a life.

History's applications

In many ways the Strong Women factoid captures some defining attributes of THS. It is made true through social processes. It circulates as both an impossible (and idealised) fantasy, and as a fully realisable actuality – a real program with real outcomes, that could be everyone's outcome with the right mixture of approach and manner. The program operates as a promissory note luring the dedicated towards the success that could be theirs if they could only speak to and form relationships with Aboriginal people with sufficient attention to inclusion and motivational information sharing. In the SWSBSC good news story, the single most proclaimed factor in public health success is that programs are driven by Indigenous people themselves, without this being a domineering inveigling.

The countering optimism behind insistent constructions of SWSBSC's success offers the promise of the resolution of what is essentially the helping white's ongoing dilemma. Namely, how does one emphasise the rights of Indigenous people to standards of living equal to that of non-Indigenous people, and insist on the responsibilities of the state to deliver this improvement, without it all being part of the colonial endeavour that originally created the problems? Partly, the bureau-professional has to imagine that the sorts of cultural difference in need of repair or reform are not the 'good' customary practices of pre-colonial yore, but rather the 'bad' bits that colonial intrusion is held responsible for. Within the public health imagination, the hope is to identify discrete 'lifestyle' differences that, with a surgeon's precision, can be isolated for excision, as long as the programs are carefully planned and delicately executed.

Living with the paradoxical diagnosis that invasion is the cause and more intervention the therapy involves breathtaking epistemological manoeuvres and the creation of a pathway out of the ups and downs of historical reference. To manage the fundamental untenability and selflessness of doing nothing and everything at once, the helping white has to call upon multiple semiotic devices to assist, including a motile form of historical referencing:

1   Aboriginal people have had no time: the pace of change since invasion has been so rapid that people have been left bewildered and perplexed, unable genetically[8] or socially to adapt to a

dramatically altered landscape and lifestyle. Explaining what is happening and changing things will take time. An ancient culture has been shattered by change so monumental that pathological and refractory behaviour, fatalism, victimhood, community dysfunction and premature decline are understandable and predictable responses.[9]

2   Aboriginal people have been given too much over too long a time: the intensity of the welfare effort has so disempowered people that they've been rendered dependent, lacking the hunger that would drive the subject peoples of other colonies to more genuine forms of self-determination (Pearson 2001).[10] After such vast investments of effort and resources, there should be more results.

3   Aboriginal people are trapped in time: kinship obligations, patterns of exchange and dependence, tethered to a hunter-gatherer mode of living (no harbouring, no rationing, no budgeting, no investing, no deferring) subverts the rational individualism required for sustainable health improvements.[11] In this formulation, culture loses its appeal as a creative resource which can be mobilised towards health gain and becomes instead just an obstacle.

4   At the same time, the benefits of the primitive time, when people were mobile across the country, wisely avoiding sustained contact with their own detritus and faecal matter, always moving on before micro-parasites could proliferate, have been lost. Fixed and unable to adapt, the new sedentary lifestyles in overcrowded dwellings admit hyper-infestation, inviting multiple and simultaneous contact diseases from an early age that are repeated throughout the prematurely shortened life course.

5   Health interventions will take time: reduction of mortality and morbidity rates requires generational transition and long-term government commitment. Health improvements 'may only be sustained on the basis of significantly changed environments, patterns of activity and consumption and household patterns which influence childcare and development' (Robinson 1996: 3). Even then, improvements may be indirect, their connection with singular interventions lost in time, thwarting the evaluative measurements of present gain against past status quo used in calculations of productive time.

6   Nothing lasts: health interventions in communities are dependent on the commitment and enthusiasm of the (high-turnover) project officers who initiate them, for lamentably, in the highly distractible hands of Indigenous protagonists, there is very little durability.

7   We are never in the right time: the Territory's diseconomies of scale, isolation and scarcity of talent put it permanently behind all other jurisdictions in the national competition for leadership status and fiscal strength.

8   In eventual utopian time, Aboriginal people will be able to assume control of their own health, socio-economic well-being and management of services. As such, a positive future obsolescence underwrites all project determinations, recruitment and training practices.

9   But there is never enough time to reach this point; our work is always incomplete.

The future perfect when interventions can be laid aside and the helping white's presence rendered obsolete is always around the corner, lurking in the wings of history.

The problem is also the answer

> To understand why the health of Aboriginal people has failed to improve (and has probably deteriorated) we need to understand how most Aboriginal people have been marginalised by the dominant culture in a land that was originally theirs. They suffer disproportionately from poor education, unemployment, poverty, poor housing, poor nutrition, alcohol, poor health services and all other ills of Australian society. These social and historical origins of poor Aboriginal health can be traced back to the time of colonisation. (Mathews 1996: 30)

Within such compact models of causality lies an entire genealogy of institutional exposure which is simultaneously self-completing and unable to imagine life outside government-led policy. Posing as universal and apolitical indicators of need, such conceptualisations simply take for granted a complete sense that for all subjects, historically and today, *all* aspects of life are propelled primarily by government policy (see Mitchell 2002). I stress the 'all', for it is a fact of bureaucratic logic that the full sweep of human experience and meaning can be distilled into categories of assumed wider import (such as economics, politics, colonisation). The pedestrian phraseology (marginalisation, poor education, unemployment, and so on) is a giveaway to the *a priori* conceptual orderings involved. Whatever else might matter to life as it is individually and distinctively lived is not attended to, or rather is overridden by an insistence that (our socially conceived) characterisations of 'social forces' are always more crucial. Such explanatory categorisations have at their heart the idea that they are not governing abstractions at all, but speak to all that is real.

Among other effects, the space occupied by Territory Aborigines is transformed into a 'symbolic pocket of poverty' which lacks, and so is able to set into sharp relief 'the gains of "our" material wealth, education, literacy, sophistication' (Stewart 1996: 118). How we valorise our own history and thus judge the circumstances of other people, even if we are critics of our own cultural heritage, is bound up in this totalising logic. In the magical circularity of interventionary perception, it is natural to believe that our past failures to be fair about resource allocation and other matters of policy necessitate greater (if more enlightened and reformed) government intervention in the present. When governmental categories are imagined as making up everything that matters for a life, it is a small step to assume that the only way forward is more governance. This is the magic of intervention.

PART III

MEETING THE STATE

ENCOUNTERING

In this chapter we confront a seeming paradox. Why, given the intense interest in Aborigines, is there relatively little effort to seek to know Aboriginal people in their lived actuality?

Thirty years ago, Hugh Brody, an anthropologist who spent his life learning the ways of the hunters of the Arctic, turned his attention to the white administrators who huddled in service settlements, employed to improve the native condition. His words make for painfully familiar reading:

> On those rare occasions when Whites and Eskimos do interact socially and casually, on occasions that are not formal and ordered by the conventions of work situations, most Whites are excruciatingly embarrassed. They do not know how to talk or what manner to adopt; they become nervous and self-conscious, they suffer from a painful shame and confusion. They exaggerate their gestures and raise their voices, showing in every aspect of their social being an acute and pervasive unease ... In such encounters, Whites show an urgent desire to please and to be sure that the Eskimo feels liked and respected. (Brody 1975: 75–76)

Among Eskimos, Whites simplify their English, talk more loudly, and seem desperate to communicate without insult. Yet among each other:

> Whites are often competitive over the Eskimo's affection. They frequently denigrate colleagues by saying, 'The Eskimos don't like

him, you know'. And they are anxious to hear from any Eskimo speakers news of whom the Eskimos may have criticized among themselves. In a general, perhaps metaphysical sense, Whites are obsequious to Eskimos: what the Eskimo says and believes about them is a matter of great importance. (Brody 1975: 75–76)

Deprived of the comforting protocols of a work context, the rare occasions of one-on-one informal mingling 'off-duty' leaves the struggling White in a situation of total unfamiliarity: 'there is no formula for handling it, no procedure whereby communication can be established, and little or no exchange between the two personalities involved' (Brody 1975: 77). Instead, the Whites see the Eskimo only as an abstraction, a generalised ideal type, formed out of a composite of truisms authorised by those with the entitlement experiences of the old field hand. Iconic stories about who Eskimos are, or what Brody calls stereotypes, circulate among northern administrators through anecdotal routes undisturbed by the social science rules of verification.

The trepidations of anti-racism

It is astonishing how accurate a portrait this also is of health personnel encountering Aborigines in the Northern Territory – 30 years later, a different mix of people, an ocean, an equator, and a continent away. As with Brody's arctic Whites, a striking characteristic of public health professionals in northern Australia is their propensity to narrate tales of adventure and near disaster in their times spent working with Aboriginal people, to the commiserative or appreciative delight of friends and colleagues. I recall one Environmental Health Officer in this light with particular fondness (and memory of punished stomach muscles from long bouts of gripping laughter). Mal Guinness's ability to tell self-deprecating and uproariously hilarious field tales made him sought-after company, and his well-timed inserts could easily knock a more serious hand-wringing 'what is to be done' discussion sideways. He once boasted to me, with happy irreverence, that working with Aborigines made 'scoring' with left-leaning female backpackers visiting town so much easier – the political credibility his exotic remote area work automatically bestowed worked a dream. At the same time, what he had to say also proved that he had authentic encounters with Aborigines to relate, and his irresistible humour made the competitive subtext of his inter-collegial displays of knowledge all the more palatable.

But for me, Brody's suggestion that stereotypes are to blame for the depersonalising of Eskimo–White encounters, while believable, falls short of a full explanation. Just as straight 'complicity' has limited capacity to explain the binds of institutional thought and action, so too the suggestion that 'stereotypes' explain the exquisite self-consciousness of whites in relation to Aborigines seems incomplete. Such a mentalist account leaves the phenomenological grip of patterned behaviours unexplained. The hold of 'stereotypes' when people are comporting themselves in the most ethical and sensitive ways they can muster is still to be reckoned with. It is the persistence of abstractions when the THS-trained fieldworker's vocabulary has been repeatedly scoured for hints of ethnocentrism, which requires closer scrutiny. How can a 'stereotype', such an emotionless concept, account for the burning figure of embarrassment Brody's description so recognisably captures? How does it explain the despondency of health professionals who feel their own lack of enthusiasm and self-doubt makes their rather uninspiring and moralistic lifestyle messages even more insipid? The misery of feeling oneself to be inept and out of ken?

It is in the very attempt to rid oneself of racial and cultural stereotypes that we can locate the breeding ground for the *not-knowing*, for the acute self-consciousness and ultimate isolation in face-to-face encounters that Brody has depicted so accurately. It is the deep commitment to the notion that Aboriginal people are culturally different, and culturally different in always enigmatic and potentially disruptive ways, that interrupts the process of engagement whereby one experiencing subject meets another and tendrils are sent out to probe and soften the edges of strangeness, there to build rapport and solidarity. Aboriginal and non-Aboriginal people alike are called on to *navigate, inhabit and replenish* a complex set of signs as they represent themselves to each other.

Like analyses which assume that policy declarations sufficiently explain the life-worlds of bureaucrats, mentalist accounts can omit consideration of how personal encounters hold within themselves effects of their own which abut and create the superstructural forces that are tracked by many social scientists (see Cowlishaw 2004, Sennett 2003). People actively produce, perform and affectively constitute 'socially constructed' abstractions. Racial categories are embodied, not simply ideational.

Since this is a story of my anguishes too, this chapter gives a closely contextualised story of me as a fieldworker beginning her work among health's fieldworkers. My hope is that by immersing myself sufficiently in the mire I can better resist the pernicious desire to depict bureaucratic anguish sardonically, as if anything noble is simply the disingenuous guilt of people denying their role in continuing relations of oppression. The more difficult task is to represent the clear desire of health professionals to work jointly with Aboriginal people in accordance with principles of social justice and mutual dialogue, collaboration and empowered action, to convey the essential dignity of this ambition, while showing its continuities with governmentality.

The cursed store

In the year 2000, remote area nutritionist Marlene Thomas was out at Numbulwar, a coastal community of Nunggubuyu people at the mouth of the Rose River in East Arnhem Land.

Marlene had returned to Numbulwar to talk to the store manager – as usual, a white man – about the opportunities for implementing a new Food and Nutrition Policy that had opened up because the store had to be completely rebuilt from scratch. The old store had been cursed, and so had been closed down for at least two years, its doors permanently padlocked, and all its stock, perishable and other, lost to rats and tropical decay; the refrigeration machinery sat idle, its internal components quietly gridlocking with rust.

Marlene was working to meet a central office policy requirement for all remote area nutritionists that by the year 2000, 80 per cent of all community stores would have formal Food and Nutrition Policies in place (Stronach, Mills & Ryan undated). Marlene was dubious about the target. She was more than prepared to work with the store managers on what constituted community development and health-maximising practices – quality fresh products, visibly displayed; a policy of employing local people to work in the store, eventually to manage it; and so on – but she resented that 80 per cent target for its clear conflict with the community development maxim of working with community people at their pace and on their priorities. At Numbulwar, she told me, there was one week when the normal store manager was temporarily replaced by Sharon, the expatriate book-keeper, who had inadvertently forgotten to order in replacement lollies. The people spent their money on other things, and store turnover didn't go down at all. So now, she says, the manager 'forgets' every week. 'And that's how local policies should go – they should develop at the grass roots, even if it is opportunistic like that.' She goes on: 'I don't know why we don't just restrict the availability of unhealthy food in the first instance. But then we would be accused of doing things for people, of being too paternalistic, I suppose.'

'80 per cent of this, 60 per cent of that, 20 per cent of the other,' she railed:

> These figures are arbitrary, somebody dreamt them up, they are not real. It is disempowering for somebody like me – what if I can't reach that percentage? The reasons why are not of concern – there is never any context asked for. All they would look at is what I did or didn't 'achieve', with a very narrow interpretation of what is to be counted. And what if I do run around shoving random [store] policies together? What about the relationship to change on the ground, to people's behaviours? There would only be interest in our ability to match the percentage improvements. And if I don't, then [I can] expect a questioning of the resources I've been allocated.

When I first travelled to Numbulwar with Marlene, nearly two years before, in July 1998, she was still new to her job, and while she was not as fiery about the ineptitude of central office policies, she was already mounting a critique of administrative inefficiency. We had met earlier, accidentally, during the orientation program in March that year, when I was participating as an ethnographer and she as someone genuinely new to THS. By chance we sat at the same hexagon table on the first day and in the way of habitual returns to original seatings, we shared the same workshop sessions over a dense fortnight of condensations and generalities impressed upon us as necessary knowledge for good operators. She had told me then that she had 12 communities to look after and that her time was totally in the hands of the community, because the nutrition program worked in a community development mode. But that there was also a lot of paperwork and organising of travel, office politics to navigate, and many workshops and meetings to attend:

It is ridiculous. I go out only one, if I'm lucky two, days a week and the rest of the time is either organising to go out or dealing with office bumph. There are so many inefficiencies. I have to get travel forms signed by Darwin office – it is very inefficient. And then because the nutrition program connects with so many other programs, you spend a lot of time trying to connect with other staff who are also doing bush work and are in transit themselves and very hard to catch. We are like ships in the corridor, you just by-pass each other coming and going, so trying to coordinate community visits – well it's just a crazy system.

Sure enough, on my first visit with Marlene in her workplace, it took an inordinate amount of time to organise another seat on the same light aircraft she was booked on so I could accompany her to Numbulwar for a field trip within a field trip.[1] There were repeat phone calls from the travel clerk with advice that I would have to pay for a separate charter. Hang on, no, won't have to do that, I could go separately on the doctor's plane for free. Nope, I could go with Marlene on her flight instead. Actually, I could only go one way with Marlene but unfortunately there'd be no return, unless a seat became available 'on spec', in which case I would have to pay several hundred dollars in cash and on the spot to the pilot … No wait, good news, it's all sorted, I can go both ways, for free, no problems, I would just have to help Marlene pick up medicines and pathology items from the hospital before six in the morning.

Then Marlene told me to fax the Numbulwar Council with an explanation of what I was doing (as an anthropologist shadowing a health professional). It took at least an hour to get the wording right. It took at least another to get the fax through as the number was wrong, and tracking down someone who had the updated version snowballed into a piece of time-consuming detective work as I found list after list in office after office, all with the incorrect number. Yet on hearing about how many times the travel clerk had rung me with changes to the travel plans and how long it had taken me to send the explanatory fax, Marlene was delighted: 'Day one and you are already in the picture! So now you know!'

She kept returning to this in a light-hearted kind of way and told others, tongue-in-cheek, that I was really seeing things how they actually happened. During the day several things had gone wrong for her as well.

When we had returned from lunch the telephones were not working, her hard drive on the computer had been broken since the morning and now her printer was refusing to respond so she couldn't print the education material she had been intending to take to Numbulwar.

It became a theme of its own, the business of 'so now you know', and it proved critical to eventually being treated as part of the furniture by other regional officers, as someone to yarn with over a cup of tea in the staff room; or to get to do a minor but time-consuming errand or two. And it allowed me to keep company with health professionals when they travelled to communities, to sit out long journeys in four-wheel drives and light aircraft and retreat to our sleeping quarters for post-mortems at night. The following comments were typical:

> It takes a thousand hours to unpack the car because someone else has left their junk in it, and then put all your stuff in there … I might think I can get away by such and such a time but it never, ever seems to happen … Like you ring up the clinic and say, 'What do you want?' and they say we want this or something or other so you collect it and get that all on too. It's tiring, and that's before you start.

'You cut all this stuff out in a consultation session when we are asked how things might improve. We say "better coordination" or "more realistic deadlines" instead,' an office worker in the East Arnhem regional office tea room told me, pleased with my interest in how things *really* worked. This was just one of the many such discussions over the sheer logistical hassle of doing bush work that I was to have over the coming months of hanging out with regional officers.

For the first few weeks before our trip to Numbulwar, I had stayed in Nhulunbuy, the administrative service centre for the East Arnhem region, sleeping in the government-issued home of another health professional, who, being away on study leave, had made his rare three bedroom house available to Cathy, a Murri woman from Queensland, and more temporarily still, to me. I'd first met Cathy when she was only three weeks into her new job as Aboriginal Health Promotion Officer. It was hard for her, she'd said then, being an Aboriginal woman, because people seemed to constantly forget that all this was new to her too. Everyone speaks clear English where she comes from in Queensland, and they're light skinned: here she was astonished and proud to see 'real Aborigines, real tribal people', not just the odd dark one in among 'the caramel', like back home, but great numbers of 'really black' blackfellas. Even so, she wasn't enjoying her work very much. It wasn't what she had been expecting, which was itself hard to put into words, but she just sat in an office most of the time, and since hers was only a temporary job, she occupied herself with looking for other positions and writing emails home.

In my meantime, I occupied myself with inveigling my way into the lives of the other officer workers in the small public health outpost of THS, discovering the rivalries and cleavages between those who saw themselves as doers and those who saw themselves as facilitators, with both claiming superior results when it came to dealing with Aboriginal people. Tucked away behind the Nhulunbuy shopping complex, or rather, to one side of the bitumen tarmac fronting the shopping complex, the THS East Arnhem Community Health Centre Building is a dowdy two-storey affair, coated on the outside with khaki brown pebblecrete, the signature adornment of 1970s institutional architecture. The entrance is obscure, accessed through a recess in an alleyway, not facing the street and not well signposted: you go up one flight of narrow stairs (there's room for only one person at a time), taking two turns, and then confront an equally narrow rectangular grid of newly painted rooms with pearl grey walls and a bluer grey enamel gloss edging the windows and doors. The effect is that of insistent geometricity: rectilinear rooms hosting office staff down one side of a narrow hallway; office equipment, the air-conditioning plant and a kitchenette down the other, harmonised by the grey tones of the wall paint and laminated office furniture.

First encounters

My first visit to Numbulwar with Marlene back in 1998 had been her first visit there too, and took place on my second day of shadowing her. Like me, she was nervous, and we were full of over-eager bonhomie with each other, our strain to create a more relaxed mode of relating manifesting itself in excessive solicitude. We kept making small jokes, a strategy for masking our initial unfamiliarity, our newness and lack of ease with each other. It was a strain that carried over into our talk with 'Willy', the Aboriginal Aged Care Worker who came to pick us up from the airstrip using the health centre vehicle. He took us straight to the Visiting Officers' Quarters (the VOQ),[2] hopping out of the vehicle to help us open the high wire gate with its stiff padlock, joking as he forcefully pried the old lock apart that 'it takes a man'. We all laughed then, Willy, Marlene and I, with feigned gusto, our eyes surreptitiously darting off one another in what I felt to be an awkwardly desperate yet curiously alienating desire for friendship.

Our gear safely stashed and locked away, we climbed back into the large white Toyota four-wheel drive and Willy drove us the 30 metres to the health centre, a square demountable building, about a metre off the ground, painted brown on the outside, with orange linoleum floors and light blue walls on the inside. It backed out onto a stunning view of the Rose River, framed by sand dunes and a few coconuts, with tamarind trees from the Macassans still growing along the edges.[3]

When we arrived, the clinic was closed for lunch. The nurses who greeted us at the side door introduced us to the two Aboriginal Health Workers, who shook our hands softly and looked down at the floor. They seemed keen to get past our phatic conversational ambits and back to their own talk and I was glad when we moved outside, where Peg Andelwar, the community health nurse who had been liaising with Marlene to arrange this visit, joined us on the back steps with cups of tea, and spoke to Marlene about the store that was to be built.

Peg was keen to take advantage of community development funding that Marlene had available for sponsoring Aboriginal nutrition workers in communities, and enthusiastically listed all the tasks such a worker might be given to do in Numbulwar. With a new store about to be built, it was an opportune time to work on what the store should stock, how healthy food could be identified with stickers and posters drawing attention to good food choices, how they could have monthly themes ('food suitable for diabetics'), and so on. As the sea breeze caught the coconut palm leaves in lazy rustles, the two got into an animated exchange. Peg seemed very task-focused and kept moving beyond generalities into next steps and tactics. She would take the idea of appointing a nutrition worker to the community that very afternoon, she said, stabbing her finger into the air as she spoke. All the important community people would be meeting then about an anti-smoking program: it would be a good time to also mention public health ideas for the new store.

Cups of tea over, Peg took us on a walking tour of some of the streets. The houses were mostly made of weatherboard. Some were on stilts; some were on the ground, with rusting wire grilles covering the windows. Some were built on plain sand dunes with scant vegetation; others were fenced with spots of greenery: clusters of lemon grass, an odd coconut palm or eucalyptus tree. Eventually we came to a stop outside the house of an elderly man called Barradginn, the inaugural Chair of the Peg's newly formed Health Council. We waited some time, enough for the back of my neck to get sorely sunburned, but when Barradginn came out he was a sight worth waiting for. An old man stepping slowly with a walking frame, white as white neck-length hair wafting outwards in all directions, snowy chin stubble against his chocolate brown skin, one mesmerising blind eye a milky blue-ice curve, sporting a crisp new navy anti-smoking T-shirt, KICK BUTT! QUIT boldly lettered in white against the dark blue. He said hello to Marlene and me but then we all said little else, shuffling our feet and grinning. Peg explained who we were – Marlene's the new nutrition lady, Tess is a student – and confirmed that he would be at the Health Council meeting scheduled for 2.30pm that afternoon, when Marlene would talk to them about good tucker.

On the walk back to the VOQ Peg explained that Barradginn was a diabetic who had lost the front halves of both feet from ulcers and now was keen to make sure that younger people knew what he hadn't as a young man. 'He tells me that if he had only known then what he does now he would still have his feet.' This led to a discussion of ways of communicating health information to Aboriginal people. Peg stressed that the material needed to be visually literal: people needed to be able to relate what they saw to what they were being told. She thought the anti-smoking posters which have more graphic representations (sponges squeezing black liquid representing tar from lungs, or listings of all the poisons in cigarettes, for example) were the most effective. Marlene commented that she had heard these were not very effective because they turned people off, being too negative. I suggested that maybe it was just middle-class sensibilities being repelled, and Peg commented that either way what worked up here would always be different. Our traffic in semi-factual anecdotes, incorporating odd snippets of 'I've read ...' or 'They say ...' continued all the way to the VOQ, where we parted company, agreeing to reconvene before the community meeting later that day. It was public health shop talk: endlessly diagnostic, relaxed and easily informative, the extent of our institutional socialisation revealed in our idle discussion. We swap and reinvest simultaneously, casually and without constraint.

All this time, our talk never made clear what had happened to the cursed store – the reason for us being there – and what was happening now. What was left in it? What did it look like inside? What were the clan disputes about? Why had it been cursed? Who by? What reparatory work was being done to lift the curse? Or was it not like that at all? Had the curse been left unchallenged on the (equally valid) assumption that whitefellas would reverentially accept the finality of a permanently cursed store, unquestionable in its deeply mysterious voodoo secrecy, and perhaps offer to build a new one? The curse, it seemed, was also exerting its magic on our powers of speculation and curiosity. I didn't dare ask questions when others didn't.

Over our lunch of sandwiches made with the food we'd brought with us by plane, I asked Marlene what she knew about the sorcery business. Not much, she admitted. People tended to be close-lipped ... and there was clearly still trouble about it, she hinted. The store had been placed under such a strong curse that all its contents had been left inside, with meat still in the freezers and no electricity. The Sport and Recreation Hall (an elaborate-sounding title for an elongated tin shed) was being used as the temporary store, and one of the reasons Peg had urged Marlene to come out was to get nutrition on the agenda while the planning for the new store was still in its infancy. In community development terms, this would mean developing a store policy at the community's pace, when they were ready for it – but it also meant that 'the community request' for Marlene's visit, dutifully noted in her travel requisition, had in fact been at the behest of a fellow THS employee, the community health nurse.

Marlene casually noted that the school principal had been evicted from the community recently, something to do with running the school canteen as a community takeaway and refusing to pay royalties to the traditional owner when this was demanded. To ward off his wrathful malediction, in which every part of the school, down to the very land it was on, would be permanently and irrevocably cursed, the Numbulwar Council President had placed a lighter curse on the school a month before, as pre-emptive protection. Amid all the spells, with the school canteen now out of bounds, a new takeaway was to be opened in a disused small tin building, another good reason for the nutritionist's visit to Numbulwar with her shadowing anthropologist.

Later I found the newspaper report: 'CURSE CLOSES REMOTE SCHOOL. Royalties demanded on tuckshop':

> A bush school has been shut down by a curse amid claims the traditional owners demanded a royalty payment from the school tuckshop. Education Minister Peter Adamson confirmed yesterday the Numbulwar school principal had been asked to leave following the row ...
>
> The 182 pupils and 40 staff have refused to return to school since a 'temporary curse' was placed on the school by Numbulwar Council President Lindsay Joshua last Tuesday.
>
> A council spokesman said Mr Joshua was forced to invoke the curse to prevent the region's most senior custodian, Albert Rami, from invoking an 'irreversible curse'. The spokesman said: 'Had the big curse been put in place, no one would have ever returned to the school and the whole place – including the foundations – would have to be ripped up and taken away'.
>
> He said the dispute began when principal Jean Gurnier 'publicly defied' the authority of Mr Rami, the Numbirindi people's ceremonial leader. (Thomson 1998: 1–2)

I had not seen Marlene asking any questions of Peg, of the Health Workers or of Barradginn about the whole dramatic affair of curses and evictions, and was struck then about the seeming lack of interest in what I 'knew' (anthropologically) to be issues of all-consuming importance in the micro-politics of Aboriginal communities (see Reid 1983).

The lack of interest appeared to contradict the anthropological material, such as it is, on the intensity of white interest in and eternal gossip about Aboriginal behaviour (see Koster 1977). It seemed to me that our gossip as health personnel, whilst still centring on Aboriginal issues, was related to problem diagnosis, program opportunities, and points for intervention. We were not trying to piece together coherent narratives about what might be going on for people on a day-to-day basis, as perhaps I might if I were being differently anthropological (when like as not I'd have nothing to do with health professionals except parasitically, accessing their hospitality and data). Rather, we simply accepted strange events as happenings taking place on the periphery of, and yet needing to be incorporated into, the routine of our own activities. Like others who learn on the job, it seemed I was learning the severe limits to bureaucratic inquisitiveness and simultaneously, the silence which reinstates the opacity of Aboriginal culture.

We stopped our sandwich discussion when Peg arrived at the VOQ door to tell us that the afternoon's community meeting was cancelled: the people had apparently gone fishing, so we'd be having that meeting tomorrow morning. Instead, there was time now to go to the community Town Council office[4] to meet with the Council members. This was going with the flow.

Again, we drove the very short distance – 50 metres! – to the Council Office in the Health Centre Toyota, to find Barradginn waiting outside.[5] The Council turned out to be Steve, the Town Clerk, who was not there yet – hence Baradginn's patient wait outside. Steve turned out to be a brown-skinned fellow, short of stature and rangy of build, dressed as an outback man: faded jeans, cowboy belt, red checked shirt, rough speech. There was a strong smell of tobacco and a confident roll to his hips when he swung out of his vehicle. His girlfriend Linda, a local Aboriginal woman, slim in brand new jeans and a bright yellow singlet, and with long straight black hair, climbed out as well. She was attending the meeting as the proposed new manager of the soon-to-be opened takeaway.

Steve was carrying two cans of Coca-Cola balanced in one broad hand. 'Health food drink!' he called out provocatively to the trio of health professionals awaiting his arrival. Sharon, a white woman of fair skin and demure manner, also joined us. We had met Sharon on the road earlier in the morning, when we were looking at household yards on our way to see Barradginn. She had made a charming and unusual sight ambling slowly in her smart gear along the dusty Numbulwar roads – she wore a straw hat with sky blue band, tailored navy trousers, a camisole top with a pretty floral pattern and a pale blue over-shirt to protect her fair skin from the sun. On the morning's walk she'd had a romance novel tucked between the index and forefingers of a well-manicured hand, and a wicker basket tucked in the crook of the opposite arm. Like an English maiden *en route* to a picnic, she was a real contrast to ruffle-haired Peg, tanned as a berry and wearing a simple 'mission dress' (an A-line cotton dress with two large square pockets at hip level and a zip up the front), and to Marlene and me with our loose-fitting cheap Indian cotton gear (our own more dishevelled attempts to keep the withering tropical heat at bay). Since Sharon was the Town Council accountant and placed orders for the store, Peg was keen to ensure that Marlene and Sharon had the chance to meet.

The meeting could now begin.

When Marlene finally spoke, after Peg's explanation for why Marlene was in town and what the newly formed Health Council was trying to achieve, I was surprised at the stiff public health formality of her words. She did not say what she wanted to see happen in the community, as she had with me, but rather said things like, 'It's important that the knowledge that I have about food business doesn't just stay in my head – it has to be community knowledge, the ideas have to come from the community', and she evaded Steve's insistent prompts for specific tasks and actions. 'Well, what would you like to do?' he kept asking. 'When do you want to do that?' At other times he simply dug for straightforward information: 'We would like a list of the sorts of things we should or shouldn't be using in the takeaway. Can you provide us with something like that?'

Linda, the takeaway-manager-to-be, had been collecting recipes she wanted to try out from *New Idea* magazines, and now wordlessly put a bundle of cut-outs on the table for us to see. She quietly murmured 'milkshakes'. Steve nodded proudly and declared that his girl Linda had a lot of good ideas. Marlene hemmed noncommittally. Debriefing after the meeting, Marlene said she was horrified at the very suggestion of milkshakes. The machinery would be difficult to clean, the milk would have to be kept cold; the whole thing could be a real bacterial nightmare! She wanted to encourage the use of prepackaged fruit juices and diet drinks but hadn't wanted to quash Linda's tentative enthusiasm or directly contradict Steve in public. She would talk with Linda alone and separately some time in the future.

Barradginn had remained quiet through the whole discussion, except when Marlene had pulled out the 'Store Book' from her hessian bag. It was an A3 sized spiral bound and laminated set of photographs of stores and food displays, which he asked for by silently holding out his hand. While the others continued their meeting talk he paged through it, stopping at a full-scale photograph of fruit, vegetables and nuts, a bountiful still-life of healthy foods, to suddenly comment forcefully, stabbing the picture: 'This one, this one we want at the store now! We need this kind of tucker!' The others looked up, nodded and smiled, and briefly allowed their discussion to divert to the Store Book and whether Steve could keep the glossy copy in Barradginn's hands for the full Council board to look at. Marlene said she could leave it with him for a short while and could certainly get them a smaller version (A4 and black and white), but she would have to go back to the Nhulunbuy office to see whether she had a spare of the larger, more glamorous full-colour version Steve now insisted they wanted. Later she told me that this had been an acute moment for her. She had felt ridiculous showcasing something which was ostensibly a community tool but which she had also been told cost a lot of money and was in short supply in its high-gloss form. She was tempted to just leave it with them and deal with the bureaucratic consequences later, but in the semiotic sabotage of office politics that risked making other things more difficult.

Still nothing was said of the padlocked store. I daydreamt, idly wondering whether maggots would still be at work, or would it now just be snakes, rats and spiders?

'Was it difficult working out who to address in that meeting today?' I asked Marlene as I cooked us both a scrappy meal out of tinned lentils, an onion and a capsicum later that night. It was, she responded. She had not known quite who her audience was, but in the end stuck with pitching it to Barradginn, who, after all, represented what she was there for. It was too early to be rushing into promises and Steve did not represent the full Council. She had not been able to talk to Linda alone yet, and Peg the nurse had hinted that Linda might be silenced by Steve's domineering manner. Marlene needed to build relationships first, and get a better feel for the power networks operating here. Mid-sentence, loud music erupted close to our enclosure. Looking out, I saw the silhouette of kids dancing under the glare of the clinic spotlight to the beat of disco music. Marlene turned up our television in response, but even shutting all the louvres only lightly muffled the thumping. One green and one blue light had been suspended from the wooden beams holding up the corrugated roof of the Fifty Cent Building outside (an unwalled pergola structure named for its octagonal shape). Drab during the day, with a grotty cement floor and dogs lolling in the shade, right now the silhouetted dancers and disco lights transformed the pergola into a vivid scene of rhythmic limbs knocking pure auditory adrenaline out of a tinny ghetto blaster.

Attempting to sleep despite the disco sounds, I lay awake thinking about the kids and their dancing, experiencing what I felt was a moment of real ethnographic limitation. Was the disco a spontaneous thing, did it happen often, or was it perhaps part of a well-intentioned welfare program, 'a drug-free' recreational alternative to promote 'adolescent self-esteem' or some such? More importantly, what stopped us going over and joining in? What was so inhibiting that we kept ourselves insulated inside the walls of the VOQ? I realised I knew very little about anything that was going on, either out there or in here.

But I was also aware of my role as someone wanting to know the community as visiting health professionals come to know it, and that seemed to entail being someone who doesn't inquire into things, but just assimilates disruptions – in this case a noise nuisance of the first order – as things that just happen, unexplained and inexplicable. And certainly not someone who would take up this opportunity for laughing and forming relationships with the kids, being foolish, exposed to their teasing, drinking their poisonous brew of fermented cordial and dancing into the night. So it was that on the next day, every white we met commented on the disruptive noise, the poor class of music, their lack of sleep, how it goes on all the time, and then how the kids don't attend school, how they fall asleep at their desks, it's a real problem, something needs to be done, but the parents don't or can't control them, the kids just run amok all night and then they are useless during the day. We casually kicked the complaints about as conversational fillers at odd moments throughout the day. But nothing was said of the night's, the behaviour's possible place in community life.

Oranges and apples

The cursed store was near our outdoor convening place for the delayed community meeting the next morning. We were meeting in the Fifty Cent Building, returned to ordinariness in the daytime light, Coke cans and other debris the only hint of its moonshine alter-life. The cursed store sat there, on the other side of the road, a corrugated iron building with padlocked doors and kerosene drums blocking the entrance way, brooding in the growing warmth of the sun.

The members, about 20 in all, were mainly either children, or old. People stood, or sat on the ground; a few were seated on the plastic stack chairs scattered about. No young adult men attended, and there were only three young women, all with new babies. Any particular kinship patterns were not entirely clear, and notably, as I became more attuned to what was not seen as important, nor was it a subject of any post-meeting commentary. Peg, Marlene and I sat cross-legged on the sand out in the sun, dutifully leaving shaded space and seats for the Aboriginal members.

We had no idea where all the young men were. But if this had been Wadeye (Port Keats) on the eastern side of the Territory coastline, poster community for dysfunctionality in bureaucratic assignations, we would know to think they were all on the grog somewhere, or sitting out gaol sentences, neglecting their young children and their almost equally young wives, leaving it all up to the tired old grandmothers. We would know to know that social policy interventions were critical for teaching the too-young mothers how to parent and for building the self-esteem of the young men, so that they feel less estranged from their own culture and adopt healthy pursuits and 'training pathways'. We would also know the semi-anthropological terms with which to categorise Wadeye as an artificial community, formed for administrative convenience by assembling seven (or nine or fifteen, depending on who does the telling) warring tribes together.

And if I were with anyone but Marlene, the fact that the old people outnumbered the young here at our meeting in the Numbulwar Fifty Cent Building would be turned into a factual tidbit at a future meeting of public health officers as part of bureaucratic trade talk about communities and their problems. But this is something I know Marlene will try to resist. Unusually for a public health worker, she is determined, as far as she possibly can, to shed the values and synopses others would give to her as fixed truths about Aboriginal people and places. In fact, when I returned two and a half years later, when she was already one of the longer serving white professionals in the region, she told me the very term 'cross-cultural' was misleading in its inherent homogenising:

This term 'cross cultural' – forget the 'cultural' business, we're dealing with distinct groups of people. There's a woman who was employed here to do a job because, based on work she'd done with Eskimos (laughs). Don't get me onto that! And she couldn't cope, yet she was employed because she had that 'cross-cultural experience' and, I mean, yeah sure, I've worked in Africa, I've worked with Aboriginal people in Redfern, but hey, I'm working with Aboriginal people here and they're vastly different. As is every culture in different contexts. As are we! I mean let's just put everybody who's not Balanda[6] into one cultural grouping!

Marlene had told me she wanted to come to Numbulwar to form an *independent* relationship with the community. Reading her predecessor's case notes, she had been struck by the clear insistence that Numbulwar was unsuited for nutrition interventions, that its internal politics made it impossibly problematic for successful community development work. She thought she should see for herself, and not accept the harsh external judgment. Yet despite this desire not to be swayed by the prescriptive verdicts of others, a desire I share, at the same time, whether we like it or not, we will both later speak with the authority of having 'been there', an authority few fieldworkers (health professional or anthropological) can resist invoking. Like it or not, we will absorb and contribute to the interlinked resignifications which animate classificatory discourses. There will be misrepresentations from ignorant others to compel our corrections and the professional need to assert our 'bush cred'. And it will later be hard to distinguish what we ourselves have witnessed in communities from what we've been told at one or more remove from Aboriginal lives, in case notes, casual talk, meetings or workshops, where so much depends on adept participation in the circulation of fragments and factoids.

Back at the Fifty Cent Building, Peg introduced Marlene to the assembly (obscurely, they proceeded to call Marlene Cathy after that[7]) and went through her agenda: an item about a doctor visiting from Sydney in the last week of August to look at kids with pus-filled ears; news on attempts to recruit a male GP to live and work in Numbulwar; and a forewarning of the planned visit of another THS public health officer, coming soon for a week to talk to anyone who wanted help quitting the smokes, prompting a conversation about how many smokes that disabled girl on respite care was getting from her carers. 'Six packs a day, Peg, maybe more!' someone interjected.

'And them people looking after her they bin gettin *gunja* wit that respite money.'

'Yo.'

And then hilarity as one woman imitated the wheelchair-bound girl in question, miming her spastically throwing a rock at her imaginary carers in irritation at being deprived of her smokes.

People chuckled, repeated the joke and the exaggeratedly disabled throwing actions, chortled some more, then the discussion petered out.

Peg waited for a time, building a little space of silence before saying, solemnly, 'And now we got a big question.'

Pause.

'What question, Peg?'

'We need to talk about getting good food into this town, how to make Numbulwar a place for good tucker, good food for skinny kids, or diabetics, to make everyone strong and healthy. Marlene there is a nutritionist and she is here to help us. So can everyone just take some time now to think of ideas for what we might do, and then let's talk.'

After another pause, one of the older women suggested that a list could be given to the workers at the Women's Centre, so they could know what sort of things to cook for the old people. The Women's Centre need a list from Cathy, the old woman said, stroking Marlene's arm.

Peg was not impressed with the deviation from her focus on the store, suggesting perhaps Marlene could stop by the Women's Centre later, but for now, what about the store? But the men thwarted Peg's countermove by listing the healthy sorts of things that could be included in the old people's menus, chanting paired terms like 'rice, chicken', 'oranges and apples', as if reciting rote instructions.

'Not too greasy, not too dry,' interjected Billy, on how chicken and rice had to be.

'Green beans, carrots, lettuce, milk. Apple, damper, that baby ... wad its name now? ... Farex!' said Peter.

'Orange, potato, turtle,' chimed Billy.

'Yeah, turtle! Those old people bin need that meat and fat too. Yeah.'

Barradginn mischievously said the old women could do all that cooking, the men could go fishing: the women snorted and chortled.

A woman from the left called out: 'We're diabetic here because we bin eating rubbish food la shop.'

'Yo,' affirmed the group.

Peg seized the opportunity: the shop was back on the agenda. 'The

Women's Centre feed old people and that's good, but we need to think about how to feed everyone now.' Someone interjected helpfully, 'in that shop too, that big one now'.

Peg: 'Well, I've been talking to Marlene about how to get good food in the shop and she says we can think about setting the rules and have a workshop with the store workers, and the people who prepare food, at a meeting in the first week of September. Do you want to talk about that now, Marlene?'

Silent up to this point, this was Marlene's opportunity to present herself. She pulled out the high-gloss Store Book from her hessian bag. Resting it on her lap, tucked under her chin so that it opened outward, she explained: 'This book gives us ideas about things we can do when there is a new shop. On this side are pictures and this side, this writing here (pointing) gives suggestions about what can be done and who you can talk to, because Numbulwar doesn't have to try to do everything on its own – there is help.'

Barradginn again gestured for the book and Marlene once again handed it over.

Peg: 'One idea I'm thinking of, you know how we weigh the babies at the clinic? We could do that at the Women's Centre and talk to the young women about nutrition and how to give those babies good food so they're not skinny kids, because to grow up strong for culture and community you have to be strong as a baby.'

Her public health moment was interrupted by the arrival of a truck bringing stores up from the barge into the area dedicated for the soon-to-be-resurrected takeaway. The men were noisy, shouting at each other as they dragged heavy crates off the back of the truck, their racket louder than the rumble of the truck motor, which had been left on to power the cassette music blasting from the cabin. Peg looked up at me as I scribbled notes, laughed drolly, and rolled her eyes: 'Tess, you getting all this down?' I sure was.

When the noise abated and people were less distracted, Peg resumed.

'One idea that Barradginn came up with yesterday for putting good food in the shop ... (turning to Barradginn) you wanna tell them?'

Barradginn leant forward from his plastic chair:

What I bin decide when they shop here they tell you this bin kill you. My decision to, make you understan, Monday you can get him onefella, not two, not three will kill him. Just Monday, Wednesday, Friday, one packet won't. What you people think about that?

(Standard Written English translation: *My suggestion is that when people go to buy cigarettes at the new store they be told at that moment that smoking kills. Sales should be rostered to every second day, and then should be sold only one packet at a time, not in bulk. Do you agree?*)

A discussion in the local language erupted. There seemed to be some antagonism towards Barradginn's proposal to restrict cigarette purchases to one packet every second day, particularly from the people grouped to his left – one late arrival, an old man in a smart blue Akubra hat and leather riding boots, was leading the protest. The talk went on, with participants overlapping each other all at once, no longer attempting to speak in English, and Peg sat, watching us, us watching her, her eyebrow raised, three bemused whites left behind in the language mire. Barradginn erupted in English, asserting the need to balance people's individual autonomy with collective restriction:

Health government say, we have a list, just one smoke! Else government close'm that shop. Policy him say – like that poster, all types of poisons, ten thousand different ones [referencing a federal government anti-smoking poster stating the different toxic chemicals in tobacco]. When you decide I take'm to Council tomorrow. You decide, those smokes, they put him underground but his choose, but one packet, okay, go around ask, people don't give. This stuff killim you. That's true. I'm no liar – I'm dreamin that. You can order yoursell, you can kill yoursell. You gotta make the rule. I take la meeting tomorrow. I smoke, I gotta but him mysell.

(*We could have a policy that has the endorsement of the health department, specifying the restriction on cigarette sales. If it is violated, the government will close the store. The policy will reflect what we know about the dangers of tobacco. Remember that poster showing all the toxic chemicals contained in one cigarette? Of course, people can still choose to smoke, even if it kills them. That is their choice. But we should also restrict sales to one packet. We should consult with people, but tobacco is lethal. I know this to be true. You are free to buy cigarettes; you are*

*free to kill yourself (we cannot stop that). But we have to make
this determination. I will take it to the wider community meeting
we are having tomorrow. I smoke too. But I have to give up by
myself.)*

A woman called Flora spoke up, defending Barradginn's outburst
against the muttering from the people to his left. 'All that country that
talkin' all around now we low,' she said, gesticulating with hands high
and low, then tracing a diagram of bar graphs in the sand in front of
her, describing morbidity and mortality rates. 'They show us now at
Darwin Hospital ... (moved into language ... reverted to English) '...
for your health and your body.'

Barradginn, pointing to Mario, a little boy who had just wandered
into Flora's lap:

> Like Mario now – we gotta look after him properly way.
> Language, ceremony, culture, language. Tobacco bin made in
> America and Norway,[8] not Aboriginal culture, it's white culture
> alway just kill you ... (moved back into language) ... Bob Marley
> culture not for us, not for Australian people ... (language) ...
> Think about this Monday, Wednesday, Friday can buy smoke ...
> (language)

During one of the pauses, Peg suggested quietly to Barradginn that
perhaps people could come to him at night to give him their decisions.
Barradginn nodded and said to the others, 'You come see me tonight.'
Peg wanted to move the discussion on. 'If we talk about nutrition at the
school, what should we say?'

Flora: 'Old ways, bush tucker, new ways, gotta be both ways.'

'Yo,' confirmed the old women beside her.

Peg: 'There's money for health promotion, if there's young people
around who could do things, maybe plant foods in top camp or water
cooler in the shop. Think about young people who would really like to
do some work and have ideas. Let me know, OK?' Nods.

Peg closed the meeting then, and we all went our separate ways:
Marlene and I to visit the Women's Centre, Peg back to the clinic,
others to whatever they had in line for themselves. Joining us in our
VOQ, Peg devoured our leftover lentils, cold from the fridge. We
discussed the problems of staffing the Women's Centre now that federal
funding had been removed and how the community would prefer a

white coordinator who could more easily avoid the humbug of kinship obligations and just run the place fairly. How the task of community development is to try and give expert information and suggestions, but also to allow sufficient space for people to form their own decisions. (As another public health worker put it to me, describing the need to sit back while being an expert resource, 'We need to be on tap, not on top.') Adult education is a real challenge out here, we agreed, and in our amplification of this as a problem, we necessarily left unspoken the unstable mimesis demonstrated in today's public meeting, where the voice of the proselytising health professional was echoed in chants about apples and oranges and the clear bilingualism in health facts revealed in bar graphs in the sand (see Lea 2005).

Interrupted again by the blaring sounds of the disco in the dark of the later night, I helped hurriedly slide the windows shut and draw the curtains, as Marlene turned on the ancient air-conditioner in the Numbulwar VOQ, its overworked rumbling a poor match for the insistent midnight thump of the ghetto-blaster booming from the Fifty Cent Building outside. Falling asleep to the repeat refrain of 'JO-OHN-N-N-EEEY, JO-OHN-N-N-EEEY, JO-OHNN-N-EEEY', an exuberant love jingle broadcast to the sand dunes, mangroves and mud flats of the Rose River, I was left to mull over the power of our silences. Our lack of speculation in some areas, yet clear and unarguable causal analyses in others (as in, whites are needed to justly administer principles of access and equity where blacks cannot), both feed a lacuna which refuses to yield to straightforward co-presencing (meeting people as they are, without prejudgments; being together in trust and quiet acceptance). To the extent that silence is its own form of tacit communication, our non-curiosity preserves Aboriginal strangeness inside the fastness of our own routines. Avoidance keeps our normative schemes for assessing Aboriginal life intact: our judgments remain inferential and culturally bound. Our silences speak about what we do not need to know in order to already know Aboriginal communities.

Conclusion

It is an arresting image, that of the cursed store, requiring our silence for its potency. That it does not speak back is ultimately reassuring, at once affirming the merits of our exclusion from the everyday of

Table 7.1   Extracts from nutrition action plan (THS 2001)

KEY FOCUS AREA 1: COMMUNITY STORES

Implementation Plan	*Approx Cost*	*Performance Indicators*
Store Workers Project		
• Community meeting to inform that funding has been secured and to identify workers	Continued employment of substantive Nutrition Workers	• Workers identified
		• Completion of course modules
• Commence training, development of resources and evaluation tools		• Attainment of competencies for Cert 1
• Negotiate food supply modifications	$24244	• Number of nutrition promotion activities
		• Number of people participating in nutrition promotion activities
• Report completion and dissemination of results		• Core food consumption
		• Vegetable and fruit consumption

KEY FOCUS AREA 3: COMMUNITY NUTRITION WORKERS

Implementation Plan	*Approx Cost*	*Performance Indicators*
• Meet with interested women to discuss job description, wages, hours, support structures/plan		• Meeting held
		• Workers employed
• Commence training		• Course modules completed
		• Attainment of Cert 1 competencies

Aboriginal social relations and further exoticising and mystifying them. It is through *not knowing* the quotidian detail of Aboriginal life, through not knowing the mundane micro-politics of sorcery and such like, *through distance* that we can maintain our claim to cultural sensitivity and ethnographic authority. At the same time, we retain a sense of the mysterious depths hovering on the edge of our knowing. We are not attempting to change any of *that* deeply cultural stuff, unlike our interfering colonial forebears. We are only amending the burdensome deficits that have accrued under western influence. So it is that we will later be able to explain the conflicts of 'implementation' (for Marlene and Peg, of inclusively developing a store policy, but it could be anything, really) using irrefutable vocabularies about the need for time and non-dictatorial processes. We will deploy equally powerful rational explanations of the distress, dependency and low self-esteem produced by colonialism among Aboriginal people and which therefore necessitates our greater enthusiasm, commitment, resourcefulness and resilience; and we will be intensely interested in showing our knowing about Aboriginal people for all these purposes – all without moving beyond an essential instrumentalism and external purview in our actual interactions and thinking.

Such are the community development efforts that are dot-pointed in activity reports as irrefutable actions that have been or are still needing to be taken with, on behalf of and for Aboriginal people. Consider one such implementation plan (Table 7.1), produced to document the actions required in community stores southwest of Katherine (Timber Creek, Bulla, Kalkarindgi Yarralin, and Lajamanu), in which we see in Key Focus Areas 1 and 3 the formulation of the tasks being pursued by Peg and Marlene (THS, unpublished work document 2001).

It all seems so purposeful, so blithely confident, when actions are re-presented in a grid, where the casually omitted discrepancies allowed (or indeed required) by stable dot points are able to hide the real life uncertainties of community work. But can dot points and silences contain everything? What of the physical and emotional discomforts, embarrassments and distastes which cannot be immediately accommodated within such rational public health framings (see Povinelli 2002)?

Where do they go?

SUPPRESSION

Unlike academic scholars who seem only recently to have discovered that whiteness is a racialised embodiment, administrators in the Northern Territory have been race-conscious for quite some time. Even though bureaucrats have attempted to erase 'race' from their texts by removing racialised terminology from their written and formal language, preferring such seemingly neutral demarcations as 'cross-cultural', 'urban and remote', 'Indigenous and non-Indigenous', it is nonetheless continually reinserted into the professional's everyday consciousness as a matter of pressing concern (Butler 1997, cf. Cowlishaw 1998). Beyond the reporting deluge immersing the health professional in problem diagnosis and suggested repair, there is also a consciousness of one's white privilege which comes from confronting the spectre of epidermal difference in the flesh. There is a subjective 'more' which continues to escape the semantic elisions of policy texts and is carried in the self-conscious bodies of white health professionals into the field.

The disequilibrium many health professionals admit to feeling when they first meet Aboriginal people can only be spoken in private, secure moments of shared reflection and mutual empathy. This is when colleagues might tell me how their sense of personal sanctity was threatened when a scab-encrusted mutt of a dog rubbed itself against their leg; and I in turn admit to not wanting to use the margarine I've watched just such a dog licking. And they tell me how distressing it can be when they're hailed in a town supermarket by someone they know from out bush, now drunk and incoherent, being aggressively demanding and threatening to the kids. How secretly anxious one man felt when a black friend, his adopted brother, picked up his newborn white baby for kisses and cuddles and he inwardly thought 'fu-u-u-ck' but refused to let himself look alarmed as he watched what he described as scabies-infested skin with a smattering of streptococcal sores rub up against the silken chubby smoothness of his new and most dear little one. Or how another wanted to give up after spending month after exhausting month consulting widely for a project, cajoling and pleading with Aboriginal people to contribute and participate, only to be belligerently told by the same mob that she'd not consulted sufficiently and was simply out to exploit them for 'black dollars'. Or when fieldworkers try, day in, day out, to 'get something up' and it all comes to nought when their own energy wanes after too many setbacks. How hard it is to proceed when they do not receive any cues from seemingly impassive black faces that any of what they are doing is even being heard, let alone understood.

As this new public health doctor put it to me, as we left an evening workshop which focused on ways of improving Aboriginal adherence to treatment programs:

> I'd say the most important issue is to have patients taking control of their own disease. In remote communities it is really difficult to have two-way full and frank conversations with Aboriginal people, even with the Aboriginal Health Worker there translating for you ... Having the Health Worker there doesn't really make a difference because you don't know how much they understand of what you are saying and how well they are translating it. I find with the older patients, especially women, that they just sit there and don't offer you anything at all. Their facial expressions stay the same, everything, they sit there and don't look at you, they don't say a single word and then they get up and go. It is disheartening.

In quiet and empathetic safety they speak of the strain of being eternally polite, of being 'beggars at the table of sociality' (Bauman 2001: 218), trying to be their best selves by suppressing what they well know to be bourgeois anxieties and donning a more rugged attitude to their culturally embedded senses of bodily pollution and personal hygiene. They hide their concern for smooth white skin behind shirts and lotions, and in the isolation practices of sleeping few to a bed, unable to place thick social relations before a concern for lice, sores and scabies (Povinelli 2006: 61).

Bureau-professionals who deal with Aboriginal issues fall over themselves to use the most correct terminology, insisting on the capitalised term 'Indigenous' as opposed to 'Aboriginal' as the latter is said to exclude Torres Strait Islanders; or, a new refinement, 'Warramanga people' as opposed to 'Indigenous', as the latter is said to homogenise. They try never to imply that people who do not lead 'traditional' lifestyles (however ill-defined) are lesser indigenes.

That upholding these constructs requires active self-policing becomes clear in moments of transgression, in the slips and cracks of factoid exchanges. One rumour, circulated with a full relishing of its delicious suspension of the normative genuflecting, had it that the Arnhem Landers from Galiwinku had taken to calling all sojourners 'Balanda' (meaning whitefella), *including* the brown-skinned Aborigines (alternatively, 'urban blacks', 'halfies', 'coloured mob', 'yeller-fellas') occupying identified positions in the public service. Even bureaucrats who normally treat the Aboriginal colleagues they work alongside with extreme respect and deference revelled in the anecdote. It provided momentary release, when the work of suppressing a widely shared but rarely spoken distrust of people who powerfully claim Aboriginality in institutional settings but seem to lack 'authentic' customary knowledge, could itself be temporarily suspended. There is a consuming strain to being diplomatic, hyper-privileging the contributions and presence of Aboriginal colleagues who operate in brokerage positions as project and community liaison officers, and yet judging behind their backs – unable to relax into the innocuous duplicity of their otherwise ordinary bad-mouthing and mild running critique of each other because race, everywhere denied, exaggerates the interpersonal sensitivities and the issues become those which are known but not named.

Double layers of self-awareness destroy naturalism in the vexed presence of race that has been signed as oppressed (see Sennett 2003). Bureaucrats have had their habitual body postures thoroughly critiqued by well-meaning expositions on the nature of Indigenous cultural distinction and the extent of bureaucratic intrusion, with the result that their ordinary ways of being in the world, known to be arbitrary and power-laden, become forced and unnatural. The frustration, the weariness and disappointment, the unease and repression, and most especially the emotional and bodily disgust, may stem from stereotypes, but they are much more than that. As this public health worker put it to me:

> There is a tension in withholding or suppressing your own cultural horror when you go out bush. I would come back just absolutely rooted. It is not only that you are trying to be careful about what you say and how you say it and what the messages need to be, which is fraught enough, but you know, I used to sit there and have to pretend that the horrible, scabby, mangy dog which was rubbing up against me as I was sitting down talking to people wasn't filling me with absolute horror, while in the meantime being handed a baby that pukes up on you and you smile and pretend nothing is happening in the name of 'cultural sensitivity'. If I was in my home I'd leap up and get something to clean the puke and I'd shoo the dog away. So I'd come home, absolutely *rooted* and open the door to find Steve [her husband] had just let the kids go wild. There'd be toys in the hallway, dishes piled high in the sink, kids tired from being left to go feral and the only thing I could do was go straight to the sink and start cleaning because there was no way I could relax without some order. You come from chaos to chaos. Steve would say, 'Hey, you just walked past me! I'm here too, you know!' and I'd say, 'I can't stand this; I *have* to *have* some order!' We eventually got a cleaning lady, and I know it sounds like a joke, but I still say, to this day – although Steve says I'm exaggerating, I know I'm not – that lady *saved* our marriage! She literally *saved our marriage*!

Things might be thought, but they are seldom, and even then, very guardedly or ironically, said. And if health professionals perchance do confess to feelings of frustration, to experiences of 'cultural horror' in one of their many group sessions, the work of being ordinary demands ahead of time that these will be careful worded admissions: the confession would reinstate the extraordinariness, arduousness yet ultimate do-ability of their tasks – given enough commitment and displays of the right attitude. The more fraught dimensions of encountering will remain hidden from view. In fact, after many years, I have never heard such formulations as 'I hate to sleep like that' or 'I detest the running snot in kids' noses' or 'The drunkenness horrifies me' put so straightforwardly in any public forum. Instead, as part of learning about public health success stories, suitable approaches and thus the vocabulary for recoding one's own private anxieties as the problems Aboriginal people would like to have rectified, participants would quickly learn, for instance, that curing dogs of their skin diseases, despite its essential irrelevance to human health outcomes,[1] is a critically important community development task. Action is justified on the basis that dealing with dogs is an important entrée for forming relationships with Aboriginal people: if dog-loving community people can see us doing a good job with their animals, they will trust us to deal with the harder issues much closer to home (see Territory Health Services 1999: 2.32–2.34). The scabby or maimed dog that is such an offence for the bleeding heart remains a target for intervention, delivered via an entirely defendable community development platform.

Such productivity helps overcome the feeling of irrelevance that the pressure to make everything appear participatory can otherwise induce. At the same time, truly negative emotions and visceral responses remain suppressed, because admitting them runs the risk of allowing oneself to be seen as (peculiarly and idiosyncratically) unable; it also makes people feel that they are themselves as racist as everyone else, when a key aspect of the public health presence, purpose, pleasure and satisfaction, lies in its politically rehabilitative intent.[2] The rules of class, race and professional authority are complexly inhabited within liberal progressive circles: the public health rationales are honed and refined, mobilised to keep up with changing situations, 'as texts that people perform rather than read' (Sennett 2003: 52).

But the point I really want to draw attention to is that this *terribly private* business of confessing discomfort is in fact a *most social* phenomenon, dependent as it is on the presence of like-minded witnesses (Biddle 1997: 227). For by being unmentionable (which means entirely admissible but only in hushed tones and among like-minded friends), the private admissions assume the veracity and authority of a confessed, secret truth and as such, reinforce the shared sense of sacrifice and ordeal which bonds public health professionals. It is also seductive for ethnographers, perpetually beguiled by the seeming candour of the 'I shouldn't be telling you this, but ...' confidences of their informants, into believing that they are getting to deeper, more truthful levels of information, when all along these secrets are ever-present as public secrets: known, shared, and meant to be (m)uttered (see Foucault

1990, Taussig 1999). All along, our getting through the façade with each other was meant to happen; it was an expected (ordinary) moment in the privately engineered creation of the extraordinariness of public health endeavours.

Let's not delude ourselves about this matter of the private admission and its powers of disruption in the public formulations of public health. Should there be some kind of emotional outpouring, a collective display of people's felt senses of risk and jeopardy in, say, a debriefing workshop, the task of the facilitator will be to help people 'get through it', to sensitively manage 'the situation' so that participants can reframe themselves for future helping acts. The group may well join in narrating tales of hardship, invited to attend to these aspects of their experiences by the compulsion introduced by other revelations, taking up each other's affective responses and reciprocating in kind as mutually supporting professionals are wont to do. But the expectation that these discordant tales will be restored to their proper order, with whiteboard and butcher's paper strategies developed for 'dealing with it', will frame the confessional space. Participant flailings would be quickly insulated by a rush of constructive analysis and the inclusive, supportive pressure of co-participants intent on smoothing things back into a restorative practice, recoding 'problems and difficulties' as 'challenges and opportunities'. Everyday and ordinary bureaucratic referencing would be restored through collectively formed narrative unifications that contract the possibilities of critically reflexive interpretation into remedies for future approaches. The work of talk would retranslate uncontrollable feelings into therapeutic dot points about the need for better preparation of fieldworkers, for more organised opportunities for networking, for more time for project development and consultation, for more institutional support for public health approaches as a whole, for greater coordination of effort and so on.

There is a gap, a space created by the non-correspondence between the (countable, measurable, knowable and unfortunate) Aboriginal object of bureaucratic talk and rules for comportment and the particular, subjective, lived-in experiences of racial ('cross-cultural') encounters, which health professionals are left to fill; if they don't, or can't, they are seen to have failed. So fill it they do. Professionals compensate for what they struggle to comprehend with all kinds of theories and explanations (reverential silence included), juxtaposing personal viewpoints with accounts from others, anthropologised texts and bureaucratic guidelines, health facts, social scientific theory and colonial histories – all of which point to continued Aboriginal misery and white responsibility as indisputable realities (Jordan 2005: 59–60). Professionals must tiptoe around a reified traditional culture and view all bad habits as introduced. As anthropologist Trinh T. Minh-ha remarks: 'the invention of needs goes hand in hand with the compulsion to help the needy, a noble and self-gratifying task that also renders the helper's service indispensable' (1989: 89).

The current national intervention offers double reinforcements. Not only does it accelerate the speed at which the process of dire depiction/diagnosis/more-of-the-same travels along the spiral routes of institutional recursivity, but in its abhorrent overruling of core principles of community development, the emergency provides a deep and unifying point for objection: the progressive whites who are tangentially deemed part of the problem are strengthened with new and satisfying resolve around a clear and present external enemy.

Incorporating the corporation

All this might explain how the organisation gets to repeat itself and truisms become reinstated, restored by new experiential material, but the phenomenological and seductive pull of simplifications remains only partly explained. The obsequiousness noted by Brody and others,[3] which makes public health workers so desperate to please and be liked, is a complex mix of colonial guilt and psychic projection. It is also, to put it very simply, an outcome of institutional embodiment, of our incorporation of the corporation. When whites are operating in Aboriginal communities, or in workplace events featuring Aboriginal participants, they are excessively keen to create a connection, 'a relationship', an ambition about which they are placed on an almost permanent workplace trial. To achieve the desired relating, they have first to overcome the wariness that all strangers or slightly acquainted people potentially exhibit with one another.

More excruciatingly, the grounds for automatic connectedness, which visually and behaviourally similar people can at least take for granted, must also be transcended. This is not just about phenotypical sameness, to contradict the august explanations of an earlier generation of race theorists, who expounded the virtues of liberal tolerance with the argument that difference is really only skin deep (see Benedict 1983). There is a micro-language of racialised inhabitation that is expressed in gesture and glance and which is conveyed from body to like body in little acts of mundane and unverbalised mutual comprehension, and these acts and understandings, whilst not static or unbending, at the very least facilitate companionable dialogue (see Goffman 1971).[4]

In contrast, even when public health professionals visit Aborigines within spaces that are (tacitly) designated for joint use, their encounters are marked by a simultaneous withholding and involving, a vigilant watchfulness and an excessively careful control of bodily movements. To form the desired relationship, professionals have to reach through the shrouded models of Aboriginality they're mentally carrying, construed out of all that they've seen, heard and learnt, to construct dialogue. But professionals are not simply interacting from the subjective state of their habitual white selves to the Aborigines they form out of 'stories created by former colonists' (Langton 1993: 33), which might be fraught enough. When professionals and their Aboriginal interlocutors meet, it is as prefigured bodies: their own, and the ones they are employed to help change. They meet Aboriginal people not as they might meet each other, as strangers who are each individually potentially friend or foe, slight or intimate acquaintance, but as generic representatives of programs and advocates of approaches which aim to reorder the most intimate aspects of Aboriginal life, lives which are themselves understood as types.[5]

At the same time, and this really is a rarely spoken secret, it is the very everyday rituals and mundane concerns through which individual people re-form their thick and distinctive socialities, these encultured ways of being in the world, which administrators 'know' to be 'faulty' and in need of improvement through supposedly neutral health-conferring practices. Indigenous practices of being together, side by side, sharing sores, 'one cup, food that travels from mouth to mouth' (Povinelli 2006: 57), little acts of co-presence that drive infection and kin relatedness at one at the same time, have to be recast as the unjust sins of racist administration, overcrowding, and poverty, of long waiting lists for housing upgrades and then only getting an uninhabitable shack. While public health goes to the heart of how people eat, sleep, prepare food, keep house, rear children, have sex, order their time and finance their activities, the community development task is one that must deny its colonising and betterment aspects. To explain phenomena as requiring improvement is necessarily to distance yourself from inhabiting them. The extent of creative artifice in this process, even in the face of clear mismatch in the ways health professionals and their Aboriginal interlocutors perform the desired forms of 'community-led' diagnosis and response (one group calling out 'oranges and apples' while the other manoeuvres to have the look of community action around the development of a store policy), cannot be explicitly recognised.

When you stop to think about it, being able to screen so much of one's surrounds out of the picture while being so intensely engaged is itself a magnificent testimony to bureaucratic inhabitation.

Professionals are speaking and perceiving as representatives of their profession and administration, as well-intentioned community developers, and, in their own bodily constitution, as ideal ambassadors of their culture's abstracted knowledge about health and well-being. On this last point it's important to recall that public health professionals are relatively young (some are in their forties, most in their thirties and twenties), represent both genders and alternative sexualities, are middle class and, by definition, tertiary-educated and fully employed. They are usually of sound health and lack intrusive physical disabilities. Some have taken lessons in Aboriginal languages – most commonly Yolgnu Matha for the East Arnhem region and less frequently Kriol in the Katherine district and Murrin-Patha southwest of Darwin. As Aboriginal-oriented public health personnel, all have been exposed to various Aboriginal Studies texts and courses, either as part of their own further studies (towards a Masters degree in Public Health or Community Studies) or through the medley of formal and informal professional tutelage opportunities constantly available throughout the organisational network. Few public health professionals spend time in Aboriginal homes (see Chapter 9), and their discipline-specific specialties (as Environmental Health Officers, nutritionists, Women's Health Advisors or people concerned with ears and eyes) will determine which community residents and organisational representatives they are most likely to come into contact with.

When extending the help of THS beyond the office workplace, professionals experience bush travel and anxiety-laden community work as nervous outsiders, intent on mobilising the efforts of

Aboriginal inhabitants who often do not seem to want to know. Few claim any ability to fully overcome the self-conscious outsiderness that being positioned to wield interventions and give expert advice confers. Despite the bravado stories within officer-to-officer talk that impute easy command of relaxed relating, only a small number seem able to slipstream through the two-way power relations embedded in their dependency on Aboriginal consent and participation for their relating (see Bauman 2001, Conley 2000: 86–87).

Doing 'bush work' is considered both an honour and a burden. Symptomatic of this is the syndrome of 'burnout', an explanation for high turnover which has produced its own genre of prescriptive literature (see Edelwich 1980, Jones 1982, Maslach 1982). In practitioner formulations about the hazards of fieldwork, one hears many reasons for burnout, including the shortcomings of government policies, the insufficient fieldworker support and preparation, the poor accommodation facilities, the family toll of time-consuming travel, the physical arduousness, the high cost of remote area living, the isolation and lack of entertainment, and even, in the words of one fieldworker, the dominance of married couples in regional townships. Less frequently, some will mention the financial benefits of earning wages where there is little to spend money on. Mal Guinness, for example, told me his first investment property was purchased out of travel allowances and an unknown number of free flights earned through frequent flyer award points.

Interestingly enough, there is seldom any analysis of where the ever-changing job holders go to next (equipped with the cultural capital of remote area experience), nor whether the rapid movement is restricted to regional office holders alone, let alone any attempted deconstruction of reasons for mobility. High turnover is simply proof of burnout. The equation – remote area work is beset with difficulties which lead to burnout, which leads to high turnover – has solidified into a commonplace. Meanwhile, on the rare occasions when it is noted, the high turnover that is equally, if not more, true of senior management positions in central office locations is ascribed to the corporatised need for managers to constantly replenish their careers, to refuse stagnation by frequently reinventing themselves.

It would be unwise to make more of this than it deserves. Turnover is high everywhere in the Northern Territory, which is of course an impediment for all sorts of actions. The point is simply that there is a pattern to the talk about bush work, of which the romance of burnout is but a small part. Professionals greet their projections of Aboriginal neediness with models of themselves as iconic helpers, the repudiating converse of a silent alter-ego, the iconic oppressor. The contradictions are inscribed within the professional's very body. In the field, public health professionals act out an impersonalised representation of themselves. They become their program in spite of themselves. The mimesis which is ordinarily attributed to Aboriginal people as they are enjoined to create western management regimes with an indigenous patina (Merlan 1998: 150) is not one-sided. Professionals introduce themselves to Aboriginal people in terms of their name, position title and program purpose. They retreat into their directives and project plans (though not without complaint). They mime the organisation in their representation of it.

It is not only the fact that Indigenous people seem so deeply mysterious that makes professionals in communities hyper-aware of being in a community, even when the encounters they have are so partial and disjointed. It is also, to paraphrase Taussig (1987: 78), our personality absence even in their presence, our deeply personal maintenance of impersonality, that wears professionals down.

Conclusion

In remote area public health work, and not just in Numbulwar, there are odd silences, and a curious lack of speculation about the everyday concerns of Aboriginal people.

It would be less surprising to find an abundance of rumours and speculations about Aboriginal affairs in efforts to supplement what is not fully known with fragments of second-guessing and supposition. After all, as we have seen, that is what so much administrative work is based on: being in the know, splicing an account of action together from a patchwork of snippets and deductions. But while there is endless interest in pinpointing Aboriginal issues and cultural habits, in no way does this entail crossing the borders that anthropologists bodily wade through, moving inside cultural forms and imagining them with detached intensity. This is a key methodological difference between anthropological and health fieldworkers, and important to note in the context of the very many overlaps between anthropology and things bureaucratic – although let me quickly add a caution to this romantic image of the rapport-striking anthropologist and recall the haunting words of W.E.H. Stanner, who, reflecting on what earlier generations of anthropologists urgently and earnestly involved themselves in, similarly shows how an early distancing kept anthropologists aloof from everyday life as lived:

> The young anthropologist ... wanted to understand what was then being called the 'functional system' of social life, how institutions help to maintain each other and contribute to the whole process of human society. We were beginning to speak about 'social structure', the system of enduring relations between persons and groups. Where a society was breaking down (as with most Aborigines) we thought it our task to salvage pieces of information and from them try to work out the traditional forms of social life. Such were my interests. They help to explain why an interest in *'living actuality' scarcely extended to the actual life conditions of the Aborigines*, and why in referring to those conditions I did so in a sidelong way and in anything but a firebrand's words. But it will hardly do as sufficient explanation. *What was missing was the idea that a major development of Aboriginal economic, social and political life from its broken down state was a thinkable possibility*. How slow this idea came to all of us. (Stanner 1968: 203–04, emphases added)

Our silences also reflect the extent to which we instinctively embody our institutionalised selves. We are clearly able to fall into relaxed communion with fellow institutional actors at a moment's notice, and in fact routinely seek one another out in small 'expat' clusters for this purpose. Yet when health professionals encounter unfamiliar Aboriginal people, they move from normative inhabitation to a racialised self-awareness which manifests itself as hyper-civil behaviour. We are politely, reverentially silent in the face of sorcery; passively acquiescent when alien vocabularies lock us out; deferent and watchful in the presence of 'community people'; careful to use as non-threatening a language and bodily posture as we can possibly muster; over-eager to laugh and appear at ease; committing to little except possible return visits and the supply of information materials – and we later call it 'going at the community's pace'.

Controlling speech and committing to little also ensures that one cannot be criticised for doing nothing ... or worse, for doing the wrong thing.

In this excruciating context of 'disimpersonation' and deliberate non-specificity, it is useful to consider the advice from a document produced by the Department of Local Government (augmenting insistences given in many other settings, such as orientation sessions) to assist officials who may be visiting an Aboriginal community for the first time. Following cautions such as that answers to questions should not be rushed, as 'English is probably not their first language', readers are reminded that 'As always you are representing "the government" and will be assessed in that context. What you say is what "the government: says' (Department of Local Government 2001: 2).

As such injunctions demonstrate, health professionals occupy a position already marked by the inscriptions of others. At one level, they are positioned as translators of an abstracted health knowledge which, whilst having a poor correlation with the complexity of influences through which westerners actually attain good health, is nonetheless meant to represent the core and transferable items necessary for good health. They are standards created on paper, and which exist only on paper. No actual body is where the ideal health-promoting body is at.[6] Health professionals attempt to 'share' this iconic information in the most helpful yet non-prescriptive manner possible. Caringly produced graphics and guidelines assist them in their task. But on another level, they must beware of exercising any false authoritativeness, as they cannot prescribe any actions or commitments without the intensive consultative and authorising footwork required to rehabilitate 'interventions' so that they instead appear to be community-determined goals.

These are the more obvious ways in which professionals clearly take their corporate settings with them into remote geographic settings. But I have also argued that there is an institutionally authorised perceptual registry operating in black–white public health relations which powerfully determines individual experiences. Wanting desperately to help, but prepared via an insistent tutelage on the depths of Aboriginal mystery, saturated with verdicts which make sense of everything they may witness and hear through the benign explaining rationalities of colonial depletion, social injustice and economic scarcity, and repeatedly alerted to the possibility of upsetting Aboriginal sensibilities through a wrong look/dress or a too-directly stated dialogue, health professionals cannot help but stumble through interactions hamstrung by 'cultural sensitivity'. They become excessively self-aware, left not so much 'with no formula for handling [their unfamiliarity], no procedure whereby communication can be established' (Brody 1975: 77), as with an excess of procedures and formulaic rules; a surfeit which ensures that their interactions are always already mediated by existing genres of interpretation.

The incorporated self enters a pre-problematised encounter with a projected other, against which the incorporated self is defined and returned back to interventionary logic. Creating stability in dot-pointed representations out of this truly fraught yet magnificently human context of service delivery is, I believe – and will now go on to argue – a testimony in own right to the power of bureaucratic magic.

MASTERY

Emma: The fact that the Army worked out so well, it pulls you up short on assumptions. Because for me that would have been too full on, too regimented, all the things that everyone tells you not to be.

Tess: Where do you think those philosophies, of not being too regimented, not being this or that, come from?

Emma: It's probably a response to the way things used to be … that whole missionary culture.

Tess: Like a backlash?

Emma: Yeah, almost. Nobody likes to be connected to that history, but there are some Aboriginal people who were brought up with that [mission culture] and who view that quite happily, you know what I mean?

    I agree with the philosophy behind community development. Theoretically it's the best approach, but a lot of it is really airy-fairy and based on talk and talk and talk, and people get damned well sick of all the talking. People in communities, they just want things to be improved; they don't necessarily want to talk about how. Because a lot of Aboriginal people say to me when I ask, 'Is that OK? is that OK if I do that?', they just look at me like I'm a maniac and just say, 'Of course you can do such and such.' That real sense of (exaggerated hand wringing, hunched shoulders, fawning expression) 'Is this the right thing to do?'

Because I dunno – somebody's figured that out for the communities as well. Communities didn't say, 'Well I think the community development approach is the most appropriate.'

Just because it looks good on paper doesn't mean it works well in reality. I think we're so concerned about what looks good on paper that we'll have to keep on doing that, because even if there's something else that would work better, if it looks politically incorrect, well we'll never be doing it ... we are so hung up on what is the right thing to do and all the process and all that, that we'll keep on doing it even if it doesn't work. (Environmental Health Officer, outside Katherine, no longer in position)

Sending in the Army

Among the people charged with turning rhetoric into practice, as the saying goes, are many who question the self-evidentiary nature of community development categories, turning instead to other forms of logical interpretation: perhaps Aboriginal people liked being ordered into line military-style in the good old mission days. What if being bossed around is more in tune with their *real* cultural preferences? Could it be that the non-committal uncertainty and respectful deference that health professionals have learnt to exhibit confuses more than it involves? Maybe a dictatorial approach that just gets in and does things is what Aborigines require from their helpers. Might they just want to be well governed? How would anyone know when 'true' community development, like self-determination, is never perfectly in place, is just another idea and is always so confounding?

Public health field officers are left with many puzzles to solve. Sometimes they pursue the conundrums to the outer limits of derivation: if self-determination isn't the answer, maybe overt assimilation is. Mal Brough called it 'normalisation'. Maybe that's all anyone has been up to anyway, disguising the takeover bid in the language of participation and community control and doing a half-assed job in the process. Maybe that's why the Army were so successful in doing the work of Environmental Health Officers when they were first sent in by John Howard back in 1997,[1] getting community people involved in the building of houses and latrines, when they were the last people you'd expect to have what it takes to build cross-cultural rapport with Aborigines. Someone else says blackfellas work well with the Army because they make a lot of sense in terms of Indigenous culture: mostly all-male groups with clear rituals and ceremonies, men who muck about in the scrub and affect to live off the land. It all makes sense.

An imagined convergence is thus created out of what is imagined about an Aboriginal imagining of the Army, with the Army itself standing as a mix of the assumed and the known. A junction is formed where what is taken to be institutionalised Aboriginal and what is taken to be institutionalised white society are seen as merging in unexpectedly fruitful ways. The Army were organised, they came in with resources, not just words. They delivered results, which is just like what happened in the mission days. And they had energy enough to mobilise a listless group of people who otherwise seem to have so little to do:

Emma: I seriously thought the Bulla project [with the Army] was going to be this huge big disaster. I seriously thought that. I could just see all these Army people strutting around. But the community people loved the Army, they seriously did! They just thought it was great. All the young boys thought it was great, it was like a big hero thing, people were really interested, this exciting thing. The Army put on morning teas and stuff, the Army came with money and provisions, to entice people to get involved, and they were enthusiastic themselves, and there was enough people to make it 'An Event'.

I think that's what's lacking out there. That's why they get so much into those evangelists and stuff when they go out there: it's An Event! People don't realise how bored some Aboriginal people are. They're just sort of young adults. When there isn't that much traditional connection – like there might be connection to the family that live out there and stuff, but you know they're just hanging out, people are bored, really bored.

So yeah, things went OK. It went fine. But of course when the Army left it all fell to bits, you know, and that's what we always said [would happen]. To start with, when it was thick with Army guys, wow! Energy! Energy! People got into it. I think that's what I find hard: when you go into a community, that's what is often required. It's not your knowledge and it's not your skills, it's your motivation and just that energy. People already know a lot of [public health] things; they've heard a lot of these things before. People can say to you exactly what they should be doing, using public health talk.

But it's to do with motivation and energy. It's like going anywhere, I suppose. It's like going to some poor, bloody economically depressed suburb where everyone's on the dole and no one's motivated. And it doesn't just come down to money either. It comes down to motivation, and that's what is not there [in communities]. Sometimes you see, where there is one person there who is generating some interest and motivation, what does happen then, because they fire [up] other people – but then as soon as that person goes, things start to disintegrate. Which is a sad thing. And that's why it's hard going out, because if you go out to a community and you're feeling tired, depressed, or anything, like you could just be feeling a little down, then in some ways, there's probably not much point in you actually even being there, because you know you're missing the essential ingredient – your energy.

Judging by the look

Sitting at the Formica table in the Visiting Officers' Quarters (VOQ) at Galiwinku, Ivan Church and I are crunching on breakfast muesli, our travel bags already packed for a later return by light aircraft to Nhulunbuy.

Galiwinku is our last stop on this mid build-up,[2] sticky September tour. We've been judging by the look of things the quality of the houses

Outside view of Visiting Officers' Quarters

and waste disposal systems, shower recesses and hydraulic pumps in remote communities – remote to us, near and close to our Others. It is hard, this looking at; it is draining and disconcerting simultaneously. Draining first. Flying in turbulent air in single-engined aircraft, fighting motion sickness and dehydration, bouncing for long hours in hard four-wheel drives, the tropical heat melting our sun-cream into rivulets of oil. And disconcerting. Witnessing and participating in encounters with Aboriginal people, not so much harsh collisions as gently fumbled, excruciatingly enunciated glidings past; such relief when it's over.

Before I returned to Darwin as an adult professional armed with an honours degree in anthropology and five years' experience as a federal policy officer, in my mind's eye the people who worked in community development roles operated something like the classical anthropologists of yore: dossing in local houses, learning languages and forming relationships through the sharing of food and lodgings. Of all the work choices on offer, I was drawn to prevention and public health, to the young turks of the biomedical system, precisely because of the kinship I fancied they had with anthropological work.

But in my years of alternately shadowing public health field officers as they move in and out of communities and office-based activities, we have never once set foot inside a lived-in house. Only, and then only occasionally, the shells of houses, too new to be occupied yet; or, much more rarely still, houses temporarily evacuated for the purpose of an environmental health inspection or a scabies expulsion. Sometimes we might stand outside a lived-in house, and sing out the name of who we want to see – this being the culturally respectful way to attract attention, they say. But we never go inside, commune in silence, or sit on the ground in the outside yard, trace sorcery intrigues, join in the teasing and the fighting or gamble over a game of cards, *despite* injunctions to take the time to build relationships. The interactions to be had seem always to involve trips with four-wheel drives.

Dealings with community-based people are usually on-the-job and task-oriented, and while it is hard to maintain a work/not work distinction in the increasingly mobile lifestyles of Aboriginal and visiting professionals alike, the general practice of professionals keeping themselves clear of non-institutional Aboriginal people at night and off-duty remains more or less the case. The places we do inhabit – our Nissan Patrol troop carriers and Toyotas, the VOQ, the council chambers, the health centre, the school, the nurse's home for dinner should we command sufficient interest and status – these places that bear our presence also mark *our absence* from the Aboriginal lives we fear might also be refusing us. In the softening, excusing logics of public health that are ever available, I am told the reason we don't cross into houses is that Aboriginal people are already so prevailed upon. It would be a reversion to the bad old ways of the bad old days to extend our intrusion into that last bastion of privacy, the domestic abode. Describing her fieldwork practices, an Environmental Health Officer explained the limits of after-hours interaction in this way:

> I haven't ever; I would almost always be separate from the community. Like, I might go out for a walk or something in the afternoon, but I wouldn't go out at night. [I might] have a bit of chat with whoever is in the health flat, but I don't go out … Most people seem to do it that way. Most people do think really differently about coming out to a community. There's no socialising at night time or anything. Maybe sometimes some people do, I am not sure, but I've never really felt comfortable enough to do that.
>
> And also the intrusion factor. I sometimes think – like I think public health is a good thing and everything – but sometimes I imagine myself in that situation and someone like health promotion coming in and coming over to your house and [saying], 'Come on, clean up, do this, and feed your kids this, and DON'T SMOKE!'

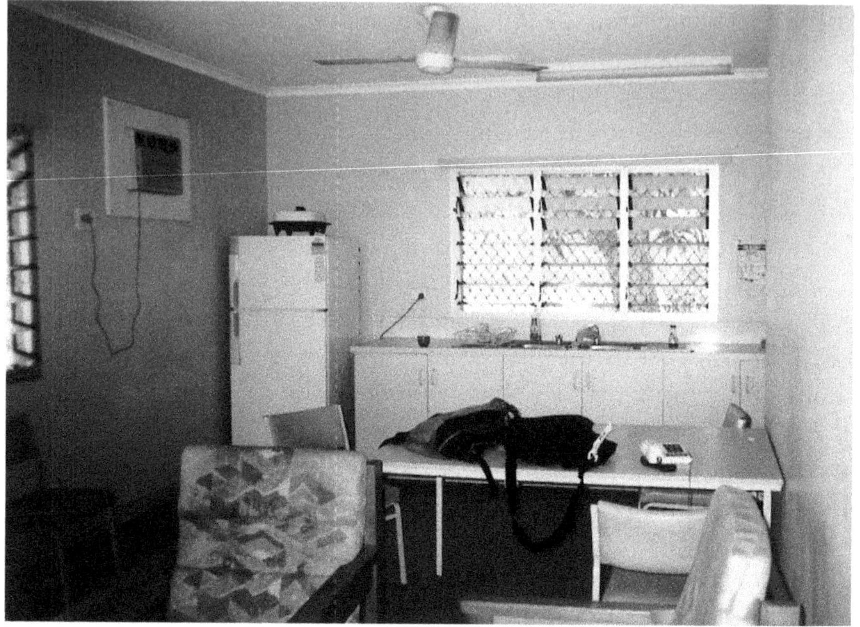

Interior Visiting Officers' Quarters

> Imagine if in the evenings you go over to be [in their faces] all the
> time! We wouldn't put up with it!

Instead, a situation of mutual avoidance has become commonplace. During the day, visiting professionals will follow a polarised route, from our temporary home base at the VOQ, to the Town Council office buildings and thence to the Health Centre, with the possibility of a rendezvous with the Aboriginal employee we've come to see, if they show, in some previously agreed open space.

At night, in the VOQ, the few intrusions from Aboriginal people cadging money or smokes or wanting to sell art and craft products are hurriedly dealt with. Instead the television and other outsiders form company; writing field notes for future file records restores a sense of interventionist progress and helps keep loneliness at bay. Field officers sometimes pursue tertiary studies by correspondence while doing bush work, often tailoring their subjects around specific work problems, as a means of usefully filling in the time.[3] It makes you think: perhaps the boredom which is so often nominated as a problem for Aboriginal youth may well be yet another institutionally generated projection, inverting anthropologist Clifford Geertz's warning that we should not regard 'ethnographic miniatures' as little everywheres, as 'wall-sized culture-scapes of the nation, the epoch, the continent, or the civilization' (Geertz 1973: 21). In THS, my now = their world.

Judging by the look of things, our interactions with Aborigines 'out bush' reduce to this: walking lines between the outposts of the THS and the wider Northern Territory and Federal Government-funded organisational empire. By the look of things, the trusting unguarded relationships that are so insistently dot-pointed as key to effecting change in the Aboriginal domain are experienced by very few; in truth, our well-worn tracks in this supposedly more direct encounter and experience zone of 'the field' merely reproduce racialised suburban boundaries.

On the inside looking out

Interventions, as Australian cultural theorist John von Sturmer has observed, are by definition always extraneous. They are always opposed to immersion and co-presence. They always come from the outside and always 'presuppose a position of otherness' (von Sturmer 1989: 137). What stands out here as we literally personalise the desire for close and meaningful relationships with Aboriginal people in our very bodily presence in live-time remote area communities, is how *tenaciously* our externality is maintained. Even while pursuing our timorous attempts to enlist Aboriginal people to self- and community-betterment projects, we suffer a self-imposed isolation from the lived actuality of their lives.

The VOQs impose their own brand of in-community exile. Available within all East Arnhem communities (excluding homeland centres and outstations), they are defined in advance by their exact duplication of each other. Clean and modern, equipped and bounded, no matter where we go, the VOQ is the same: the same allocation of yard space, high wire fence, locked gates, small verandah out front. The same internal layout, security-screened windows, pastel internal wall paint, hard-working furniture, a fridge, a microwave, a range oven, two bedrooms, each with two spring beds, each with access to an ensuite bathroom, meant for separate men's and women's sleeping quarters.

When we visit communities, we bring and affirm our own little

Layout of Visiting Officers' Quarters

world: we import our own food, meet with other visiting personnel, travel in corporate vehicles. There will be crackers, a loaf of bread, sandwich spreads, something to cook for dinner, pasta with pre-made sauce maybe. Inhabiting these spaces after a day of roaming through the community in our four-wheel drives (our 'Toyota Dreaming' as many will cynically remark), little everyday tasks – preparing an evening meal, taking turns to do the washing up – reinforce our cultural separateness. The domestic structures we set up within communities reinscribe our habitual patterns, with the very objects we find available or bring in our luggage linking us to our homes, our histories, our economy, our systems of mass production and global trade networks.

Regional offices in service centres – the towns of Nhulunbuy, Katherine, Alice Springs and Tennant Creek – likewise mark the distinction between the orientation of the public health professional and that of the communities being 'serviced'. At the moment of professing an outward, Aboriginal-directed orientation, the inwardness of THS is mirrored in the interiority of the narrow regional office blocks. An architectural defiance of public health's avowed claims to partnership-building and client–professional boundary erosion is embodied in the rigid forms of the office block with their air-conditioning, pearl-grey paint and bright fluorescent lights. An unscheduled community person visiting here would have to be handled delicately, like the unwanted nocturnal visitor to the VOQ. Physical co-presence and 'real acquaintance' with 'real Aborigines' is mediated through highly circumscribed spatial arrangements.

True, for many public health officers, community work is not a world of ease and institutional comfort, but something which is grappled with emotionally and physically. It is exhausting, gruelling, stressful, seldom yielding the reward of 'tangible results' and, as they say, you need coping strategies if you are to survive long in the job. Yet this very formulation presupposes an ability to detach oneself from the field one is entering and constitute it as an object of reflection (see also Argyrou 1997: 162–63). The portrait of hardship presupposes that one is entering into, and thus also later retreating/returning from, zones of pathology, non-modernity and cultural distinction.

Earlier I suggested that it is this detachment, this bodily removal, which enables concerned health professionals to disembody the disease and illness of others from the somatic position of their own mind/body (see Leder 1990), to imagine illness as fundamentally an issue to be responded to intellectually and pedagogically. Being able to remove oneself from and yet intellectualise the domain one is sojourning through is, in Foucauldian terms, the position of 'the eye of power' (1978). It enables us to reimagine Aboriginal people as *tabula rasa*, without individual materiality or deliberate alterity; all there is is an overlay of cultural difference that belongs to surfaces alone, that we frame by pre-analysis with dot points on cultural difference. It is thus possible to be interacting with people in the most jocular and affectionate of ways without ever losing one's (encultured) institutional self, nor the perceptual screen that guides our interpretation of the encounters we are participating in. The analogy here is with the intellectual study of anthropology and anthropology in the field: through physical removal and intellectualising, separations are reified.

It remains for me to show how our various modes of inhabiting an institutional self are not a form of ignorance, which can be corrected with more 'authentic' immersion and orientation processes, but an exhibition of cultural mastery in its own right, and rather magical at that.

Reinventing by venting

Back with Ivan, our breakfast talk returns to the anxieties of his work, a subject we've relentlessly canvassed over our time travelling together. He is concerned at the history of poor housing design and shoddy workmanship, the failure to incorporate Aboriginal living preferences, the inadmissibility of the heavy claim of kinship on patterns of cohabitation within the public housing-designed three-bedroom layouts. Yolngu don't live as Balanda, he rails, in three-bedroom houses with fixed nuclear families. He grows angry thinking about what he assumes is a lack of consultation with Aboriginal people and, equally culpable, a lack of consultation with people on the ground like himself – people who would be able to tell those town-based project managers and engineers exactly how long copper wiring and small shower heads can last before they corrode; exactly how badly sited a sewerage drain in a dry swamp will turn out to be in a wet season deluge; exactly how culturally important it is to have separate ablution facilities for men and women.

He is scathing about the means available to Aboriginal people for living healthily. Take the issue of refrigerators, he says, as we sit comfortably in the VOQ, our government-supplied whitegoods humming in the background. They are designed to cope with open and close rates based on the use patterns of urban families who are absent during the day at school and work, are inactive through the dark of the night, and are not living in tropical climates. Washing machines are the same, he says, retelling the *exact story* Jimmy Kneeler told his audience of inductees (Chapter 5), warning public health folk how important it was that they learnt about what really happened, so they could correct the myths that circulate beyond THS about Aboriginal dysfunction. If washing machines out here were used in the same way that the average-sized middle-class households use them, Ivan now tells me – as I know he too was once told – they would break down at about the same rate. But because they are used much more frequently by a greater number of people with far dirtier clothing, the engines collapse much more frequently. Vandalism soon follows. Even more appalling, he laments, Aborigines are then held to blame.

In my notes, it is clear that I don't think to ask who blames like this: who exactly are THS bureau-professionals warding off with the talisman of counter-stories? In fact, THS bureau-professionals never make it clear whether they've witnessed or heard such insults themselves, or when or who by – but we all know how to relay the offences. We know to be solemn with worry, and in our worry we manifest what anthropologist Basil Sansom might call an 'honest ethnocentricity' (Sansom 1995: 309, n.13), seeing the intermingling of sweat and dirt among too many kinsmen living together as terrible problems indicating injustices to be eradicated, and not as potent signs of the alterity Ivan intends such deference towards. I am easily able to assume, with Ivan, a general racist and conservative enemy and worry with him about how to get better functionality out of whitegoods for Aboriginal people so they can better store our healthy foods and better rid their clothes and bedding of any lingering, disease-causing traces of human use. For I too have mastered and am mastered by the allure of institutional logic; I too am held in the thrall of the magical promise of government-led improvements.

Feuding

The day before our departure from Galiwinku, Ivan and I had been taken by Roy, an Army sergeant, to Gawa, Gulmarri, Nanyingburra and Banthula, all part of the group of Marthakal Island outstations, to inspect the capital works being installed there by the Army.

One outstation had flowed into another, each house, kitchen, shower block and fibreglass septic pod exactly alike, site placements the only variation; this standardisation, like that of the VOQs, means you get more for your money.

Roy's a chippie by trade and a big man. His khaki shirt stretches over a distended belly, forcing his breast pocket to tighten like well-stretched clingwrap over the cigarette packet wedged in there. He's here to oversee the installation of health-conferring houses on nominated outstations and to ensure that they are built to the government's environmental health codes. Ivan's task is to check on Roy's work: to find out whether or not the installations have in fact been built to code, to make sure the effluent disposal trenches are wide and deep enough to do their work of transpiration, and so on.

There is a perceptible strain between the Army sergeant and the Environmental Health Officer, and not just because the Army has already

An Army-installed house

made its own inspections, using its own qualified men and are thus resentful of the second-guessing and the seemingly arbitrary standards being imposed. 'You're paying a lot of money for shipping air,' Roy had disdainfully pointed out, gesturing his thumb in a curt backward move towards the giant (but code-compliant) septic pods awaiting removal to the outstations and so, with Shakespearean eloquence, giving the thumbs down to the environmental health regulations Ivan and others had fought such hard cross-institutional battles to have mandated. As the two stand each other off with their polite but tight talk, I watch Roy sceptically raise an eyebrow at Ivan's hints that his (Ivan's, that is) being left out of so much of the Army's work on this extended infrastructure project demonstrates the Army's overall cultural insensitivity, and I note Roy's unmoved silence when Ivan talks of the immense privilege, the profound sense of honour and gratitude Ivan felt when approached by a community elder here at Galiwinku to discuss 'the importance of dogs to ceremony'.

Still, whilst not enthusiastic about Ivan's enthusiasms, Roy was courteous, and seemed happy enough to drive and show us around, even inviting us to later join his men for lunch at their base camp on one of the outstations.

At each stop Ivan marks where things are sited on a hand-drawn

Inspecting health – a buried septic tank

map he has sketched in his notepad and asks construction questions of the site personnel, taciturn Army men with rolled sleeves, tattoos and sunburnt skin. There is little else he can do, as an inspector of hidden end results. What's he going to do, tell them to move a concrete slab already laid (see above)? As self-appointed advocate, the fact that he is the last person brought in to look at things is a sign for him of bureaucratic indifference to Aboriginal welfare. He tells me that in Victoria he would have been called out before the men started, called back again to look at the equipment, again when the trenches were dug, and again when the project was ready for sign off. 'Things are so slack here,' he says, bitterness burdening his words with grave emphasis. But I recall that a similar firmness weighted his objections when he joined his colleagues, at a meeting in the Darwin central office, in their emphatic critique of management calls for a reliable environmental health presence at the outset of projects funded by other government agencies. The group imperative then had been to claim overwork, under-resourcing and professional demarcation boundaries; the job of environmental health being to promote health through community development, *not* to inspect buildings.

In conversation with me, Ivan reinforces the contradictory nature

The outstation view at Nanyingburra

of his community development advocacy: 'I keep saying, "I'm not a housing inspector, I'm not a housing inspector – I go where the people want me to go." I don't think we should be doing houses for people, it just imposes our ideas on them.'

Such unacknowledged contradictions are at once fascinating and typical of public health accounts. They reflect not hypocrisy, but people's best efforts to wade through the inherent paradoxes of externally driven empowerment projects and retain some sense of professional integrity. The evidence used does not need to be consistent to fill this need: people draw on various anecdotes, conflicting or not, to reinforce the 'authentic' nature of their advocacy.

At Nanyingburra, after Ivan's redundant inspections, we follow Roy into the base camp itself, where the soldiers have been living for the last three months. A new house, with khaki green iron cladding (surely an Army coincidence) has been erected for the traditional owner of the area. It sits on a windblown peninsula overlooking a stretch of white sandy beach the soldiers say is stalked by a rogue crocodile.

'I hate it,' the blunt sergeant says to our expressions of delight at the beauty of the setting, refusing to be drawn into our sentimentalising of the landscape (see Weiss 1996: 1–2). 'I dunno how these people can live out here. Give me a spa, access to the TAB, a cold beer, a comfortable hotel any day!'

In the middle of Roy's hot and humid nowhere, the Army have

installed a virtual community: one canvas tent with rows of bunks for sleeping, another with a long trestle table and bench seats as the mess hall. I am told to be careful: 'I'll go in and tell 'em to behave. You stay here,' Roy gruffly warns me. 'They've been here for two months straight and there aren't many women out here.'

Embarrassed by the clichéd allusion to hungry testosterone, I attempt dismissive mockery: 'How primitive can they be?'

'If you had ever been to Mitchell Street[4] in one of their civvy breaks you wouldn't ask,' says Roy, adjusting his girth, my wince confirmation that his rebuke has made a mark.

The tent is full of people feeling self-conscious but assiduously pretending that nothing is awry. Ivan and I sit down at one end of the trestle table, unintroduced and clearly out of place. Every time I look up from the table I meet a pair of eyes, quickly averted back to metal plates piled with meat stew and deep-fried chips, while we delicately prepare sandwiches from a wee tin of low-fat salmon and a loaf of wholemeal bread. Ivan is as conspicuous as female me, with his bright blue long-sleeved shirt, gold ear stud and little terry towelling hat. And in this place the Army has temporarily made its own, with us surveying the Army's work to reorganise Aborigines into more healthful places, there are no Aboriginal people at all. Their rearranged landscape can be surveyed in their absence, binding us to them, them to us, in wordless exchange.

Is this the Army's Energy, Energy! that Emma saw catalysing so much Aboriginal interest? No matter. The stories never do quite match. They are instead infinitely adjustable, which only seems to enhance their spellbinding effects in creating momentary certainty out of the otherwise inconclusive drift of public health effort, and verifying the shared social knowledge, registered in our bodily habits, that such sense-making gives rise to. It can grate, though, this complementary sense-making. Where Marlena is tentative, Peg is bold (Chapter 6). While Emma suffers doubts about the hegemony inherent in community development, wondering whether decisive forthrightness and mission-style discipline are the way to go, Ivan thrashes about in the agony of doing too much *for* rather than *with*. Yet there's no torment in organising down-to-earth solutions for straight-shooting Roy. He knows what he's there to do, then he wants outta there, mate!

The little disputations about manner and approach – well, not so little really: they assume momentous import in the cataloguing of who sins most against Aboriginal people – the *inflated* disputations, then, mask fundamentally shared epistemic positions of interventionary superiority and competence. They form what anthropologist Dominic Boyer calls, describing how the binary East/West is constructed and inhabited in contemporary Germany, 'a fundamental diversity of individual permutations of broader social knowledges [that] gravitate around preferred, dominant typifications of identity and alterity' (2000: 462). Amidst the intense factionalism about approach and political commitment, there is a tremendous standardisation in the logic which explains the need for our interventions, for our very positioning as concerned helpers. It is, as we have seen, such a readily (I will not say 'easily', for its fraughtness is essential to the constructions of our extraordinariness) generalisable logic that it can be inserted into any situation, without the need for specific knowledge of these particular people, their place, their contemporary context, specific histories or intimate local concerns.

Discrepancies R Us

Health professionals are not stupid. Far from it. 'Off the record', many admit to a discrepancy between their own subjective struggles and the dot-pointed protocols for interaction and formulaic homilies on cultural difference they have been immersed in and find themselves regurgitating. Many reflect on how little they really know, often within the same conversational breath as declaring that relationships have to come first:

> It does seem crazy that you have clinic staff out there but you don't have public health staff based in communities, and I think that that is – not that I'm volunteering to go and stay in a community – but I think that until there is that real tie, unless you're a really amazing communicator, you're not really getting to know anyone, and in a couple of years you're gone and you still didn't really get to know that many people. How many of the old ladies and the young girls with their babies really trust who you are? And half the time you didn't get to see inside anyone's house or you didn't get to talk to people about it, you know? (Environmental Health Officer)

They are well able to identify the discordance between the fractious complexity of Aboriginal existences they glimpse and the alternately uplifting or melancholy dot-pointed abstractions that they conscientiously reproduce as explanations for Aboriginal pathology. Their representations of their work are imbued with contradiction. Simultaneously multi-layered and reductionist, full of detail about the infinite variety of local personalities and practices and just as instantly codified into simplistic and universalising character traits: Aboriginal people/we are like this; they/we don't do that; they/we used to be such and such. For instance, Marlena and I had many discussions on what she saw as the need to build on what people know. One time, she told me with some anger that her fellow THS nutritionists preferred learning about Aboriginal women from the written accounts and anecdotes of other whites than from the women themselves. If they took the time to talk to the mothers, she told me with some vehemence, they would find out that the women already knew about healthy foods and when and how to wean their children. Others, like Emma, have spoken with considerable self-irony about their own initial romanticism, how Aborigines were not the ideal victims their liberal imaginations were originally expecting, echoing Povinelli's observation that the assembled artefact 'Aborigine' is 'never wherever an actual Aboriginal subject stands and speaks' (1999: 34). In such reflective moments, bureau-professionals insist on the need to meet people as individuals first and the templated category of 'Aborigine' last.

Yet in the shift from relaxed exegesis to workplace formulations, when public health officers are consulted, perhaps for their input into some small-scale research project or for their expertise in developing action plans and evaluation reports, empirical complexity transforms into a form of capital which supplements and verifies conventional diagnoses of the need for more intervention. They supply practical evidences which re-prove the need for such formulaic remedies as more relationship-building/time/collaboration/debriefing. Even within self-critical dialogue, when professionals subject their practices to critical and reflexive scrutiny, the switching from intellectually complicated to simpler prognoses is evident. While Emma challenged the arrogance inherent within the participatory processes that community develop-ment theory takes as an inconsequential given (unorthodox move), she also posited a commonplace nostalgia that the mission times were better for Aboriginal people than the mess of today (simplification).

But how dissimilar are these discursive modalities, really? They share a fundamental metaphysical assumption that things have a beginning and an ending, that fault can be found and therefore corrected, that the teleological lessons of history need only be sounded to be short-circuited, leaving the original interventionist logic intact. It is a metaphysic which cannot for a moment entertain an order of socio-economic co-existence with Aboriginal people that *excludes* institutional intervention; a metaphysic which would ask, as pre-emptory response to even this critique, *but what else would you have us do?* For doing nothing has now become unimaginable.

Emma is also able, without fear of contradiction, to retell the social work truism that unemployment leads to apathy, that Aboriginal people are bored and have project fatigue; that they need to be energised by the energy of helping professionals if they are to get involved in health activities. In the easy manner in which middle-class anxieties and their logically derived behavioural consequences are assumed to be forms of psychic motivation for everyone, all people of all cultures are assumed to need work, market-economy style, to create self-worth and a sense of purpose. It is of no matter that Aboriginal conceptions of work value and self-esteem seem so poorly known within the bureaucracy: the psychic satisfaction of self-support through paid work is simply taken for granted as universal.

That participants continue to reproduce culturally embedded conventions of understanding and enactment in spite of what they know, at times refusing to admit their empirical knowledge into the policy frame, reveals something of the power of institutional articulations to make convenient sense of discordant social relations. It reveals something of how thoroughly formal diagnoses are ingested, how useful the abstractions are to smoothing the infinite diversity of actual practices into an artificially static taxonomy of known characteristics. And it suggests something of how satisfying prescriptive discourses are: they have the allure of conclusive termination points ('this will all end when we/they …', or 'unless and until we/they …') while building on the trade routes of institutional talk to reaffirm alliances and enmities. It seems that, once absorbed, well-meaning cause and effect analyses become key devices in showings of knowings to other professionals, part of the easy exchange in the deceptively transparent authoritative assessments that mark professional talk. As organisational ethnographer David Mosse would put it, 'development projects work to maintain themselves as systems of representations as much as operational systems':

> unruly practice is stabilized, and the gap between policy and
> practice constantly negotiated away ... policy designs also provide
> the framework of self-objectification for project actors accounting
> for themselves to each other and to outsiders. (2006: 940)

And while there are clear demarcations between kinds of helping whites (the gruffness of the Army soldier, the softness of the educated professional), indexing social idioms of identity distinction (Bourdieu 1984), the key axis of classification – the very different absent Aborigines – create the shared interpretive frame to which we all commonly orient our discordant talk.

Effortless and voluntary

At our breakfast of healthy muesli before our flight back to Nhulunbuy, after we've done all the inspecting we're expected to do, Ivan tells me about his wife's frustrations, attempting in her spare time to get a Women's Centre to function properly in another Aboriginal community. She has been doing it for about a year now, and like Ivan, struggles with the meanings and the fascinating, frustrating processes of 'getting Aboriginal people to take control'. They often talk shop. He says, 'I say to my wife all the time – in this business there is no such thing as leaving your work at the office.'

He told me that from the outset his wife refused to be the one to clean up at the Women's Centre. She knew that if she took that on, it would establish a precedent, when the women need to learn how to run it for themselves if they are to ever have full say about how their lives are organised. So she let the place get unsightly, and resolutely ignored admonitions from other whites about the growing dishevelment. Even when she was told by the CDEP Coordinator to clean it in readiness for a visit from the Health Minister, who would be arriving soon to have discussions with the people about how to regulate kava, she steadfastly refused. But when she came to work that next week, concerned Balandas had gone in with their mops, buckets and disinfectant, attacking the filth anyway, which left her furious at the short work made of all her hard work, now spiralled back to the beginning of her attempted instruction of the black women in the arts of gaining control of their own environment.

It is an effortless thing to be drawn into the conspiracy of white concerns (see Sansom 1995: 277). It must be very difficult, I commiserated, easily picturing myself gut-wrenched with the same dilemmas of sparking work motivation and navigating the clashing of wills with other interfering whitefellas about how best to help Aborigines. It is an effortless thing to be so drawn, and this is critical, given the simultaneity of our mastery of and accession to institutionalised logics; given the way such logics, elaborated in so many registers of interaction and action, constitute such a salient, dominant form of being. Our incorporation is so complete that we even voluntarily and automatically rehearse forms of bureaucratic doing and worrying with only each other as pillow-talking audience, and will deploy the structure of managerial argumentation in the moment of railing against managerial intrusion.

Mastery

> The spectacular alliance of so much nobility and so much futility ...

> *Roland Barthes (1957: 31)*

One afternoon I was walking past the office of a Nhulunbuy public health officer and saw him buried in a sea of computer printouts, with yet more charts on his computer screen. There was Ian Goodman (a colleague Ivan Church despises for what he sees as Ian's gung-ho, know-it-all, action-man arrogance), furiously marking up copies of a survey form which gave a matrix listing of all the things to look for in community houses so that inspectors can objectively assess (and so objectively prioritise) their level of disrepair. Seeing me, he immediately launched into a summary of his activities and of his troubles with not being understood by those idiots in Head Office.

'The government is not concerned to do things properly but just wants to shovel the money out and pretend that is the addressing Aboriginal issues,' he railed. He was particularly irritated with some recent initiatives emerging from the NT Department of Local Government (DLG) in relation to the development of a housing repair and maintenance survey form. He said it was developed without any input from people such as him, people at the coal face. He has developed his own version, a more concise survey protocol he claims is easier to fill in and to interpret, to replace the overly complicated DLG version (which, having been through three iterations of field testing and multiple institutional negotiations, now includes 95 questions).

'I thought – Jesus! They must just want to stuff this up! They will end up with a questionnaire that can't be completed and data that's just not valid.'

I asked if he had raised his concerns with anyone. 'Have I ever!' he exploded. But his inputs were received with antagonism, so now he was just going to use his own forms and they could all just go to hell. Yet here he was, annotating the DLG forms with his suggestions anyway, making a last-ditch effort to renegotiate the technical terms of the matrix and to amalgamate the complicated questions. 'Why did they ignore you?' I asked, settling in for a long story about villains and victims, suspicions and grievances. Concluding it, he shrugged:

Ian: All I can think is that I threatened [the Darwin manager]. This is about his career. Whereas for me it is not about my career but about fixing the houses and improving the health of people, based on educated decisions. In fact, I am ruining my career by pointing these things out. About two months ago they advertised the Director of Aboriginal Housing position and like an idiot I applied.

Tess: Why like an idiot?

Ian: I was setting myself up. They didn't even bother to interview me.

Was there really a conspiracy or was his simply a poor application? No matter again. Stories such as these are indispensable to public health work, where grumbling is as instrumental as enthusiastic rallyings in giving shape and form to bureaucratic actions, and artfully crafted facts and fictions taken to be real become real because of the needs they serve.

And of course, beyond all this mundane strife and worry about money wasted and forms grown too large lie no end of real, tangible and tragic things to worry about. As a way of work public health is plagued with communication problems, travel ordeals, cancelled and disrupted meetings, stop-start projects, decisions referred to other sites for (unlikely) resolution, long gaps between the decision to act and action itself, loose commitments, few resources and many evaluation reports available that describe but do not fix the problems. Back in the regional office, professionals may be freed from the claims of heat and dirt through fresh paint, air-conditioning and scheduled meetings, but other antagonisms quickly enter. Head Office's intrusions are multiple and its policy demands are unrealistic. Colleagues can feud over petty entitlement issues and office factions can form over the most incidental matters. In disputes about good intentions, rivalries reign, judgments are instant, and the possibility of slipping up can stalk every slowed-down second of performance. Workplace gatherings can be full of veiled criticism and camouflaged invective which sustain interpersonal rivalries and alliances alike, and individuals must constantly work to maintain their reputation as progressives. But through all this, institutional actors can at least feel that by fighting for the right words and emphases with and against each other, they are saying No! to oppressive governance on behalf of and for Aboriginal people, in the same moment that they participate in a collective, if antagonistic, re-creating of the organisation and its logic of intervention.

But nor does exhibiting how mastered and masterful we are need be so tense. To the instances I've already given (the workshops; the community meetings; the ever so easy hand-wringing; the marital pillow-talk; the redundant data critique), I want to add another image, of the pleasures that can be had in reproducing the terrible burden of deciphering how best to act.

Far away from Nhulunbuy and the Martharkal outstations to the east, with Ian's and Ivan's counterparts in the rumour-filled Darwin regional office, I joined Environmental Health Officers Mal Guinness, Jimmy Kneeler, Peter Woods and Don Forster in a small informal workshop to discuss the vexed issue of community control and better housing. Don had been in the kitchenette meeting room ahead of us, scribbling across the whiteboard, trying to put the thoughts his recent postgraduate public health studies had given him into a framework of community control. He started with a stick figure, and the statement that appealing to hearts as well as minds is important for building the understanding and knowledge that are prerequisites for action (Figure 9.1).

As we suggested words to fill the spaces Don's arrows and text instantly created, with one of us suggesting an issue and another suggesting better words for little rephrasings, Mal joked about Don's clothing, about his being the worst dressed of all the men working there. Joining the banter, I told them how I had spotted an extremely good-looking woman sashaying past Don's window earlier that day and had noticed how Don's office door had then *mysteriously closed*, lacing the words with deliciously drawn-out innuendo. The tables turned. Jimmy taunted that it had been me who'd noticed and drawn the bawdy connection first: 'This is the anthropologist going native,' he teased, recalling all the locker room jokes related to a woman among men we'd previously clowned about with. So it went, inane and hilarious, our heavy-hearted participation in the whiteboarding exercise, struggling for words to describe the dimensions of the problem of working alongside (*with* instead of just *for*) Aboriginal people, leavened with small office intimacy and coffee room camaraderie.

Jimmy told us that he had received a phone call earlier that day from a doctor alerting the unit that he'd seen a poisons icon on the inside of a flour tin and asking them to investigate. 'Puts a new slant

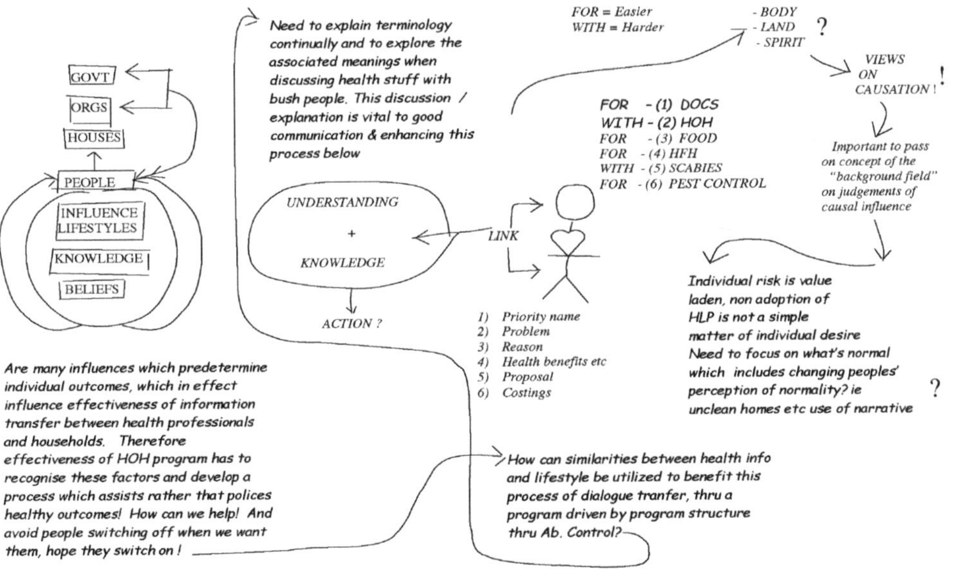

Figure 9.1 From the whiteboard: 'with' is harder than 'for'

on baiting the flour, doesn't it?' Mal wryly quipped, which segued into jokes about drugs in communities and 'Who's the dealer?' wisecracks about Willy at Maningrida, who smokes a lot of dope.

'When I first met him he said, "Oh I don't smoke that stuff any more", but that same day we went on a car trip and then he asks if I minded if he had a smoke and he lit a huge reefer!' Jimmy recounted, imitating the blissful smoking of a joint as he spun his yarn. We all laughed, especially at Mal's final quip: 'If he got busted, they could do a movie called *Free Willie!*'

Amidst our goofing, it is important to stress that coming up with responses to Don's whiteboard gaps was as hard going and as gruelling, as attuned to public health factionalisms and as subterraneanly, interpersonally competitive as it is in any public health work event. Professional camaraderie, banter and mild-mannered brinksmanship feed off each other. There are, at every moment, many nuances and trades to attend to. But these are integrated, automated, so that we can make jokes, think, worry, compete, and diagnose all in one. The hand-wringing is so second-hand, the formulations about the cultural differences and knowledge gaps to be overcome so comprehensively known, so well mastered, so sedimented into our professional diagnostic repertoire, that we can rearrange the classifications any which way, meandering with jokes and innuendoes as part and parcel of our intellectual labour. Energised by our repartee, the forms on the whiteboard resolutely took shape, our banter activating our will to proceed as effectively as alarming statistics or well-facilitated workshops have done in other contexts.

The little jokes and innuendoes spurred us on, just as they made powerful statements about relationships, intimacies and distances all at once. But having little apparent connection to the whiteboard text, they will slip quietly out of focus, from both insider and ethnographer depictions of bureaucratic processes alike. And like Ian's wasted efforts to change an already approved questionnaire, our temporary whiteboard artefacts do not produce legitimated policy, nor are they done in response to any management edict. They are as temporary as line drawings in the sand, as ephemeral as Ivan's marks on his makeshift maps, as immaterial as Ian's comments for feedback no one wants – and as impossible to appreciate without the related stories and epistemic links to multiple and recursive articulations, formally disseminated as accredited research or more humbly as conversational currency within everyday bureaucratic situations.

It is a magical, finely laced web of beliefs and justification, critique and the creation of oppositions and things to denounce – in short, a whole cultural organisation being created by people who live and feel in the space between the pen and the paperwork, with its 'spectacular alliance' of institutional embeddedness, creativity, redundancy and repetition.

BEING T/HERE

Being born in Darwin, I have always known about in-place and out-of-place bodies (see Feldman 1997: 35). Before leaving in a flurry of self-righteous young adult indignation, I remember being shy of – yet intrigued by – the flocks of black people walking quietly, always the ones not in cars, their relaxed amble a foil to the office walkers' brisk drivenness. Slowly moving between camps, hostels and doss houses in the dusk or early morning, avoiding the full blaze of sun. Like Soweto, I used to fancy, recalling images from secondary school texts. Trying to ignore the raucous women screaming 'Fuck yu, fuckin cunt!' to their men and hitting scratching kicking wildly as they staggered uncoordinated fight steps in public spaces, wary pedestrians picking out delicate detours, absorbing the familiar spectacle with stern apprehension, their bodies anxiously hunched in counterpoint to the groggy flailings of brawls in the street.

Progressive whites know to speak of these exhibitions as a problem of itinerancy ('They need public housing/to go back to their own communities/they're here to visit sick relatives in hospital/poor things, the government should provide more shelters'). This is our public secret, a naming given to a social rawness too confronting to be given other names; our very politeness issuing its own decontaminating proclamation, a deft re-securing of our liberal decency in the face of what we can only see as abjection.[1] It is all said with a certain amount of sympathy, as if to anticipate and ward off the hostile contempt of our less tolerant Territorians, as we unconsciously affirm our roles as proselytes of the helping state.

Growing up and leaving the racist, sexist, highest-violent-crime-rate-against-women-in-Australia-redneck-town, never coming back, but coming back anyway, 12 years later. 'It gets in your blood, this place,' locals will tell you. It never left mine. Back first as a bureaucrat, and then as an anthropologist, trying to make sense of living one's flesh and blood in the compromised, bureaucratised swirl of racialised encounters. Flailing in turn through the conceits of anthropology and institutional politics that were as ritualised as the ones I was attempting to objectify in the postcolonial frontier.

In Darwin today, the wild north is still much the same, only more civilised, which means its old rawness has a new vocabulary and has been visibly straightened out by high-rise buildings. Built on the back of extractive industry and defence force money, a new suit and a lick of hair cream has spruced up our unruly province. But one still gets to see the occasional black body lying prone in odd places – in the blazing sun of a workplace car park, on a street corner, in the cool cement portal of an office building. Check quickly to see – still breathing? – before assiduously moving on. Don't really want to have that broken conversation, navigating the serial demands of slurred words. Easier to instead have moralising debates with professional acquaintances about whether or not to give money to the black beggars in the street: Yes, they say, but only if it is for food, and you'll have to buy it for them; never give straight cash – it'll go straight on booze. 'So what?' I might say, to spur a new bout of aghast talk.

From the air-conditioned offices of the bureaucracy, the beckoning, alluring intensity of the mired determination to see and speak good is a familiar home. 'They come in from the communities to go on benders. They don't drink back in their own country. If the elders could only be supported to control the young people it would be all right,' I am told, have always been told, as I was nurtured in the warmly explaining liberal politics of my mother, of my reading, of my professional and academic work. And yet ... didn't my father do that too? When he would come back from nine months' survey work measuring newly acquisitioned land, subdividing mining towns, laying out roads and fencelines? Out with the Aboriginal chainmen, frugally equipped with a rifle, Keen's curry powder and Saxa salt, a camp oven and billy can, a theodolite, splintery survey stumps and a beaten four-wheel drive, rolled a few times in the scrub? Back in town to sit out the monsoon season and throw back a daily slab of beer with red- and black-skinned mates?[2]

Were these benders only the unruly and abnormal moments of an otherwise ordinary, culturally stable life? A strong memory tugs at me now of killing bullocks with him one time when he was sober. The macabre treat of being allowed, just the once, to plunge the knife into the warm soft quivering chest of the just-fallen beast, secretly proud that I knew the trick of leaping aside from the fountain plume of warm blood before it splashed across the hard hot ground. As an adult with a new identity as vegetarian anthropologist, I visit women known to me once simply as the mothers of the friends I played with years ago, now grandmothers who relate to me as woman-to-mature-woman. How fervent was their worry when my own mother had to go to work when Dad was back in town, because he always brought in a truckload of blackfellas with him. How one had checked up and found me playing happily in the bath with a black man on the toilet in the room next door and cried, 'Billy Lea, I am taking this girl now and she is not coming home until this house is safe, you hear me?' Was I oblivious then or not? I can't remember: there are no field notes available for reordering.

The aching sense of familiarity when I walk into Aboriginal spaces as I've shadowed anthropologists, then bureaucrats, is an echo of my own lifetime of straddling bush and town, for this is my doubly occupied space too (Stewart 1996). Flies buzzing over food, an axe and a rifle, a billy can for making tea, plastic salt bottles on the kitchen bench and spreading piles of junk, pitted against the neatening of filing cabinets and institutional carpets, professional introspection, managerial agonising and academic refraction.

Another memory now, of going to Nguiu, Bathurst Island, with the late Bob Collins, in the final weeks of our review of Indigenous education, after assembling case studies of over a quarter of all schools in the Territory, tracing a topography of education system failure, illiteracy rates the only indicia showing any signs of acceleration over a 20-year period (Collins & Lea 1999). Or should that be decline? Anyhow. In the place of holding consultative court my face is caressed by Tiwi women, strangers to me. They hold my chin in their hands, stroke my cheek and look at me askance.

Others stare, gesture in my direction and talk among themselves. It feels as if I've been waiting for this moment all my life. I'm told about my father's fathering of other children, two black sisters I never knew were a possibility, and the contradictions seep back into my refined practices of objectification. The bush life he had, the urban life I've tried to have, the buzz of putting on prim court shoes to literally step into bureaucracy, sandals for academia, and black women in the street: too drunk to fight properly, rank and malodorous, swinging wildly, widely, and missing their mark. Perhaps one of my sisters, perhaps not. Maybe they don't even exist, or it's a case of mistaken identity, his name being confused for someone else's. Then again, maybe it's true. It is my own piece of unfinished business.

As for what happened to Bob, well, it puts my own ordeals into a very light space. His pelvis and his right femoral joint were smashed to pieces in a car accident in Kakadu in 2004; cancer ate into his bones; and he committed suicide before facing charges of child sexual assault, said to have taken place over 30 years ago in the tropical warmth of Maningrida and the cold of Canberra. A different kind of unfinished business.

Writing the life out of things

If I assess this ethnography against the criteria of native ethnography[3] – that is, as an attempt to bring anthropological light to bear on my everyday, thoroughly bureaucratised and racialised life in the postcolonial frontier – then I have failed dismally. While my life-world entanglements – entanglements of governance, race, politics and gender – have been alluded to, much has been suppressed, and even now it is hard to put the life that has led me to this point into well-theorised words. Giving an account which respects the affective dimension in an arena conventionally thought of in purist disembodied terms has certainly required autobiographical involvement, but in this place, in my place, the frictions of postcoloniality have to be lived through, not just fictionalised. Despite the representational permissions granted by the overhauling of theories of ethnographic representation and the fictional plays with factual accounts over the last decades, it is impossible to write back in the pulsating life that sustains and subverts the projections of order and rationality that we insistently overlay onto 'the data'.

I am not raising these issues as prelude to an overview of the much-vaunted identity crisis in anthropology,[4] but to identify the almost too obvious fact that authors who attempt to re-enchant their ethnographic portraits tend not to turn to bureaucratic fields to make their case. Or rather, if they are depicted, bureaucracies are used to give greater relief to the magic of the non-bureaucratised, non-rationalisable modes of existence that are being ethnographically reclaimed. The bureaucratic *modus operandi* is *a priori*, automatically, disenchanted. Even dictionary definitions assume an in-built alienation, with the very term 'bureaucracy' being saturated with negative meaning, opposed in every way to the wonder of life itself:

> **bureaucracy 3 a:** a system of administration marked by constant striving for increased functions and power, by lack of initiative and flexibility, by indifference to human needs or public opinion, and by a tendency to defer decisions to superiors or impede action with red tape <inveighed against the evils of the ~> **3 b** : the body of officials that gives effect to such a system <caught in the meshes of a timid and heartless ~> (*Webster's Third New International Dictionary of the English Language*, Unabridged)

> **bureaucracy 1.** Government by officials against whom there is inadequate public right of redress **2.** The body of officials administering bureaus **3.** Excessive multiplication of, and concentration of power in, administrative bureaus; a system characterised by power without responsibility **4.** Excessive governmental red tape and routine **bureaucrat. 1.** An official of a bureaucracy **2.** An official who works by a fixed routine without exercising intelligent judgement (*The Macquarie Dictionary*, 2nd edition)

For bureaucrats, reduced in most analyses to dull mirrors of their unexciting artefacts, all liveliness and excitement, mystery and enchantment are stripped away, the better to depict the (imputed) instrumentality of bureaucratic modes of being.

Even in this work, where processes of inhabitation are foregrounded, the political and the economic displace the aesthetic and the spiritual, the somatic and the sensory, each and every time. Joy, love, sex, pain, hatred, boredom, emotional display and repression, lethargy, drift and delirium, all these marvellous and ordinary modes of inhabiting the world somehow are always secondary to the greater theoretical point. Instead, I work to create, in Taussig's marvellous words, a 'duplicitous lucidity' (1987: 463). The magic of life of itself seems to intrinsically resist even the 'new' forms of ethnographic representation; the only privilege being a native ethnographer has possibly given me is a greater feel for the magnificent detail of all that's still not here (see also Bakalaki 1997, Narayan 1993).

The real irony is that if I view this conundrum as itself an anthropological intrigue – as a pattern or phenomenon to be understood – with the detached intensity of one who wants to know what it is to be *this* person or *that* grouping, I can see such repressions as ultimate homage to my mastery of bureaucratic magic, and its mastery of me.

The magic of bureaucratic creations

Welfare bureaucracies attempt to change the world, and do change it, by orienting the bureaucratic inhabitant so that she or he conceptualises the world in terms of reform and intervention. The 'real work' of 'turning around' Aboriginal ill-health is always contingent on the activities of workshopping, coordinating, consulting, drafting, creating ownership, finding the funds for more positions, recruiting and (oh! if only) *the time* for more community development, program evaluation, researching and relationship-building. At the same time, feeding into these enactments of activism and dedication, participants run an ongoing critical dialogue which might denounce these same activities for *not* leading to outcomes, for being repetitions of what's been tried before, for being no more than the stop-start white-dominated activities of their predecessors.

Mounting this critique, naming the nonsense with cynical blasts about the waste of time, the misspent monies, the poor data, the reports sitting on shelves, the ignorant policies or the useless paperwork – blending a wry knowingness with a suspension of disbelief – is a breathtaking performative act. And we all enact it. The scandal of Aboriginal health, and all the self-recriminations about the lack of time and resources available to deal with it, obliges participants to obscure the ways in which the remedies they struggle to implement speak of their own longings.

Then there's the way in which our artefacts (policies, data, charts and diagrams), the abstract forms that bring our desire for breakthrough analysis to terrifyingly logical material life, are themselves attributed magical properties. Not only do they become endpoints for action, but they are seen as in and of themselves 'making a difference on the ground'. Like icons, a high value is placed both on the correct ritual processes for their assembly and on their inherent motivationary power. Even a footer on a document can be subject to days of deliberation and exquisite craftsmanship. As we have seen, such institutional artefacts are familiar and abundant. For the sake of convenience, we will call them all policies, but they could be separated into their categories: mission statements, annual reports, qualitative research, quantitative research, survey results, data summaries, evaluations, program reviews, project status reports, strategic initiatives, budget papers, workshop recommendations, political commentaries, media reports, academic papers, seminar presentations and so on. They all, in one way or another, represent the shaman-like hope that the projected world that is to be acted upon can be manipulated through its representation in policy artefacts. And in a way, of course it can.

Ethnographically, it has been vital to move from icon to performative scene and back again to examine how information (the name institutional artefacts are better known by) and actions taken on behalf of beneficiaries become seen, magically, as effective in the 'real world' of persons, things and events. So much human artisanry, effort and faith goes into the creation of these bureaucratic forms that it is impossible to separate the artefacts from the hopes of their artisans. Impossible, that is, but for the equally wondrous disappearances which hide the impassioned faith and sensuosity infusing institutional knowledge forms from both insiders and outsiders.

Which finally brings us to the ways in which the denial of life's contingencies and ambiguities, its richnesses and mundanities (of all that other magic, the magic of life itself), sustains by stealth the credibility of interventionary logic-magic. Political scientist James Scott is one who has given considered attention to the issue of what is left out of bureaucratic representations so that they can achieve 'the clarity of the high-modernist optic' (1998: 347). Taking development projects as his focus, Scott argues that orderly vision allows contemporary administration to happen. The standardisation of things like population attributes is a necessary first premise in development policies as it makes the otherwise unruly, particularised details of the 'real' world amenable to definitive, quantitative answers and therefore to systemic regulation. Order requires overview, and overview requires simplification.

But these very understandable abstractions from the more messy real are, he warns, inherently problematic. It is the eruptive details of everyday life, Scott argues, that give governmental efforts 'their intended consequences, their range of (intended, semi-intended, unintended and indeed perverse) effects, and the dissonance within and between specific strategies, programs, policies and their consequences' (Dean 1994: 153). At the end of the day, the lived details that are left out of planning efforts in the name of regulatory classification will always return to haunt implementation efforts. In other words, while it is impossible to make plans without simplifying, this very failure to capture the complexity that stands beyond the plan renders impossible the desired correlation between pronouncements and effects. The vicissitudes of everyday life among the people being improved – a life that interveners may barely even know – inevitably snag the smoothness of their interventionary imaginings.

By way of remedy, Scott urges planners and concerned researchers to consider the relevance, detail and integrity of local knowledges and non-modernist practices before leaping to override them with visions of progress and improved amenity, so as to avoid repeating development mistakes (Scott 1998: see especially Part Four). As an explanation and conclusion, it makes perfect sense. For Scott, the answer lies in paying greater heed to the people's preferred ways of being in the world, in respecting their alterity and being mindful of the everyday wisdom and expertise that informs it. As a bureau-anthropologist, I would have no argument with that. It is what I might say if I were called on to suggest ways forward for more effective health practice, or what I might say if I were defending the relevance of anthropological work – and surely this unmistakable congruence is a dead giveaway of the fact that there is institutional magic at work.

For in directing our gaze to what policies gaze at, we are once again drawn to consider the in/adequacy of their representative function, and with lightning speed are moved on to the idea of resolution through some better process. But even our critical verdict of ineffect is simply another means of buttressing an original intentionality. This is the seductive pull of bureaucratic magic. Scott's analysis ignores the fundamental narcissism of bureaucratic practices, which do not suppress but feed off complexity, including full-bodied wallowing in the practical, erupting complications of the imputed worlds being worried about. Scott's 'real' (the space 'out there' where life is inhabited in rich detail) does not flatly precede the diagnostic techniques of institutional actors; neither is it their badly managed product. One is always inside the other.

All around the creation of bureaucratic forms is the active social role played by uncertainty and second-guessing, experiences from the field, multiple adversarial inputs, and the need to gain footholds by declaring clear pathways for actions which self-sustain by never being satisfactorily fulfilled. There is a mutability to the communicative moments in which state representations are deployed, a context-dependent dynamism to how they are expressed, which is as much a testament to professional creativity as it is an indication of complete immersion in and accession to institutional logics. It is an ultimate act of intellectual objectification to discount the tremendous work of imagination invested in academic and bureaucratic rationalities alike, to not acknowledge the creative doublethink both critic and native use to render such lively sites of human interactivity, image-making and meaning creation somehow dull and lifeless or, at best, helpfully (or blightingly) instrumental.

Snag-free governance has no traction. If there were no problems to be amended, organisations to create order would not be required.

An image of action is the real

Of course there are deformations of the world of practice in bureaucratic representations, and not just of the sort Scott has in mind. Consider, as my final example, the following diagram, produced as an outcome from the Fifth Annual Chronic Disease Network Workshop on the theme 'Making Work or Making IT Work?' held in Darwin in May 2001.

The workshop gathered into itself representatives from the many organisations concerned with Aboriginal health. THS policy officers and public health field staff were there; doctors and nurses too. There were NGOs and Aboriginal community-controlled health services, researchers and advocates – representatives, one and all, of 'the real world'.[5] Concluding the day, the key themes of the workshop were

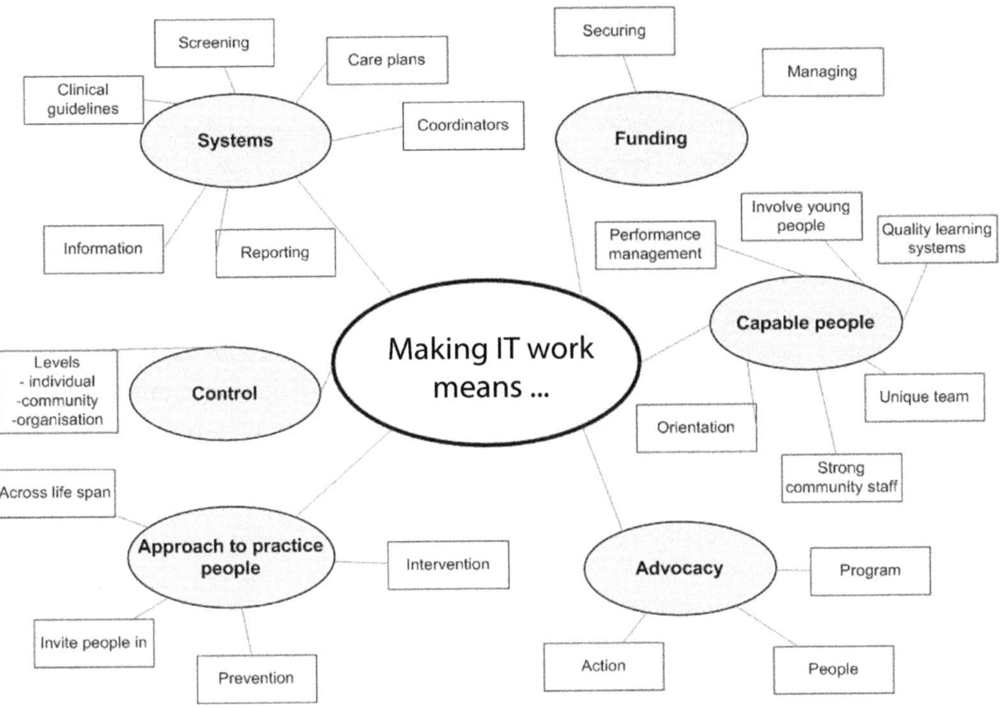

Figure 10.1 Making IT work means ...

represented diagramatically, a formulation task which simulated the look and feel of action in the drawn-out arduousness of whiteboard constructing in the tired afternoon (Figure 10.1).

I stress the tiredness of the afternoon. Participants were lacklustre after a day filled with accounts of program activities limping along in the field and the myriad ways in which projects were struggling to achieve 'runs on the board'. One survey conducted in the Katherine region had found that Aboriginal men with chronic diseases were not aware that they were meant to be on case management plans. This despite the immense investment in the technical systems needed to encapsulate health records electronically and, more worryingly, after establishing an Aboriginal-run health board to oversee proceedings. Another participant, a self-declared member of the 'stolen generation', berated attendees for their whiteness, claiming that those present were deliberately holding on to their professional positions in order to exclude Aboriginal people from them. It was a strained proceeding, a failure of this, a misrepresentation of that, exclusionary processes and power differentials duly confessed and weighing down professional shoulders.

As the afternoon wore on, the diagram and associated dot points listing the workshop's recommendations for 'Making IT Work' juggled participant inputs into caption points of 'good practice', the magic of intervention being that the very act of listing these attributes made us at once more accountable, striving, in control, compassionate and full of propriety, in the face of all-round and curiously reaffirming adversity. It was a nonsensical and typical construction. We could contest it on the grounds that for Aboriginal control (individual, community, organisation) to be real, it should be more than dot points over to one side, but that would still be obeying the silent edict these forms send out to the viewer to participate in the ill/logical constructions, as if there really are outside referents being empowered or not through our aesthetic efforts.

Let's think now of what such forms deflect in order to draw attention away from themselves as culturally embedded artefacts. This deflection doesn't just depend on the 'magic of style';[6] it depends on the removal of the magic of life itself in order to achieve an institutional look and feel, which is no mean feat, considering the passionate and in-worldly circumstances in which these forms are actually made. All around, as groups worked through the formulation process of 'Making IT Work', there were plentiful distractions. There was another angry Aboriginal antagonist, periodically standing up to rail against the racist government and the lack of proper representation for Indigenous people (other institutional players like himself, that is), forcing all subsequent speakers to apologise for their expert qualifications and wrongfully gained positions and, hours later, provoking restless shuffles from an audience grown impatient with a ritual flagellation taken too far.

There were exasperated sighs, giggles, whispered asides and little notes, flirtatious or complaining, passed from one person to another; idle doodlings in the margins of notepads; the background hum of the air-conditioning (a problem on that day, as it was intermittently too hot or too cold and delegates needed to keep repeating their complaints); and the disruptive sound of doors opening as intruders barged into the wrong conference room only to loudly and apologetically disappear again. There was the corridor talk between sessions, mini-meetings, quick assessments of both the presenters and of the usefulness of the workshop, and dismissals of/support for the ritualistic accusations of racism, combined with endless variations on a theme of all-round lack of support for public health from all-powerful 'thems' (the general 'state', including the Federal Government, THS management and so on).

And yet, in the newsletter which later reported the workshop event (White 2001: 3–5), only our flowchart and an account of the systems required to make our identified interventions sustainable survived as the material evidence of our gathering. As Latour has put it, 'only finished products have an essence' (2002: 48).

An entire universe of bureaucratic imagining is thus built on a life-world, a surrounding 'real', which everyone takes completely and utterly for granted. Even participating in the workshop, suspension and attention, fact and fantasy, real and unreal, nourished and blended into each other. Being there, the objective conditions of our participation – the institutional surrounds, the actors, the air-conditioning – blurred into our tacit, becoming, as philosopher Mikel Dufrenne puts it, 'no longer truly real for me' (1987: 5). Conversely, the 'unreal' – the collective conjuring of an abstract representation of the problems to be fixed – was paradoxically 'not truly unreal, because I can participate in the play and allow myself to be lost in it without being duped' (Dufrenne 1987: 5). It was not unreal, because it was materially conjured and jointly authored. Through being so seriously moral and purposeful as we produced our incantations ('involve young people', 'provide funding'), transformational qualities were magically conferred into our whiteboard artefact (Sartre 1971: 66–67). And it was not truly unreal, because the representation we collectively created became the most real product, the tangible thing the event was archived by, one more institutionally crafted thing among the many. One that at first glance glides over the eyeballs, because of the grandest and most magical of all its achievements, its quintessential banality. This is bureaucratic magic, sweet and pure.

Blurring in and out of view

The way in which bureaucrats are instrumentally depicted and sensuously evacuated resonates with how professionals foreground a projected Aboriginal (or general public) neediness in order to background their own fears and desires. The bureaucrat, forgotten in the insistent foregrounding of the kinds of project-led improvement everyone has learnt how to yearn for, nonetheless has sensory experiences, in every single moment of every single day, that need to be reframed within the interpretive grid of interest-free, depersonalised, betterment-oriented service delivery. It is the compulsiveness of being involved (the magic of participation) which paradoxically whisks life-worlds out of sight. The impersonality of caption point diagnoses of problems and solutions triumphantly displaces the din of everyday affect. Wording yourself out of the picture, 'disimpersonating' some things yet being conventionally earnest about others, takes considerable, practised personal (physical, emotional, visceral, cultural) investiture.

To make this concrete, consider the question of sex. As Hearn and Parkin observe:

> Enter most organisations and you enter a world of sexuality ...
> This can include a mass of sexual displays, feelings, fantasies, and
> innuendoes, as part of everyday organisational life, right through
> to sexual relationships, open or secret, occasional sexual acts, and
> sexual violations, including rape. (1987: 3)

Yet if the vast amount of material on matters organisational is to be believed, organisations are 'inhabited by a breed of strange, asexual eunuch creatures' (Hearn & Parkin 1987: 4).

The way people allow themselves to be kept by the secret of sexuality at work is but one aspect of the larger cultural phenomenon being traced here. Not only is it the case that bureaucrats leach out the specific characteristics of specific persons in order that they may become manageable population groups (*pace* Scott 1998). Bureaucrats also exclude themselves from their own writings. For these are the screenings that we have mastered and internalised, in order to perceive the world as one that constantly invites an interventionary response, to be mediated through the aesthetic refinements of policy. This bodily repression is a key experiential source for the widespread perception of the professional world as the counterpoint to 'real life', however nonsensical such segregation has to be.

I've met the state ...

In trying to make of bureaucratic practices something of a testimony to forms of human creativity, I have tried not to lose sight of the hegemonic quality of a logic which cannot imagine betterment without some form of government intervention. Of how the artfulness of institutional actors is directed at working backwards from a verdict that Aboriginal people are suffering to create an unarguable rationale for further interventions. Nor have I denied that lives are being lost, that pain is real, that much ill-health is preventable, that (in)justice exists, that professionals bring an honest commitment to their work or that improvements can and must be achieved.

I've simply tried to follow an anthropological path of appreciating the ingenuity and multi-dimensional processes which feed into expectations of rightness and order, which give magnificent human form to institutional rituals, and which explain their compelling attraction as systems of thought and action, for both myself and others likewise encultured within interventionary logics of our own devising.

Paradoxically, it is *as an anthropological pursuit* that the surrounding life of bureaucrats, and the surrounding life that has supported and sustained my ethnographic capacity, are both made irrelevant to analysis. Writing ethnographies, we perform within the representational norms, play within the parameters available, create a pretended order for things and experiment at the margins of being an eye-I-witness, without being able to undo the meaning-finding, order-imposing whole. As for writing oneself in – well, it's all a bit like 'fessing up to negative experiences in the workshop encounter: there are rules about making ethnographic experiences tellable. There's an ordinariness to when and how to claim the extraordinariness of our accounts. Inserts about the life of the ethnographer strategically reveal how one's subjective experience pressed into the fieldwork and its writing up, told in ways which are themselves authorising, authenticating, and destined to showcase the capital of the fieldworker.

There are two issues I am intent on merging here: what one has to do to be a bureaucrat among bureaucrats, and what one has to do to be an anthropologist among anthropologists. Bureaucratic language undeniably demands that we speak of the world in terms of 'authoritarian reason' (Taussig 1987: 133), which seems to require that we sacrifice the life that goes on beyond the objectivity assigned to it so as to create the image of a manipulable reality (Dufrenne 1987: 64–66). This is also the practice of anthropology, and for not dissimilar reasons. To inhabit one's ethnographic self requires the same bureaucratic ability to deflect the full sentience of lived environments out of the account, replacing it with something other, a knowable (predominantly language-based) object. A performance requirement of anthropology is that we further transcend what people do and say to seek the larger (wider, deeper, occluded) answers lying beyond and behind the (culturally construed) everyday concepts we say are shared by ourselves and our subjects.

That anthropologists revert to administrators when thinking through what the beliefs, theories and actions of western professionals may mean is not accidental. There is something essential being brought out by this replaying of bureaucratised perception within admonishing accounts of bureaucratised perception. For all that it may be an unintended mimesis, it is nonetheless accurate.[7] As if to affirm this, there is only a limited vocabulary available to ethnographers to describe the seduction of the tragic occupation, to evoke the sensory dimension of being animated by the urgency of the (institution-spreading) question: what is to be done? The unarguable forms of liberal rationalism enacted by the benevolent 'we' that feels compelled to act, the very subjects of this ethnography, are much easier to define in terms of complicity, conformity, governmentality, because 'we' anthropologists are ensnared by the same (institution-spreading) desires for order-from-disorder and further, by the same belief in the power of representation to bring the misconceptions of others to correcting light. We share the related need to disavow our self-interest in a continuing subalternity that needs our representational championing, in order to continue our research (see Kulick 2006). As people's advocate, the anthropologist's job is to chide policy for its poor effects, not to comprehend the cultural habits we share with the formulators.

It is a hard labour, trying to make sense of people whose job it is to produce sense, until we see this very effort as evidence of the problem at hand. The flood of bureaucratic knowledge forms send out an enticing challenge to decipher the truth, or the proper approach, out of the confusion of programs, projects, theories, research, professional and intuitive opinion. It is hard not to want to clarify and evaluate, hard not to demand, in response to the circularity and repetitions herein described, advice about real programs which can be shown to work. Surely there are tangible improvements that can be claimed? Occasions where we've undeniably 'made a difference'? Recommendations that can be made for helping things improve? Policy shifts which led to seismic historical change? Surely you don't mean there should be no services at all? Or that we should leave things as they are?

People become passionate about 'the issues', which makes taking part and contributing unavoidable. Reasoning gets confounded, which sets up its own mind-bending intrigues. The very act of trying to pin causes to solutions, problems to interventions, real outcomes from claims of intent, good representations from bad ones, draws one into the process – which is why it fascinates, frustrates and pleasures, which is how its magical power is exerted. It is the compelling nature of this appeal that this book tries to understand.

For instance, I am often asked what I would recommend for helpers who acknowledge their inevitable embodiment of the state but want to know how to proceed in a way that minimises harm. I say simply: forget the agony of trying to be pure; concentrate instead on being as technically proficient as you possibly can. Dare to draw upon evidence to inform your interventions, resist the reflex disavowals of scientific approaches on the dubious premise that participatory action research is less oppressive (see Cooke & Kothari 2001). The field does not need more good-willed generalists mouthing safe platitudes; it needs people who are competent at their profession and dignified in their analysis. Perhaps this might help break through the choreographed routes of public health discourse. It would certainly make for higher calibre policy formulation.

My answers suggest the point of this book: I have met the state ...

... and she's an anthropologist

I hope by now the ordering of this ethnography has become clear. It would not have been enough for me to describe the faults of governmental policies. This is a book about the existence of the state within the self and the self within the state. My subject has not been the artifice of bureaucratic constructions but their social life, and how they are brought to life by social beings. This is art and artisanry, artifice and facticity, coalescing into powerful systems of cultural reproduction that come together in the orchestral work of upholding the developmental state. A sense of wonderment is called for, even if the cultural mastery at play here remains uncelebrated within anthropology, which only sees a non-fantastic rationality in need of correction. Indeed, it is just as fascinating to think about what kinds of self-denial anthropologists must exert to be left with so little wonder at forms of bureaucratised incorporation, but that's a whole other story.

Finally, knowing that the magic of intervention (synonyms: statecraft, remedial circularity or bureaucratic socio-logic) lies in the malleable ways it can shift itself to adjust to and if necessary recuperate any configurations that might challenge it, why would one knowingly be a bureau-professional? I ask this question because it is frequently asked of me.[8] Of all the many possible explanations this ethnography has already suggested – Brenneis' 'conventional self-interest' (1994: 33–34), the compulsiveness of doing good, the witty sociality of like-minded company, and the allure of rubbing up against the societally acknowledged decision-making money-allocating power of the sovereign state – I want to isolate the same answer that is available to anthropologists to explain their own labour. However slim the margins and narrow the cracks for influencing or altering the course of institutional events away from their colonising intent, however befuddled such an undertaking is from the outset, there is still the hope that participating from the inside at least offers opportunities for such deflections to be identified and fanned.

In the same way, if a bureaucratised life-world is the ground for our thinking about, among other things, bureaucracies, how can one get 'outside', 'above', 'beyond' (*pace* Nader 1972)? One of the few options available to anthropologists who sense how overwhelmingly encultured they are within the 'great circularity' of (interventionist) liberal reason is to use anthropology against its own grain to help sense what the master forms of sense-making habitually expel. Anthropology is at its best, or more accurately, is at its least bureaucratically socio-logical, when it tries to understand and resist falling into culturally familiar conventions of explanation. A complete epistemological break is not possible, for being native means never being able to fully leave. As anthropologist Daniel Miller argues (1995: 11), the point of anthropological studies of global-to-local capital, bureaucratised society and postcolonial practices of consumption 'is not that [such things are] good or bad, but merely that [they are] increasingly the inevitable cultural process[es] in which we find ourselves'. Being fully immersed, then, the evaluative commentary and muted promise of correction that has inflected this book is both an accurate depiction of the domain and a signal of my (academically honed) bureaucratised inhabitation.

To live with the prospect that as intellectuals, bureaucratised-being-in-the-world is a naturalised inhabitation, not an imposed one, may be for many politically driven thinkers a frightening, repulsive apprehension. But it can also be liberating to gain some sense of the lived-in, externally driven and consensual limits on our own agency. Or at least that is my hope, a hope which is the ultimate honouring of bureaucratic magic and the faith it sustains in the power of description to amend conceptualisations of how the world 'really is', and with that improved perception to somehow yield a better outcome ... for whom and about what no longer seems to be the point.

NOTES

1 Introducing the helping white

1 This term was introduced by Mintzberg to encapsulate the predominant location of academically trained professionals in government-funded organisations (1993). Welfare workers are also 'bureau-professionals' in a second sense: of combining notions of professionalism with bureaucratised ideals of fair and just administration (see Llewellyn 1998: 26). The alternative words used in this book are 'interveners' and 'developers'.

2 A growing body of literature in anthropology dwells on categories of insider and outsider, native and exotic anthropology, making something out of the emergence of ethnographers who look and sound other than the products of mid-century Euro-American academia. As Ahmed and Shore sum it up, '[t]he natives are likely to be educated, often with a university degree or PhD from a Western University' (Ahmed & Shore 1995: 19) ... and they might even be anthropologists. Like many vogue genres in anthropology, 'same culture' research, the anthropology of home and native anthropology constitute a bundle of practices searching for a coherent identity (see Kuper 1994, but see also Strathern 1987). Adherents have moved from their earlier concern with questions of bias and authenticity (for example Firth 1981, cf. Ryang 1997) to consideration of the impossibility of ever fully displacing westernised perception from the underpinnings of anthropology (for example Bakalaki 1997, Narayan 1993). Others have stressed that ethnography in one's own geographic area (however defined) is not necessarily same-culture research (Brown 1994, Gupta & Ferguson 1997, Morton 1999, Passaro 1997, Visweswaran 1994). Whilst theorising on the implications of nativity appears to have passed its peak, I have appropriated the politically invested marker 'native', originally devised to resist the oppressive weight of 'we' within anthropological discourse (Appadurai 1988a, 1988b, cf. Haraway 1998, Rosaldo 1989), in preference to other possible tags (the ethnography of home, of policy, organisational ethnography, or even, if we stretch the point, medical anthropology), because essentially, this book interrogates epistemologies of insiderness.

3 While this is a deviation from standard Australian approaches, this perspective

converges with a number of contemporary approaches to institutional ethnography and anthropological accounts in the international arena which take both development and policy as an object of study (for inspired examples, see Latour 2002 (1996), Mosse 2005, de Sardan 2005).

4   Whilst roughly correct, 30 per cent and 70 per cent are clearly anecdotal weightings. This said, health expenditure data are also in a constant state of revision and speculative interpretation. The Australian Institute of Health and Welfare's journal publication, *Health Expenditure Bulletin,* is the source most frequently used within government for reliable cross-jurisdictional comparisons and is recommended for those interested in tracking financial attributions.

5   His full lament goes like this: 'Let me tell you a story. The Governor-General was up here just a while ago to highlight the problems in Aboriginal health and he graciously went around to meet the people in the field while he was out in Arnhem Land. And he met this person, a PhD linguist, who told him he was studying the health of Aboriginal languages. I could tell the Governor-General was stunned. I mean, the people are dying like flies all around, and this guy is studying the health of languages?!!' (field notes, July 1997).

6   Arguably, the new age in the office continues a longstanding tradition where abstracted forms of transnational spiritualism form a romantic menu for western cherrypicking. The explosion of interest in new age lifestyles, the invention of occult rituals building on a pastiche of so-called native practices and ancient rituals, can be read as signs of the disenchanted west reclaiming a suppressed need for spirituality in the everyday.

7   Like as not, for instance, mid-ranking policy officers with little technical depth or subject expertise are assigned topics to write up in haste, at most drawing upon a precommissioned and sanitised digest of social issues, at worst quickly googling for research content, blending such content material with cut and pastes of safe words that have survived the editing processes of previous writing efforts. Much of the inanity of policy can be explained at this level alone.

2   The passion in policy

1   The NT Parliamentary Sittings are scheduled occasions when the full House of Parliament meets. In the Territory, these occur six times per year, and last up to two weeks at a time. Whilst the major priority for the elected government during these periods is to see its policy legislation passed, the Sittings are also occasions when Members may employ the mechanism of the Ministerial Statement to give particular issues air space. Ministerial Statements are essentially speech documents that can take up to 40 minutes to be read aloud to the Assembly. They are in no way considered routine; rather they are seen as opportunities for Ministers to have uninterrupted periods of critical parliamentary time to showcase their polemical command of the issues within their particular portfolio/s. For bureaucrats, it is an opportunity to have the arguments surrounding key initiatives sounded out in more detail than legislative discussions ordinarily permit, knowing they will circulate to a wide audience of other institutional players – unions, non-government organisations, companies, media outlets, other bureaucracies. To have a Statement listed for attention is equally no minor matter. A specific-purpose Cabinet Committee adjudicates the apportioning of speaking time – matters outside immediate legislative concern must be argued and lobbied for, with the more senior Ministers putting the case for their juniors. The ease or otherwise with which a Minister can command Ministerial Statement time is thus a signifier of his/her standing within the government. In sum, they are not seen as opportunities to be squandered, either by the Minister and his/her staffers, or by the bureaucrats

charged with providing material for the political performance.

2   The argument mooted here is that with the right incentives, private operators would either refurbish or replace the moribund old public hospitals with fee-paying client-attracting boutique layouts. Deploying the more flexible debt-financing capacities of the commercial sector, the private sector would bypass the clumsy budgetary processes for major public sector capital works that befuddles and increases the expense of government purchasing. Within the public sector, major capital works are ordinarily purchased in moments of electoral largesse, which bureaucrats capitalise on by entering into a game of over-bidding and over-building (that is, of maximising projected usage or exaggerating anticipated growth in 'need'), knowing it will be a long time before they get another bite at any new major works cherry. (For detail on the problems of hospital 'overgrowth and redundancy' for governments, see Nesmith (1995: 8) and O'Brien (1997). On hospital topography and the changing nature of surgery in relation to building styles and the need to exploit health's luxury potential, see also Hamer (1988)).

3   'Coughs, colds and little holes' is a common diminutive used to describe the non-critical ailments which people present with in casualty wards, 'little holes' being cuts or small wounds which require simple suturing.

4   Indeed, early in the following year, Health Minister Dennis Burke became Chief Minister, breaking the five-year reign of Shane Stone. Burke remained as leader until August 2001, when the Australian Labor Party gained power for the first time, ending the CLP's unbroken reign since the Northern Territory was granted self-government in 1974.

5   In its capacity to contain infinite and contradictory meanings – from the promotion of domestically amenable work practices through to a justification for mass sackings – 'flexibility' is itself a key policy word as well as a desirable attribute. Anthropologist Emily Martin provides a historicised and careful account of the ascendancy of 'flexibility' as an objective for healthy bodies, nimble managers and responsive organisations alike; Barley and Kunda give a devastating account of flexibility in the form of the mobile and ever-vulnerable contemporary professional (Barley & Kunda 2004, Martin 1994, see also Perin 1998).

6   Schwartzman (1989) provides a thorough analysis of the range of speech-curtailing modulations in meetings in her ethnography of a mental health facility, *The Meeting: Gatherings in Organizations and Communities* (see in particular 76, 80–81, 124). See also the work of Myers (1986a, 1986b) and Brenneis (1984, 1987, 1988).

7   Such reflex concern for proving inclusivity is characteristic of most bureaucratic discourse, explaining not just the wording but also the elaborate consultation steps taken to be able to claim democratic authority in and for policy texts. All formal proposals and submissions, such as might be presented to the senior management team for endorsement or to the Minister for final ratification, are required to demonstrate evidence of widespread need or demand, which symbolically attests to the reality of the problem and the value of the proposed solution. Amidst the standardised structure of subheadings within Cabinet Submissions – which, it should be remembered, have legislative force if enacted – there is space for mandatorily summarising the 'Consultation and Coordination' actions associated with the particular proposal. As Mosse explains, 'the more interests that are tied up with their particular interpretations, the more stable and dominant development's policy models become' (Mosse 2004: 646).

8   At the time of writing, the Northern Territory is still not a full state in the Australian Federation, a source of some frustration to local politicians. During 1998 it was hoped that Territory residents would vote for statehood in a referendum that was coincidentally held with the national elections of 3 October.

Despite polling showing strong support for statehood, the question was defeated. Subsequent attributions laid the blame squarely on the shoulders of then Chief Minister Shane Stone, saying his consultation processes had been heavy-handed and out of touch with 'the people'. This verdict was sustained by both members of the Opposition and disgruntled members of the Country Liberal Party, providing room for contestant Dennis Burke to manoeuvre a leadership spill in the following months.

9   For instance, an undated letter from the Leader of the Opposition admonished the Country Liberal Party's 'agenda to privatise everything from our hospitals to our water supply' and added that, 'Territorians do not need or want an American style health system where only those with expensive private health insurance get decent health care.' Another leaflet, hand-delivered to all mailboxes and turned into posters for mural and shopfront displays, listed '10 Good Reasons to Keep Territory Hospitals in our hands'.

10   Povinelli's ethnography of the labour actions of Aboriginal women in Belyuen makes a similar point (Povinelli 1993a). Authority and status are contested and negotiated interactively and recursively, a point which may seem obvious for all social formations, yet is glossed over in representations of bureaucrats as alternately static and process-bound or slippery, complicit and self-promoting.

11   People often have such sentiments critiquing the status quo and repetitions of the 'same old, same old' written as homilies on their office whiteboards or magnetted onto a filing cabinet, and manually underscore the concept of inane repetition when it appears as a finding in management texts. As later chapters will show, reciting formulaic diagnoses is itself an important and repetitive feature of bureaucratic practice, a returning that is fed by the liberal-humanist faith that identification equals eradication, operating as something of a talisman against 'reinventing the wheel'.

12   Had we delved into this case study with standard techniques of policy reconstruction, we would also have found that what gets released both within 'final' policy products and in retrospective straightenings has by far the greater prescriptive and historic authority, directing our attention to the accomplished facts, even whilst anthropologically, the drift, the compromises and the uncertainty of the just happenings and adjacent meanings in the elusive 'before' are equally deserving of critical attention.

3   The self-replicating organisation

1   Patients are transported to the Darwin and Alice Springs hospitals or interstate through direct medical evacuation (Medevac), by Inter-Hospital Transfer and through the Patient Assistance Travel Scheme. However, patients must also travel extensively within the Territory. Chillingly, research conducted in an East Arnhem community estimated that all Aboriginal infants will be evacuated in a life-critical state at least once in their first year of life (Wright 1996), while for an increasing number of adult Aborigines, certain treatments for chronic medical conditions, such as end-stage renal dialysis, require permanent residency and machine-bound life away from family in Darwin, Alice Springs or Adelaide.

2   The frequency of visits to communities invariably drops off in the monsoon season in the Top End, and it is commonly noted that the highly picturesque coastal and wetland communities are more frequently accessed than those in the simmering hinterland, which correspondingly have fewer on-site visiting officer amenities or departmental service outlets. Conversely, the Tiwi Islands, being a short flight from Darwin, are visited on a daily basis by a wide range of government and other institutional representatives.

3   For a more detailed discussion of these points of critique and schism, see Nettleton and Bunton (1995).

4   Consider, for example, the following analysis of the strategies most likely to yield 'excellent outcomes in contemporary primary health care in Australia'. Following an investigation of 185 published accounts of practice, a closer evaluation of 99 of these and detailed study of 25 of the most highly cited cases, 'Eight broad strategies of primary health care practice were identified which appeared to have contributed to excellent outcomes in the cases studied: consumer and community involvement; collaborative local networking; strong vertical partnerships; inter-sectoral collaboration; integration of the macro and micro; organisational learning; policy participation; and good management' (Legge et al. 1996: 12).

5   In mathematics, fractals are any of a class of complex geometric shapes that commonly iterate the same pattern yet are capable of holding infinite variation (as with a fern leaf), and in which the form of the whole can be seen in the isolated part. It is the relationship between classes of phenomena that matter in fractal equations. Within anthropology, Wagner deploys the metaphor of fractality in his analysis of Melanesian big men as a means of describing the simultaneity of being both individual and group, or, in his paraphrase of Strathern's work, to describe a subject who is neither singular nor plural (Wagner 1991: esp. 162–63). Here I am using a fractal metaphor to indicate both a singular object and a rapidly reproducing formation with different coordinates that at any point of drilling down has its own particularity within an overall pattern of sameness.

6   In many situations, 6–9 months is more likely to be the norm, either because the project itself is short term or because a permanent position experiences rapid turnover (as is the case with remote area nursing positions which, in some parts of the Territory, have a life of three months, or teaching positions, where eight months is the average). It is difficult for bureaucrats to render this precisely in charts or statistics, as electronically tracked 'position separations' cannot distinguish whether a person is lost to the system altogether or has simply moved locations to reappear with a different title elsewhere within the organisation. One can know turnover at the level of the whole domain (overall appointments, resignations and retirements) or at a magnified level of local area detail, but not both at once.

7   A whole other book could look at Australian Government's (pre-national emergency) plan to 'fix' Aboriginal communities by establishing Indigenous Communities Coordinated Trial (ICCT) sites across the country – to be overseen by the Council of Australian Governments (COAG), itself a cipher of coordination. But it would take more than Kafka to honour the ruses of rationality feeding the constitutive absurdity of such operations.

8   By this I mean that if the meeting is not a standing committee but formed through diary appointment, it will always have an ostensible purpose towards which participants will specifically orient themselves, despite the lack of a written agenda or any formalised recording of the decisions reached. Presence at the select 'mini-meetings' that surround official meetings is directly proportional to the influence of the officer.

9   Don Dale Juvenile Detention Centre is a prison for teenagers on the outskirts of Darwin. Extracts have been randomly selected from a two-day public health coordination meeting featuring program managers from across the Top End, held in Darwin.

10   This earmarking itself borrows from the reputational schemas elaborated above. Determining which communities to approach for permission would itself have been the topic of coordinating discussions, with such criteria as council management stability, proximity, population size (for sampling purposes), level of upheaval, likely willingness to participate etc used as the yardsticks.

Some communities, such as Alpurrurulum (formerly known as Lake Nash), are predefined as impossibly problematic and are ruled out, thus reinstating the uneven distribution of resources that development projects are meant to ameliorate. A defendable response to this point is also at the ready in the logic that bureaucrats should concentrate resources in a fewer number of areas to build 'real successes' that other communities would be inspired to emulate, rather than failing equitably by spreading too thin.

11 Not spending funds that have been hard won through argument and passionate constructions of need is regarded as poor management indeed within service agencies (see Munro 2001).

4 Learning the arts of helping

1 Hummel's work, *The Bureaucratic Experience* (1994), reprinted four times since its first release in 1974, is a sustained example of this argument. Hummel argues that the bureaucracy systematically stifles humanitarian impulses among employees, and transforms individuals into clients and cases. As he can allude to the myriad nightmarish encounters with blinkered administrative stupidity and heartlessness that we all have in our repertoires, his typecasting holds up too well to be dismissible. But I have been at pains to argue that the incitement to bag bureaucracy in both popular and scholarly literature is part of the analytic problem. Among other things, it ignores the equally myriad encounters with bureaucracy in which a blind eye has been turned, ambiguities exploited and inconsistencies mined for the benefit of clients. Yet even this counter-critique (a defensive promotion of 'the good guys' working on the inside) simply upholds the original framework and its methods of apprehending the bureaucracy as the site of either good or bad practice, when these are the binaries that need to be overturned in the name of analysing it as an enfleshed and cultural domain.

2 An immense body of organisational literature defying easy summary is relevant here, although comprehensive overviews can be found in Boden (1994: especially 28–54) and section one of Schwartzman's seminal work *The Meeting: Gatherings in Organizations and Communities* (see also Bauman 1977, Garfinkel 1984 (1967), Paine 1981, 1989). For work explicitly focusing on the work performed by storytelling within institutional settings, see in addition Jefferson (1978), Kunda (1992), Maynard (1989), Munro (2001), Schwartzman (1984, 1981, 1993, 1994), and Van Maanen (1979, 1988). The range of approaches represented within even this highly selective sample vary widely, from the high empiricism of ethnomethodology and its enchantment with questions of communicative involvement and storytelling in conversations, to disembodied linguistic treatments of institutional talk as formal texts to be analysed for the structural logic of the words; severed from but isomorphic with the structuring of the organisation itself. Workplace stories themselves may be analysed for their internal narrative patterning and rule-governed grammars (for an innovative analysis which – unusually – draws on literary criticism to look at storytelling and performance genres in organisations, see Czarniawska 1997). Note also that several authors have pursued Schwartzman's injunction to 'see with meetings' (Schwartzman & Berman 1994: 66) specifically in relation to Aboriginal groupings, by asking what meetings accomplish, not so much in terms of their resolved outcomes but in terms of their sense and structure-making (Myers 1986b, Rowse 1992: especially Chapter 3, Williams 1985). Other authors who have focused on black–white interactions using town or citizen meetings as part foci include Cowlishaw (1988), Kapferer (1995) and Morris (1985). For a sustained ethnographic analysis of the role of white brokers among Aboriginal fringe-dwellers in Alice Springs, see Collman

(1981, 1988: especially Chapter 1). However, despite this abundance, it remains the case that the behind-the-scenes talk work of bureaucrats as they ponder how to deal with Aboriginal people among themselves and within their own organisations is far less represented in the anthropological literature, except by way of conjecture.

3   Surprisingly, given their dominance as a mode of interacting in many contemporary organisations, workshops are almost completely untheorised within the anthropological canon. Schwartzman's work on meetings remains one of the few serious anthropological treatments of gatherings in a welfare-oriented organisation (see Schwartzman 1989).

4   As Sansom argues it, the evasion of answering direct questions with the disclaimers 'dunno' or 'caan say' are not so much statements of ignorance, non-cognisance or even reluctance, but rather are evidence of the questioned person disclaiming his or her competence to speak about the subject at hand, regardless of whether or not the matter is 'known' (Sansom 1980: 21). That is, a person may know the subject but may feel herself not to be the rightful person and so choose not to transmit. The capacity to promulgate knowledge of events or people is collectively licensed, policed by intersubjective scrutiny and minute counter-practices, such as rejections and rejoinders (see also Povinelli 1993b, Sansom 1988, von Sturmer 1981).

5   In THS, circumspection in the Aboriginal knowledge economy is not appreciated so much as part of wider and more complex dramaturgy but as a set of expressive codes that are more appearance than substance, that exist as part of an opaque world knowable through a set of abstract rules, codifiable into prescriptions for proper etiquette and strategies for negotiating. 'Not things-in-themselves but things-for-us', as Taussig has put it (Taussig 1987: 78), or, as von Sturmer would say, a complex existential world is reduced to the 'dum-de-dum of the most pedestrian prose — "One hot day in October ..."' (1989: 127). See, for example, the East Arnhem cross-cultural manual (Devitt 1995).

6   Rearranging tables and claims for informality, comfort and respectful disclosure are ritual openings in the health sector (see Strathern 2006: 191–92). Workshops will commence by visibly rearranging the tables into a circular or U-shaped pattern out of their former grids – not before participants arrive, but *after*. Another ceremonial ritual in almost all collective gatherings in THS is a requirement to turn-take self-introductions, specifying 'who you are and where you're from' – implicitly understood to mean work titles and position descriptions, not other possible identities. This is a democratising routine ostensibly aimed at 'breaking the ice' but which reinforces the voluntary adoption of depersonalising tactics in committed health work.

7   For anthropological work which sees the analytic task as locating the trace of the primitive exotic in the institutionally familiar, see Durrenberger and Erem (1997) and Trice and Beyer (1984).

8   See Hanson-Berman's account of meetings in her joint article with Helen Schwartzman (1994: 78–85) for an extended discussion of the similar tendency to discount workplace meetings – negations which are as likely to occur within meetings as side-talk (and, I would add, in such unspoken forms of communication as eye rolls, doodled notes and grimaces) as in meeting post-mortems and other after-the-fact accountings. In THS, it is institutionally de rigueur to involve oneself in dialogues and processes with a for-the-moment-intensity but to afterwards declare it all a waste of time.

9   The inherent assumption that such tellings represent moments of truth, that this is when people are being their least performative and manifesting their most authentic selves, is widespread in THS. Yet, as the late feminist social analyst Iris Young notes, 'The assumption of a consciousness immediately present to itself, which

can know itself and its contents with apodictic certainty unlike any knowledge of other things, is illusory. It exhibits what Derrida calls the metaphysics of presence, the idea of consciousness as self-originating, a metaphysics that is possible only by taking speech, or voice, as the model of thought, wherein one can deceive oneself that speaking and hearing oneself are simultaneous and unmediated. There is, however, no originary position of the subject with respect to language or the world' (Young 1990: 12; see also Scott 1991).

10 In his analysis of the depictions of terror in the rubber colonies of Colombia in South America, Taussig makes different use of the notion of the ordinariness of the extraordinary (1987: 39). Taussig's concern is more with the mundanities of daily life that emerged in reports of the atrocities that were being committed. There, in accounts of floggings and tortures, vicious mutilations, rapes, mass murders and executions, are tropes of rationality (a rounding out of numbers flogged in record books, for instance) and signs of universal petty irritation – a comment, say, on the beastliness of the mosquitoes. My point is that public health professionals create an aesthetic out of their practice as caring and daring which, in its purported radicalness, is heavily procedural. In public health discourse, emotional display is just as much a routinised, institutionally informed posture as is the call for greater coordination. It is part of the work involved in presenting oneself as an entitled (ordinary) member of the extraordinary and special public health profession.

11 I am grateful to Jon Marshall for pointing out that since, without practice, introductory martial arts will not be of much use in any such situation, the responsibility for coping is once again put back onto the field agent.

12 For a critique of such open-ended attributions about the holism of Aboriginal health, see Brady (1985). For an insightful analysis of the 'spiritualising' of Aborigines which speaks of the west's own alienation, and the burden Aboriginal people bear as representatives of western idealism beyond health, see Lattas (1992, cf. Li 2000). Langton (1993) describes the pressure placed on Aboriginal people by other Aboriginal people to represent themselves in iconic terms in her essay on representations in film and media; and Povinelli (2002) describes the existential pressure of shaping oneself around the eligibility criteria of a wide-ranging set of institutional demands for authenticity.

13 The existence of an entire body of managerial publications on this very issue – making friends and influencing people – should be marked at this stage, although the deliberate formation of alliances through techniques of politeness and flattery is only partly to the conscious fore here. Instead, it is the maintenance of an optimistic outlook and confidence in the power of decency to make a better (more literate, employable, healthier) Aboriginal subject that is the project of greater note.

14 This kind of stylistic compulsion rendered by collective analysis is also described by Schwartzman (1989, 1994). She argues that the necessity to build on what others say by referring to already established points and exchanging in like manner, is what makes meetings, like those of the Pintubi 'polity' described by Myers, 'collaborations for the production of congeniality' (Myers 1986b: 439). Trying to find rational decision-making based on evidence is not the real point.

15 Top End Remote Area Health Orientation Package, final section.

16 Needless to say, violence against nurses happens. It is the ways we are being taught to frame the expectation of violence into blameless acts by pitiable victims who are thus, by analytical fiat, in even greater need of our sympathy and help that I am highlighting here. For a more functional accounts of violence and remote area nursing, see Fisher (1995).

5 The social life of health facts

1 The burgeoning concept of health literacy pursues this idea of unequal education backgrounds and the particular role of literacy-related barriers to health service access and self-care (see, for an overview, Zarcadoolas, Pleasant & Greer 2005).

2 As Rowse puts it, 'a crucial question in welfare colonial theory and practice [is]: how can the state deliver human services which are congruent with, rather than destructive of, the most valued features of Aboriginal social organisation?' (1996: xv).

3 The verdict that pie charts are more effective (Weeramanthri n.d.) has since become a widely cited truism that is retold and reworked in other encounters between 'old' and 'new' health professionals. One relative newcomer told me once that a key challenge was the need to revise the generic, well-intentioned, nationally produced public health education media (posters and diagrams) about nutritious food groups. She said: 'One of the problems is we need to constantly change the educational information: the pyramids [of healthy food] are not appropriate. People relate better to round things. A lot of things are round – damper is round, stories are round, you sit around the camp fire in a circle, it makes sense.'

4 The paramount concern with aesthetic layout as crucial to achieving transparent meaning in development work is briefly explored by Riles, here commenting on a newsletter produced by the International Women's Tribune Centre: 'The newsletter consists of a series of cheerful, uplifting images of feminism and feminist activism that aim to counteract negative stereotypes of the women's movement and to inspire women in the developing world to an activism of their own. It contained little text and few specifics; the principal contribution is the images' (Riles 2000: 132).

5 Like simplifying cross-cultural texts so as not to make people with poor literacy feel inadequate, health professionals commonly assume that their messages must be uplifting, emphasising positives and successes in order to be both inspirational and to counteract racist stereotypes of pathology. For a savage critique of such 'behalfism', see Rushdie (1997).

6 Pholeros, Rainow & Torzillo (1993).

7 Consider the dilemmas of counting Aboriginal people for the Census, a regular subject of both intense bureaucratic wrangling and annually updated official explications of its impossibilities. Heroic efforts are required to overcome or at least mediate the difficulties. Preceding major data collection efforts are exhaustive processes of designing, testing, skirmishing, field piloting and dress rehearsal. Appropriately named processes of 'skirmishing' for Indigenous collections (taking the preliminary formulations outside the Australian Bureau of Statistics [ABS] central office and into other agencies) require negotiation with Aboriginal representative bodies and meetings with variously placed 'user advisory groups'. Aboriginal volunteers need to be recruited and trained, and more intense than usual efforts need to be made to 'clean' the data. Every time the survey instrument survives an initiation sequence, it is automatically considered more robust. Suffice it to say, the confessions of difficulty serve to reinforce the possibility of methodological resolution while reinstating the incessantly provisional nature of the data collections, ensuring that critique is synonymous with revitalisations of the same processes. (I would like to thank Professor Tony Barnes for his help in clarifying ABS procedures for me.)

8 In addition to the required linkage to science as the authorising device for health facts (however indirectly stated), there are specific rules of fact talk, traced by Dumit (2000) in relation to the work of socio-linguist Austin, and also specified by Latour (1987). Further, as I have previously shown, there is technical skill involved

in producing factual reports (with rules specified in style guides); however, there are also still ritual disclaimers and confessions concerning data inadequacy (its unrepresentativeness, non-comprehensiveness, non-universality, poor specificity, etc), and these are a critical part of the narrative performance, always indicating the further work that has to be done to truly nail the issue.

9   I am familiar with the rhetorical deployments of statistics, having myself called upon epidemiologists and health researchers to deliver dramatic statistics to 'heat up' a political speech or spice a policy document.

10   There are other emic (that is, 'native' or insider) twists to Brownian metaphors in the use of chaos and fractals in financial analysis and management theory (see also Lea 2001).

11   Ministerial Statement, August 1999, 'Preventable Chronic Disease Strategy' (Eighth Assembly First Session 10/08/99, Parliamentary Record No. 18).

12   This is well established as a syndrome in the sociology of medicine literature. Although the subject of extensive revision and critique, Talcott Parsons' classic original concept of the 'sick role' (Parsons 1951: Chapter 10) firmly established the idea that the sick person has to perform unwellness and proactively comply with the injunction to noticeably desire improvement to attain legitimacy as a genuinely sick person. Post-Foucault, this notion has been expanded to a cover a more continuous set of rights and duties, captured by Bunton and Burrows in the plural term 'health roles' (1995: 208). For a thorough overview of the sociology of illness, see Gerhardt (1989).

13   This is a more important question than may at first be obvious, given the dependence on a presenting patient-body for clinical diagnosis in ordinary contexts (see also discussion in Mol 2000).

14   Leder is quick to add that there are limitless pleasurable, painless or neutral means of returning to body awareness ('I revel in the strength of my body during a race and the glow of well-being and relaxation that follows ... I check a passing mirror to see how I look ... In meditation I set aside times where I carefully follow my breath' (Leder 1990: 91), but argues that these modalities do not exert the same strength of experiential demand and sensory intensity as do disappearances; these intensities in turn have skewed our cultural reading of the body towards the negative.

6   Manufacturing optimism, maintaining faith

1   Note that this program has been evaluated twice. The first evaluation, cited here, was conducted internally by researchers employed within THS, and came up with the result of 140 grams increased birth weight (THS 1996: 48). The second was commissioned through the Menzies School of Health Research (MSHR), a biomedical and public health research and training institute established in 1985 to conduct work particular to northern and central Australia. Conducted by MSHR employee Dorothy Mackerras, a nutritional epidemiologist, it confirmed the findings of the first, albeit with a less generous average increase (79 grams) compared with surrounding communities who did not have the program (see Mackerras 1998 and 2001, and for long-term follow-up see d'Espaignet et al. 2003).

2   The Indian hemp plant *Cannabis sativa* or, more commonly, marijuana.

3   Lorna Fejo was her real name, used here because of her clear association with the early marketing of the program. Indeed, it is worth noting how individual identities become so significantly aligned with programs or processes which classically claim to be impersonal – or rather, in processes which ostensibly aim to make programs operate on principles that are independent of the individuals that run them. That

they do not is frequently lamented and recorded in diagnoses of program success and failure aetiologies ('enablers and inhibitors' in the language of evaluation focus groups), with 'dependency on key individuals' routinely dot-pointed as a problem that more intensive future effort to include whole communities and train more locals will rectify, even as the reinstatement of a singular representative is required to provide a definite point of reference and public personality for the program.

4   The word 'Yolngu' is what inhabitants of northeastern Arnhem Land call themselves and are in turn collectively called by Euro-Australians wishing to signal their respect. Yolngu can be taken to mean 'person' in the common language group of the region; *Yolngu matha* (*matha*, literally 'tongue' and by extension 'language') comprises all the dialects of the northeast Arnhem region).

5   A former Methodist mission settlement, first established in 1934, only a short (approximately 8 kilometres) trip from the bauxite mining town of Nhulunbuy (Gove), Yirrkala is famous in Aboriginal legal history for bringing forward the first land rights suit heard in an Australian court of law. For a detailed history of the land-holding clans and their survival of missionary and government order, see Williams (1986), and Peterson and Langton (1983).

6   If they are repeatedly starved via recurrent bouts of diarrhoea and an impoverished diet, the stricken velvet villi eventually and permanently stunt, unable to perform their nutrient-absorbing function with any efficiency, consigning the growing child to a lifetime of under-nutrition regardless of future diet type or volume (see Kukuruzovic et al. 1999, Ruben & Walker 1995).

7   Microcephaly is the generic term given to any manifestation of small head size for age, gender and gestation. It is generally equated (but not automatically correlated) with mental retardation or, at the very least, with fewer brain cells and reduced counts of brain DNA, as it is always caused by microencephaly (a small brain), and the two terms are used interchangeably. As a generic phenomenon, microcephaly is caused by many different abnormalities, both genetic and non-genetic. In NT paediatric material, attribution is usually given to low birth weight; in its post-gestational guise it is called 'failure to thrive', which is in turn associated with infant under- and malnutrition. All prognoses point to maternal education combined with nutritional and lifestyle interventions as key remedies (see, for example Ruben & Walker 1993). The term replaces one in previous use, 'dysmaturity', to refer to full-term but small-for-date babies.

8   For contemporary medical theorising on the relationship between genetic preparedness and morbidity patterns, see work by O'Dea on the genetic thriftiness of attributed insulin resistance of Aboriginal people (O'Dea 1991, also discussion in Scrimgeor, Rowse & Lucas 1997: 1–2).

9   Rob Moodie (1991: 35), former Medical Director of the Central Australian Aboriginal Congress, has written movingly of the plight of formerly mobile and economically vibrant and self-sustaining populations who, in being reduced to a forced, dependent sedentarism, face continuing 'upheavals ... superimposed by an overwhelming burden of virulent racism resulting in tremendous social and cultural dislocation. This has led in many cases to a breakdown in social controls and laws that has impacted upon and marginalized urban Aborigines in particular.'

10   Comparisons between Aboriginal Australians and other 'underdeveloped' people (Asians and Africans when talk is of Aboriginal mendicancy, Innuit and Maori when talk is of comparative Aboriginal pathos) are casually made in the diverse accounts of Indigenous inequality and its amelioration, reminders of the broad imperial field from which the remedial white draws her habits, processes and frameworks (see Stoler & Cooper 1997).

11   Terry Bullemor, former Town Clerk in Wadeye (Port Keats) in the Daly River region, provided exactly this historical encapsulation: 'Also unlike most fair-

skinned Australians they [Aboriginal people of the area] have not been subject to the winter syndrome which has resulted in them [white people] having a built-in instinct to "save for a rainy day" or "store up supplies for winter". [This absent value] is not understood by many non-Aboriginals' (presentation at 'Generating Service Delivery Opportunities and Outcomes for Aboriginal Communities' conference 11–12 April 2000, Alice Springs). Recent publications by Sandall (2001) and Sutton (2001) repeat the factoid in a more academic framing.

7   Encountering

1   Opposite Groote Eylandt and so on a flight path, mainland Numbulwar becomes extremely difficult to access by road in the monsoon season, as the way in becomes intermittently impassable because of floods. Whatever the time of year, most administrators still travel by air, for the speed and convenience. Charter flights to Numbulwar are augmented by a weekly barge service that brings in fresh provisions, not only for the store but to fill the orders of resident professionals, who receive freight and grocery allowances, together with travel subsidies, to ease the burden of their isolation.

2   The phenomenon of Visiting Officers' Quarters is discussed again in Chapter 8. In brief, they are duplex buildings available within all the larger East Arnhem communities for visiting administrative personnel.

3   Maccassan trepangers are said to have planted the tamarind trees centuries ago (see Macknight 1976).

4   Town Councils are accurately described by Myers as institutions created by government in the 1960s, to represent 'local Aboriginal communities to the branches of the Australian government' (Myers 1986b: 433). In addition, they were envisioned by white Australians 'as the authoritative and legislative representative of those communities ... expected to help preserve order and regulate community life, to decide on how to deploy community resources, and to decide on employment' (see also Collmann 1979, cf. Das & Poole 2004, Fisher 1997). Today they form an important port of call for all visiting professionals to Aboriginal communities, with these visits often becoming the 'community consultations' that authorise policy pronouncements back in Head Office.

5   The inexplicable business of travelling in four-wheel drives over walkable distances deserves brief comment. Several reasons have been suggested to me, including the need to keep much-coveted vehicles secure from vandalism and stealing. I would want to explore the issues beyond such means–ends explanations, however. It is truly peculiar. Heaving in and out of large vehicles for short distances makes driving far more exhausting than walking; indicating to me that more is at symbolic stake. For a brilliant analysis of the importance of *murtakas* (motor vehicles) in white–black relations from the Kimberley perspective, see Redmond (2006).

6   'Balanda' is a generic term for non-Aboriginal in *Yolngu matha* and has become a commonly used term in public service parlance as well.

7   Reading this chapter, 'Marlene' told me 'Cathy' was the name of her predecessor nutritionist.

8   The Norway reference seemed bizarre until I later went into the store and discovered stacks of sardine tins with 'MADE IN NORWAY' in large red print on the packaging and boxes.

8   Suppression

1   Most canine diseases are canine-specific (Currie 1996). A public health rejoinder to this would be that dogs act as vectors for human contagion, particularly by eating

and stepping in human faeces and then playing with children and walking through food preparation areas (see, for example, Pholeros, Rainow & Torzillo 1993).

2   This concentration on professional perceptions suggests many questions regarding how Aboriginal people might be interpreting these same encounters. Though it does not affect the relevant points here, the fact that Aboriginal people are often extremely sensitive to and aware of the suppressed reactions of disgust could be explored. For more thorough accounts of Aboriginal reactions to bureaucrats and their meetings (how officials might be mocked but also can't be avoided), see in particular the ethnographic work of Bauman (2001), Cowlishaw (2004) and Sansom (1980, 1995).

3   See, for varying discussions of this in an Australian context, Michaels (1990: 83–86), John von Sturmer (1989, 1995), Cowlishaw (1998) and Biddle (1991).

4   Describing his own upbringing as a white kid in a large poor black and Hispanic neighbourhood in New York, Danton Conley describes lessons in race as learning comportment, 'like learning a language. First we try mouthing all sounds. Then we learn which are not words and which have meaning to the people around us' (2000: 37).

5   As this business of typing of Aboriginal people seems to me a well-understood phenomenon, I make short work of it here, concentrating instead on how individual professionals participate in transforming themselves into collective ciphers. This said, it remains a significant sub-theme that bureau-professionals project onto and measure Aboriginal communities against an idealised and iconicised model of their own best and worst features. For an account of this from a sojourner's perspective, see Mary Ellen Jordan's *Balanda: My Year in Arnhem Land* (2005).

6   In an essay critiquing the assumptions of a health promotion campaign run among the coal miners of the Hunter Valley, anthropologist Andrew Metcalfe (1993) argues that public health promoters universalise a body and sense of self that wants to be acted upon. In their concern to prevent the inequality of preventable chronic disease that seems so unfairly concentrated in lower socio-economic population groups, health promoters assume and project a subjectivity that covets a health-consciousness. Accordingly, the actions of coal miners who resist being turned into anxious calorie counters, who instead revel in lots of beer and fish and chips, are discounted as the deficit behaviours of those lacking the knowledge to behave differently.

9   Mastery

1   In 1997/98 (as again in 2007) the Australian Defence Forces (ADF) were engaged to undertake a number of infrastructure development and upgrade projects in NT communities. This assignment was at the behest of Prime Minister John Howard, and then as now, it created the look of decisive new policy action. But the dramatic announcement that the Federal Government would 'Send In The Army' to do major capital works obscured from public view the fact that the ADF would simply operate as a commissioned group of project managers, implementing a pre-funded program that was already well underway. This wider program was managed through the former Aboriginal and Torres Strait Islander Commission (ATSIC) and was known as the National Aboriginal Health Strategy Environmental Health Program. Ordinarily, ATSIC called on private sector organisations – engineering firms and the like – to tender as project managers. The ADF simply bypassed the tendering process and substituted as one of these project managing teams.

2   'The build-up' is a local term for the humid but scorching rain-free period before the monsoons start, when hot air and moisture from across the equator replace the

cooler southern winds of previous months.

3 One informant also mentioned joining a pen-pal group, which enabled him to meet people overseas when it came to using the generous frequent flyer points accrued through his bush work.

4 Mitchell Street, in the Darwin Central Business District, has become the entertainment zone for the town, with multiple bars, discos and, late at night, the buzz of a small red light zone.

10 Being t/here

1 Indigenous leader Noel Pearson frequently growls at the technical non-specificity of what he disdainfully calls 'progressivists' – the helping whites who facilitate discussion through consultations (and workshops), and offer lenient excuses and diffuse explanations of current pathology. Yet, in the same way that bureaucracies are able to co-opt critique and continue apace, in the bureaucratic domains I am familiar with, Pearson's critique has simply encouraged an equally denuded counterpoint: a new, seemingly tough condemnation of people trapped in drinking families, say, but not much technical or expert substance to give effect to the one-liner diagnoses, other than more of the same service options and rationales.

2 For recent descriptions of the hard-working, hard-playing life of Billy Lea and associates, see Forrest (2007a, 2007b).

3 The debate on nativism, whilst at one level an oblique theme to this work, is, at another level, absolutely central. I have tried to avoid using Aboriginal alterity as the foil to a deeper understanding of bureaucratic culture, as an older anthropology might have done, and to instead grope towards the alterity always already existing within civilised statecraft. This has led me to view much western institution-auspiced anthropology as all native ethnography of a sort, a view which shares Strathern's verdict that the kind of sameness that matters is not ethnic but conceptual (Strathern 1987).

4 Which are better approached in such standard anthologies as Clifford and Marcus's *Writing Culture: The poetics and politics of ethnography* (1986) and Marcus and Fischer's *Anthropology as Cultural Critique: An experimental moment in the human sciences* (1986). Critiques of this literature are also plentiful: see, for example, Pearce (1990), Marcus (1990), Nencel and Pels (1991) and, from a critical feminist perspective, Behar and Gordon's *Women Writing Culture* (1995).

5 In her rich ethnography of the aesthetic dimension of expert knowledge practices and associated artefacts, Riles (2000: 154) describes the way that many institutional documents must conform to a tight, standardised template which also dictates that an outside that can be acted upon must be imagined (the forms for research grant applications in academia are a parallel). More than just a simplification in order to regulate, such programmatic demands reflect a desire by the donor agency for fixity and access to 'the Real'. In the ethnographic instance offered by Riles, the outside world for the Australian International Development Assistance Bureau (AIDAB) was represented by the NGO form-fillers, who in turn have their own external 'reals' – such as the grass-roots women they are ostensibly advocates for. See also Mosse (2004).

6 Taussig describes what many contemporary scholars, led by feminist work from at least the 1980s, are now very familiar with – the trick of objectivist fiction, 'namely, the contrived manner by which objectivity is created, and its profound dependence on the *magic of style* to make this trick of truth work' (1987: 37, emphasis added).

7 Herzfeld's *The Social Production of Indifference: Exploring the symbolic roots of western bureaucracy* (1992) illustrates this mirror imagery perfectly. In it, he

repeatedly argues that anthropology's task is to go beyond representations of state organisations which caricature bureaucrats as soulless system-servers opposed to a repressed citizenry, admonishing readers to remember that 'the official world is itself peopled' (1992: 59). Yet nowhere in his book are the subjectivities of bureaucrats delivered in their full complexity. Rather, the text is littered with anecdotes casually drawn from Nazi Germany and modern-day Greece illustrating indifference, corruption and incompetence at work, with Herzfeld's chief task being to explain the public's forbearance (their 'fatalism') about it all. Whilst rich in hovering theoretical overview, this is no ethnography of bureaucrats. Or perhaps it is a perfect ethnography, if the task is to mirror and replicate the internal logics of the cultural order being represented. Writing from an epistemology which expects institutions to be logical and fair, logically enough, he finds deficiencies. By blaming bureaucrats for their bad implementation practices and habits of classification and rigidity, Herzfeld reifies through unconsciously duplicative critique the homogenising habits he wants overturned. Is this not a classic reproduction of a classic administrative dilemma? And thus, in its own right, a truly reflective, mimetic ethnography of bureaucracy?

8   This ethnography draws on over four years of participant observation of government bureaucrats in the Health Department of the Northern Territory of Australia, then known as THS, augmented by time as a ministerial advisor in health and as a senior executive in the Department of Education. I now run an applied research centre, the School for Social and Policy Research, which fuses anthropological analysis with interventionary work of the most mired kind.

BIBLIOGRAPHY

Aboriginal Development Unit 1996 'Strong Women, Strong Babies, Strong Culture: Part Four – An Overview of the Program'. Darwin: Aboriginal Development Unit, NT Department of Education.

Ahmed, A. and Shore, C. (eds) 1995 *The Future of Anthropology: Its relevance to the contemporary world*. London: The Athlone Press.

Altman, J. 2005 'Economic futures on Aboriginal land in remote and very remote Australia: Hybrid economies and joint ventures', in D. Austin-Broos and G. Macdonald (eds) *Culture, Economy and Governance in Aboriginal Australia*. Sydney: University of Sydney Press, pp. 111–34.

Anderson, W. 2002 *The Cultivation of Whiteness: Science, health and racial destiny in Australia*. Melbourne: Melbourne University Press.

Appadurai, A. (ed.) 1986 *The Social Life of Things: Commodities in cultural perspective*. Cambridge: Cambridge University Press.

—— 1988a Introduction: Place and Voice in Anthropological Theory. *Cultural Anthropology* 3: 16–20.

—— 1988b Putting hierarchy in its place. *Cultural Anthropology* 3: 36–49.

Apthorpe, R. 1985 'Pleading and Reading Agricultural Development Policy: Small farm, big state and "the case of Taiwan", in R. Grillo and A. Rew (eds) *Social Anthropology and Development Policy*. London and New York: Tavistock Publications, pp. 88–101.

Ashton, T., Mays, N. and Devlin, N. 2005 Continuity through change: The rhetoric and reality of health reform in New Zealand. *Social Science and Medicine* 61: 253–62.

Aboriginal and Torres Strait Islander Commission (ATSIC) 1995 *Aboriginal and Torres Strait Islander Commission Annual Report 1994–95*. Canberra: Australian Government Printer.

Australian Bureau of Statistics (ABS) 1994 *Indigenous Demography, Northern Territory*. Canberra: ABS, Catalogue No. 3316.7.

—— 1999 *The Health and Welfare of Australia's Aboriginal and Torres Strait Islander Peoples*. Canberra: ABS, with AIHW, Cataloue No. 4704.0.

—— 2000 *Australian Demographic Statistics*. Canberra: ABS, Catalogue No. 3101.0.

Australian Bureau of Statistics (ABS) and Australian Institute of Health and Welfare (AIHW) 2005 *The Health and Welfare of Australia's Aboriginal and Torres Strait*

Islander Peoples. Canberra: ABS and AIHW, Catalogue No. 4704.0.

Australian Reference Service 1976 *The Australian Aboriginals*. Canberra: Commonwealth of Australia.

Bakalaki, A. 1997 Students, natives, colleagues: Encounters in academia and in the field. *Cultural Anthropology* 12: 502–26.

Barley, S. and Kunda, G. 1992 Design and devotion: Surges of rational and normative ideologies of control in managerial discourse. *Administrative Science Quarterly* 37: 363–99.

—— 2004 *Gurus, Hired Guns, and Warm Bodies: Itinerant experts in a knowledge economy*. Princeton NJ: Princeton University Press.

Barthes, R. 1957 *Mythologies*. New York: Hill & Wang.

Baudrillard, J. 1988 'Simulacra and simulations', in M. Poster (ed.) *Jean Baurdillard: Selected writings*. Stanford CA: Stanford University Press, pp. 166–84.

Bauman, R. 1977 *Verbal Art as Performance*. Prospect Heights IL: Waveland Press.

Bauman, T. 2001 Shifting sands: Towards an anthropological praxis. *OCEANIA* 71: 202–25.

Beck, U. 1992 *Risk Society: Toward a new modernity*. London: Sage Publications.

Becker, A.L. 1996 'Biography of a sentence: A Burmese proverb', in D. Brenneis and R.K.S. Macaulay (eds) *The Matrix of Language: Contemporary linguistic anthropology*. Boulder CO: Westview Press, pp. 142–59.

Behar, R. and Gordon, D.A. (eds) 1995 *Women Writing Culture*. Berkeley CA and London: University of California Press.

Beilharz, P. 1987 Reading politics: Social theory and social policy. *Australian and New Zealand Journal of Sociology* 23: 388–406.

Benedict, R. 1983 *Race and Racism* (1942). London, Melbourne and Henley: Routledge & Kegan Paul.

Benjamin, W. 1977 'The task of the translator: An introduction to the translation of Baudelaire's *Tableaux Parisiens*', in H. Arendt (ed.) *Illuminations*. New York: Fontana/Collins, pp. 69–82.

Biddle, J. 1991 'Dot, circle, difference: Translating Central Desert paintings', in R. Diprose and R. Fennel (eds) *Cartographies: Poststructuralism and the Mapping of Bodies and Spaces*. Sydney: Allen & Unwin.

—— 1997 Shame. *Australian Feminist Studies* 12: 227–39.

Boden, D. 1994 *The Business of Talk: Organizations in action*. Oxford: Polity Press.

Bourdieu, P. 1977 *Outline of a Theory of Practice*. Cambridge: Cambridge University Press.

—— 1984 *Distinction: A social critique of the judgement of taste*. London: Routledge.

Boyer, D. 2000 On the sedimentation and accreditation of social knowledges of difference: Mass media, journalism, and the reproduction of East/West alterities in unified Germany. *Cultural Anthropology* 15: 459–91.

Brady, M. 1985 'WHO defines health?: Implications of differing definitions on discourse and practice in Aboriginal health', in G. Robertson (ed.) *Aboriginal Health: Social and cultural traditions*. Darwin: Northern Territory University (NTU) Press, pp. 187–92.

Brandl, M. and Tilley, E. 1981 *Marching to a Different Drum: The uses of anthropology in the Belyuen Health Centre, Northern Territory of Australia*. Canberra: Australian National University (ANU), Centre for Resource and Environmental Studies.

Brenneis, D. 1984 'Straight talk and sweet talk: Political discourse in an occasionally egalitarian community', in D. Brenneis and F.R. Myers (eds) *Dangerous Words: Language and politics in the Pacific*. New York: New York University Press.

—— 1987 Talk and transformation. *Man (N.S.)* 22: 499–510.

—— 1988 Language and disputing. *Annual Review of Anthropology* 17: 221–37.

—— 1994 Discourse and discipline at the National Research Council: A bureaucratic 'Bildungsroman'. *Cultural Anthropology* 9: 23–36.

—— 1999 'New lexicon, old language: Negotiating the 'global' at the National Science Foundation', in G.E. Marcus (ed.) *Critical Anthropology Now: Unexpected contexts, shifting constituencies, changing agendas, School of American Research Advanced Seminar Series*. Sante Fe NM: School of American Research Press.

Brody, H. 1975 *The People's Land: Eskimos and whites in the eastern Arctic*. Harmondsworth: Penguin Books.

Broom, D. 2001 Public health, private body. *Australian and New Zealand Journal of Public Health* 25: 5–8.

Brown, B.A. 1994 Born in the USA: American anthropologists come home. *Dialectical Anthropology* 19: 419–38.

Brown, J. 1986 Professional language: Words that succeed. *Radical History Review* 34: 33–51.

Bunton, R., Nettleton, S. and Burrows, R. (eds) 1995 *The Sociology of Health Promotion: Critical analyses of consumption, lifestyle and risk*. London and New York: Routledge.

Bunton, R. and Burrows, R. 1995 'Consumption and health in the "epidemiological" clinic of late modern medicine', in R. Bunton, S. Nettleton and R. Burrows (eds) *The Sociology of Health Promotion: Critical analyses of consumption, lifestyle and risk*. London and New York: Routledge, pp. 206–22.

Burchell, G. 1993 Liberal government and techniques of the self. *Economy and Society* 22: 267–82.

Butler, J. 1997 *Excitable Speech: A politics of the performative*. New York and London: Routledge.

Buur, L. 2001 'The South African Truth and Reconciliation Commission: A technique of nation state formation', in T.B. Hansen and F. Stepputat (eds) *States of Imagination: Ethnographic explorations of the postcolonial state*. Durham and London: Duke University Press, pp. 149–81.

Carson, B., Dunbar, T. Chenhall, R.D. and Bailie, R.S. (eds) 2007 *Social Determinants of Indigenous Health*. Sydney: Allen & Unwin.

Chambers, R. and Ghildyal, B.P. 1985 *Agricultural Research for Resource Poor Farmers: The farmer-first-and-last model*. Discussion Paper No. 203. Brighton, England: Institute of Development Studies (IDS), University of Sussex.

Clifford, J. and Marcus, G. (eds) 1986 *Writing Cultures: The poetics and politics of ethnography*. Berkeley CA: University of California Press.

Cohn, C. 1987 Sex and death in the rational world of defense intellectuals. *Signs* 12: 687–718.

Collmann, J. 1979 Fringe camps and the development of Aboriginal administration in Central Australia. *Social Analysis* 2: 38–57.

—— 1981 Postscript: The significance of clients. *Social Analysis* 9: 103–20.

—— 1988 *Aboriginal Fringe Dwellers and Welfare: The Aboriginal response to bureaucracy*. Brisbane: University of Queensland Press.

Commonwealth Grants Commission (CGC) 2001 *Commonwealth Grants Commission Trends in Equalisation – Discussion Paper*. Commonwealth Grants Commission 2001/5.

Conley, D. 2000 *Honky*. New York: Vintage Books.

Cooke, B. and Kothari, U. (eds) 2001 *Participation: The new tyranny*. London: Zed Books.

Coulehan, K. 1995 Sitting down in Darwin: Yolgnu women from north east Arnhem Land and family life in the city. PhD Thesis, NTU.

Cowlishaw, G. 1988 *Black, White or Brindle: Race in rural Australia*. Sydney: Cambridge University Press.

—— 1998 Erasing culture and race: Practising 'self-determination'. *OCEANIA* 68:145–69.

—— 2004 *Blackfellas, whitefellas and the hidden injuries of race*. Malden MA, Oxford and Melbourne: Blackwell Publishing.

Cross-Cultural-Consultants 1996 *Evaluator's Report: Strong Women, Strong Babies, Strong Culture Project 1992–1994*. Joint sponsored evaluation by the Commonwealth Department of Human Services and Health, Rural Health Support, Education and Training Program, and Territory Health Services (THS).

Cullen, S. and Howe, L. 1991 People, cases and stereotypes: A study of staff practice in a DSS benefit office. *Cambridge Anthropology* 15: 1–26.

Cunningham, C., Reading, J. and Eades, S. 2003 Health research and Indigenous health: Education and debate. *British Medical Journal* 327: 445(3).

Currie, B. 1996 Dogs and Aboriginal health in Australia. *World Health* 51: 26–28.

Czarniawska, B. 1997 *Narrating the Organization: Dramas of institutional identity. New practices of inquiry*. Chicago and London: University of Chicago Press.

Das, V. and Poole. D. (eds) 2004 *Anthropology in the Margins of the State. School of American Research Advanced Seminar Series*. Sante Fe NM and Oxford: School of American Research Press.

Davis, A. and George, J. 1993 *States of Health: Health and illness in Australia* (2nd edn). Sydney: Harper Educational.

Davis-Floyd, R.E. 1998 'Storying corporate futures: The Shell scenarios', in G.E. Marcus (ed.) *Corporate Futures: The diffusion of the culturally sensitive corporate form*, vol. 5, pp. 141–76. Chicago and London: University of Chicago Press.

Dean, M. 1994 'A social structure of many souls': Moral regulation, government, and self-formation. *Canadian Journal of Sociology* 19: 145–68.

Department of Local Government 2001 'Visiting an Aborginal Community for the first time?'. Darwin: Department of Local Government.

d'Espaignet, E.T., Kennedy, K. Paterson, B.A. and Measey, M.L. 1998 *From Infancy to Young Adulthood: Health status in the Northern Territory, 1998*. Darwin: THS.

d'Espaignet, E.T., Measey, M., Carnegie, M. and Mackerras, D. 2003 Monitoring the 'Strong Women, Strong Babies, Strong Culture Program': The first eight years. *Journal of Paediatrics and Child Health* 39: 668–72.

Devitt, J. 1995 *Taking Time for People: An orientation manual for people working in the East Arnhem District*. Darwin: THS.

Dhareshwar, V. 1990 'The Predicament of Theory', in M. Kreiswirth and M. Cheetham (eds) *Theory Between the Disciplines: Authority, vision, politics*. Ann Arbor MI: Michigan University Press, pp. 231–50.

Dufrenne, M. 1987 *In the Presence of the Sensuous: Essays in aesthetics*. Atlantic Highlands NJ: Humanities Press International.

Dumit, J. 1997 'A Digital Image of the Category of the Person', in G.L. Downey and J. Dumit (eds) *Cyborgs & CITADELS: Anthropological interventions in emerging sciences and technologies*. Sante Fe NM: School of American Research Press, pp. 83–102.

—— 2000 *How to Do Things with Science: Facts as forces in an uncertain world*. San Francisco CA: American Anthropology Association.

—— 2004 *Picturing Personhood: Brain scans and Biomedical Identity Information Series*. Princeton NJ and Oxford: Princeton University Press.

Durrenberger, E.P. and Erem, S. 1997 The Dance of Power: Ritual and agency among unionized American health care workers. *American Anthropologist* 99: 489–516.

Eades, S.J. 2000 Reconciliation, social equity and Indigenous health. *Medical Journal of Australia* 172: 468–69.

Edelwich, J. 1980 *Burnout: Stages of disillusionment in the helping professions*. New York: Human Sciences Press.

Edmunds, K.S., Vanderfield, I.R. and Dearlove, T.P. 1972 *Inquiries Ordinance, 1945–1962: Inquiry into the medical and hospital services in the Northern Territory.* Board of Inquiry into the Medical and Hospital Services in the Northern Territory.

Fabian, J. 1983 *Time and the Other: How anthropology makes its object.* New York: Columbia University Press.

—— 1990 *Power and Performance: Ethnographic explorations through proverbial wisdom and theater in Shaba, Zaire.* Madison WI: University of Wisconsin Press.

Feldman, A. 1991 *Formations of Violence: The narrative of the body and political terror in Northern Ireland.* Chicago and London: University of Chicago Press.

—— 1997 Violence and vision: The prosthetics and aesthetics of terror. *Public Culture* 10.

—— 2001 Philoctetes revisited: White public space and the political geography of public safety. *Social Text 68* 19: 57–89.

Ferguson, J. 1990 *The anti-politics machine: 'Development,' depoliticization, and bureaucratic power in Lesotho.* Cambridge: Cambridge University Press.

Feuerstein, M.T. 1986 *Partners in Evaluation: Evaluating development and community programmes with participants.* London and Basingstoke: Macmillan.

Firth, R. 1981 Engagement and detachment: Reflections on applying social anthropology to social affairs. *Human Organization* 40: 193–202.

Fisher, J. 1995 *'Context of Silence': Violence and the remote area nurse.* Rockhampton: Central Queensland University.

Fisher, W.F. 1997 Doing good? The politics and antipolitics of NGO practices. *Annual Review of Anthropology* 26: 439–64.

Forrest, P. and Forrest, S. 2007a 'Joe remembers outback survival', *Northern Territory News*, pp. 28–29.

—— 2007b 'Legendary stockman rounds up new career', *Northern Territory News*, pp. 14–15.

Fortun, K. 1999 'Locating corporate environmentalism: Synthetics, implosions, and the Bhopal disaster', in G.E. Marcus (ed.) *Critical Anthropology Now.* Santa Fe NM: School of American Research Press, pp. 203–44.

Foucault, M. 1977 *Discipline and Punish: The birth of the prison* (1991 edition). London: Penguin Books.

—— 1978 The eye of power. *Semiotext(e)* 3: 6–19.

—— 1982 'The subject and power', in H. Dreyfus and P. Rabinow (eds) *Michel Foucault: Beyond Structuralism and Hermeneutics.* Chicago: University of Chicago Press.

—— 1984 'The politics of health in the eighteenth century', in P. Rabinow (ed.) *The Foucault Reader.* London and New York: Penguin, pp. 273–89.

—— 1988 'Technologies of the self', in L.H. Martin, H. Gutman and P.H. Hutton (eds) *Technologies of the Self: A seminar with Michel Foucault.* Amherst MA: University of Massachusetts Press, pp. 16–49.

——1990 *The History of Sexuality: An introduction* (1976 edition). London: Penguin.

Friedman, J. 1998 'Global crises, the struggle for cultural identity and intellectual porkbarrelling: Cosmopolitans versus locals, ethnics and nationals in an era of de-hegemonisation', in P. Werbner and T. Modood (eds) *Debating Cultural Hybridity: Multicultural identities and the politics of anti-racism.* London and New Jersey: Zed Books, pp. 70–89.

Garfinkel, H. 1984 (1967) *Studies in Ethnomethodology.* Cambridge: Polity Press.

Geertz, C. 1973 'Thick description: Toward an interpretive theory of culture', in C. Geertz *The Interpretation of Cultures.* New York: Basic Books, pp. 3–30.

Gerhardt, U. 1989 *Ideas About Illness: An intellectual and political history of medical sociology.* London: MacMillan.

Gill, L. 1995 Examining power, serving the State: Anthropology, Congress and the invasion of Panama. *Human Organization* 54: 318–24.

Glover, J. 2001 A question of communication. *The Chronicle* 5: 1.

Goffman, E. 1961 *Asylums: Essays on the social situation of mental patients and other inmates*. New York: Anchor Books.

—— 1971 *Relations in public: Microstudies of the public order*. London: Penguin.

Goodall Jr., H.L. 1989 *Casing a Promised Land: The autobiography of an organizational detective as cultural ethnographer*. Carbondale and Edwardsville IL: Southern Illinois University Press.

Gordon, C. 1991 'Government rationality: An introduction', in G. Burchell, C. Gordon, and P. Miller (eds) *The Foucault Effect: Studies in governmentality*. London: Harvester Wheatsheaf, pp. 1–52.

Grant, C. and Lapsley, H.M. 1993 *The Australian Health Care System. Australian Studies in Health Service Administration No. 75*. Sydney: School of Health Services Management, University of New South Wales.

Gray, A. (ed.) 1990 *A Matter of Life and Death: Contemporary Aboriginal mortality*. Canberra: Aboriginal Studies Press.

Gronn, P.C. 1983 Talk as the work: The accomplishment of school administration. *Administrative Science Quarterly* 28: 1–21.

Gumperz, J.J. and Cook-Gumperz, J. 1982 'Interethnic communication in committee negotiations', in J. Gumperz (ed.) *Language and Social Identity*. Cambridge: Cambridge University Press, pp. 145–62.

Gupta, A. and Ferguson, J. (eds) 1997 *Anthropological Locations: Boundaries and Grounds of a field science*. Berkeley and Los Angeles CA: University of California Press.

Hacking, I. 1991 'How should we do the history of statistics?', in G. Burchell, C. Gordon and P. Miller (eds) *The Foucault Effect: Studies in governmentality*. London: Harvester Wheatsheaf, pp. 181–96.

Hamer, J.M. 1988 *Facility Management Systems*. New York: Van Nostrand Reinhold.

Hancock, L. 1999 'Health, public sector restructuring and the market state', in L. Hancock (ed.) *Health Policy in the Market State*. Sydney: Allen & Unwin.

Hansen, T.B. and Stepputat, F. 2001 'Introduction: States of imagination', in T.B. Hansen and F. Stepputat (eds) *States of Imagination: Ethnographic explorations of the postcolonial state*. Durham NC and London: Duke University Press, pp. 1–38.

Haraway, D. 1991 *Simians, Cyborgs and Women: The reinvention of nature*. London: Free Association Books.

—— 1998 Situated knowledges: The science question in feminism and the privilege of partial perspective. *Feminist Studies* 14: 575–99.

Harris, S. 1980 *Culture and Learning: Tradition and education in northeast Arnhem Land*. Canberra: Northern Territory Department of Education.

Hatch, M.J. and Ehrlich, S.B. 1993 Spontaneous humour as an indicator of paradox and ambiguity in organizations. *Organization Studies* 14: 505–26.

Hawe, P., Degeling, D. and Hall, J. 1991 *Evaluating Health Promotion: A health worker's guide*. Sydney: MacLennan and Petty.

Hearn, J. and Parkin, W. 1987 *'Sex' at 'Work': The power and paradox of organisation sexuality*. Brighton, Sussex: Wheatsheaf Books.

Helman, C. 1991 *Body Myths*. London: Chatto & Windus.

Heppel, M. (ed.) 1979 *A Black Reality: Aboriginal camps and housing in remote Australia*. Canberra: Australian Institute of Aboriginal Studies.

Herzfeld, M. 1992 *The Social Production of Indifference: Exploring the symbolic roots of western bureaucracy*. New York and Oxford: Berg.

Hoy, W., Mathews, J., Hargrave, J. and Pugsley, D. 1996. 'Diabetes and impaired glucose tolerance in an Aboriginal community in the Northern Territory of Australia', in G. Robertson (ed.) *Aboriginal Health: Social and cultural transitions*.

Darwin: NTU Press, pp. 44–48.

Hoy, W.E., Norman, R.J., Hayhurst, B.G. and Pugsley, D.J. 1997 A health profile of adults in a Northern Territory Aboriginal community, with an emphasis on preventable morbidities. *Australian and New Zealand Journal of Public Health* 21: 121–26.

Hughes, H. 2005 Policies entrench poverty. *The Australian*, 23 September.

—— 2007 *Lands of Shame: Aboriginal and Torres Strait Islander 'homelands' in transition*. Sydney: Federation Press.

Hummel, R.P. 1994 *The Bureaucratic Experience: A critique of life in the modern organization* (4th edn). New York: St Martin's Press.

Hunter, E. 1993 *Aboriginal Health and History: Power and prejudice in remote Australia*. Cambridge: Cambridge University Press.

Hutcheon, L. 1994 *Irony's Edge: The theory and the politics of irony*. London and New York: Routledge.

Jackall, R. 1988 *Moral Mazes: The world of corporate managers*. New York and Oxford: Oxford University Press.

Jefferson, G. 1978 'Sequential aspects of story telling in conversation', in J. Schenkein (ed.) *Studies in the Organization of Conversational Interaction*. New York: Academic Press, pp. 219–48.

Jones, J.W. (ed.) 1982 *The Burnout Syndrome: Current research, theory, interventions*. Park Ridge IL: London House Press.

Jordan, M.E. 2005 *Balanda: My year in Arnhem Land*. Sydney: Allen & Unwin.

Kapferer, B. 1995 'Bureaucratic erasure: Identity, resistance and violence – Aborigines and a discourse of autonomy in a North Queensland town', in D. Miller (ed.) *Worlds Apart: Modernity through the prism of the local*. London: Routledge, pp. 69–90.

Kettle, E. 1991 *Health Services in the Northern Territory – A History 1824–1970*. Darwin: North Australia Research Unit, ANU.

Koster, D. 1977 '"Why is *he* here?" White gossip', in R. Paine (ed.) *The White Arctic: Anthropological essays on tutelage and ethnicity*. Newfoundland: Institute of Social and Economic Research, Memorial University of Newfoundland, pp. 144–65.

Kowal, Emma 2006a 'Moving towards the mean: Dilemmas of assimilation and improvement', in T. Lea, E. Kowal and G. Cowlishaw (eds) *Moving Anthropology: Critical Indigenous studies*. Darwin: Charles Darwin University Press, pp. 65–78.

—— 2006b The proximate advocate: Improving Indigenous health on the postcolonial frontier. PhD dissertation, University of Melbourne.

Krueger, R.A. 1988 *Focus Groups: A practical guide for applied research*. Newbury Park CA: Sage Publications.

Kruske, S.G., Ruben, A.R. and Brewster, D.R. 1999 An iron treatment trial in an Aboriginal community: Improving non-adherence. *Journal of Paediatric Child Health* 35: 153–58.

Kukuruzovic, R.H., Haase, A., Dunn, K., Bright, A. and Brewster, D.A. 1999 Intestinal permeability and diarrhoeal disease in Aboriginal Australians. *Archives of Disease in Childhood* 81: 304–08.

Kulick, D. 2006 Theory in furs: Masochist anthropology. *Current Anthropology* 47: 933–52.

Kunda, G. 1992 *Engineering Culture: Control and commitment in a high-tech corporation. Labor and social change*. Philadelphia PA: Temple University Press.

Kuper, A. 1994 Culture, identity and the project of cosmopolitan anthropology. *Man (N.S.)* 29: 537–54.

Langton, M. 1993 *'Well, I heard it on the Radio and I saw it on the Television …': An essay for the Australian Film Commission on the politics and aesthetics of filmmaking by and about Aboriginal people and things*. Sydney: Australian Film

Commission.

Lash, S. 1994 'Reflexivity and its doubles: Structure, aesthetics, community', in U. Beck, A. Giddens and S. Lash (eds) *Reflexive Modernisation: Politics, tradition and aesthetics in the modern social order*. Stanford CA: Stanford University Press, pp. 110–73.

Latour, B. 1987 *Science in Action: How to follow scientists and engineers through society*. Milton Keynes: Open University Press.

—— 2002 (1996). *ARAMIS or the Love of Technology*. Cambridge MA and London: Harvard University Press.

Lattas, A. 1992 'Primitivism, nationalism and individualism', in B. Attwood and J. Arnold (eds) *Australian Popular Culture: Power, Knowledge and Aborigines. Special Edition of Journal of Australian Studies*. Melbourne.

Lea, T. 2001 A benign arithmetic: Taking up facts about Indigenous health. *The UTS Review: Cultural Studies and New Writing* 7: 59–73.

—— 2002 Between the pen and the paperwork: Learning to govern Indigenous health in the Northern Territory of Australia. PhD thesis, University of Sydney.

—— 2005 The work of forgetting: Germs, Aborigines and postcolonial expertise in the Northern Territory of Australia. *Social Science and Medicine* 61: 1310–19.

—— 2006 'Cars, corporations, ceremonies and cash: Hidden co-dependencies in Australia's north', in T. Lea, E. Kowal and G. Cowlishaw (eds) *Moving Anthropology: Critical Indigenous studies*. Darwin: Charles Darwin University Press.

—— 2008 Housing for health in Indigenous Australia: Driving change when research and policy are part of the problem. *Human Organization* 67: 77–85.

Leder, D. 1990 *The Absent Body*. Chicago and London: University of Chicago Press.

Lee, A.J., Bailey, A.P., Yarmirr, D., O'Dea K. and Mathews, J.D. 1994 Survival tucker: Improved diet and health indicators in an Aboriginal community. *Australian and New Zealand Journal of Public Health* 18: 277–85.

Legge, D., Wilson, G., Butler, P., Wright, M., McBride, T. and Attewell, R. 1996 Best practice in primary health care. *Australian Journal of Primary Health – Interchange* 2: 12–26.

Li, T.M. 2000 Articulating Indigenous identity in Indonesia: Resource politics and the tribal slot, in *Comparative Study of Society and History* 42: 149–79.

Llewellyn, S. 1998 Boundary work: Costing and caring in the social services. *Accounting, Organizations and Society* 23: 23–47.

Lupton, D. and Peterson, A. 1996 *The New Public Health: Health and self in the age of risk*. Sydney: Allen & Unwin.

Mackerras, D. 1998 *Evaluation of the Strong Women, Strong Babies, Strong Culture Program. Results for the period 1990–1996 in the three pilot communities*. Darwin: Menzies School of Health Research (MSHR).

—— 2001 Birthweight changes in the pilot phase of the Strong Women, Strong Babies, Strong Culture Program in the Northern Territory. *Australian and New Zealand Journal of Public Health* 25: 34–40.

Macknight, C.C. 1976 *Voyage to Marege: Maccasan trepangers in north Australia*. Melbourne: Melbourne University Press.

Malkki, L. 1997 'Speechless emissaries: Refugees, humanitarianism and dehistoricization', in K.F. Olwig and K. Hastrup (eds) *Siting Culture: The shifting anthropological object*. London and New York: Routledge, pp. 223–54.

Marcus, G. and Fischer, M. 1986 *Anthropology as Cultural Critique*. Chicago: University of Chicago Press.

Marcus, G.E. with Hall, P.D. 1992 *Lives In Trust: The fortunes of dynastic families in late twentieth century America. Institutional Structures of Feeling*. Boulder CO: Westview Press.

Marcus, J. 1990 Introduction: Anthropology, culture and post-modernity. *Social Analysis (Special Issue: Writing Australian Culture: Text, Society and National Identity)* 27: 3–16.

Markey, P.G., d'Espaignet, E.T., Condon, J.R. and Woods, M. 1998 *Trends in the health of mothers and babies, Northern Territory, 1986–95*. Darwin: THS.

Martin Alcoff, L. 1999 Toward a phenomenology of racial embodiment. *Radical Philosophy* 95: 15–26.

Martin, E. 1994 *Flexible Bodies: Tracking immunity in American culture – From the days of polio to the age of AIDS*. Boston MA: Beacon Press.

Maslach, C. 1982 *Burnout: The Cost of Caring*. Englewood Cliffs NJ: Prentice Hall.

Mathews, J., Weeramanthri, T. and D'Abbs, P. 1995 The past is all about us and within. *Today's Life Science* August: 14–20.

Mathews, J.D. 1996 'Aboriginal health: Historical, social and cultural influences', in G. Robinson (ed.) *Aboriginal Health: Social and cultural transitions*. Darwin: NTU Press, pp. 29–38.

Maynard, D.W. 1989 On the ethnography and analysis of discourse in institutional settings. *Perspectives on Social Problems* 1: 127–46.

Menzies School of Health Resarch (MSHR) 1998 *MSHR 1997–98 Annual and Quinquennial Report (Volume I)*. Darwin: MSHR.

Merlan, F. 1998 *Caging the Rainbow: Places, politics, and Aborigines in a north Australian town*. Honolulu: University of Hawaii Press.

Merleau-Ponty, M. 1964 *Signs*. Evanston IL: Northwestern University Press.

Metcalfe, A. 1993 Living in a clinic: The power of public health promotions. *The Australian Journal of Anthropology* 4: 31–44.

Meyer, B., and Pels. P. (eds) 2003 *Magic and Modernity: Interfaces of revelation and concealment*. Stanford CA: Stanford University Press.

Michaels, E. 1990 *UNBECOMING: An AIDS diary*. Sydney: EmPress Publishing.

Miller, D. 1995 'Introduction: Anthropology, modernity and consumption', in D. Miller (ed.) *Worlds Apart: Modernity through the prism of the local*. London: Routledge.

Mintzberg, H. 1993 *Structure in Fives: Designing effective organizations*. Englewood Cliffs NJ: Prentice Hall.

Mitchell, T. 2002 *Rule of Experts: Egypt, techno-politics, modernity*. Berkeley and Los Angeles CA and London: University of California Press.

Mol, A. 2000 'Pathology and the clinic: An ethnographic presentation of two atheroscleroses', in M. Lock, A. Young and A. Cambrosio (eds) *Living and Working with the New Medical Technologies: Intersections of inquiry*. Cambridge: Cambridge University Press, pp. 82–102.

Moodie, R. 1991 STD research and programs in Aboriginal communities. *Venereology* 4: 34–37.

Morris, B. 1985 Cultural domination and domestic dependence: The Dhan-Gadi of New South Wales and the protection of the state. *Canberra Anthropology* 8: 87–115.

—— 1988 'The politics of identity: from Aborigines to the first Australian', in J. Beckett (ed.) *Past and Present: The construction of Aboriginality*. Canberra: Aboriginal Studies Press, pp. 63–85.

Morton, J. 1999 Anthropology at home in Australia. *Australian Journal of Anthropology* 10: 243–59.

Mosse, D. 2004 Is good policy unimplementable? Reflections on the ethnography of aid policy and practice. *Development and Change* 35: 639–71.

—— 2005 *Cultivating Development: An ethnography of aid policy and practice*. London and Ann Arbor MI: Pluto Press.

—— 2006 Anti-social anthropology? Objectivity, objection, and the ethnography of public policy and professional communities. *The Journal of the Royal Anthropological Institute* 12: 935–56.

Muetzelfeldt, M. 1999 'Contracting out in the health sector', in L. Hancock (ed.) *Health Policy in the Market State*. Sydney: Allen & Unwin, pp. 149–68.

Munro, R. 1999 The cultural performance of control. *Organization Studies* 20: 619–40.

—— 2001 Calling for accounts: Numbers, monsters and membership. *The Sociological Review* 49: 473–93.

Myers, F. 1986a *Pintupi Country, Pintupi Self*. Canberra: Australian Institute of Aboriginal Studies.

—— 1986b Reflections on a meeting: Structure, language and the polity in a small-scale society. *American Ethnologist* 13: 430–47.

Myers, F. and Brenneis, D. 1984 'Introduction: Language and politics in the Pacific', in D. Brenneis and F. Myers (eds) *Dangerous Words: Language and politics in the Pacific*. New York: New York University Press.

Nader, L. 1972 'Up the anthropologist – perspectives gained from studying up', in D. Hymes (ed.) *Reinventing Anthropology*. New York: Vintage Books, Random House, pp. 284–311.

Narayan, K. 1993 How native is a 'native' anthropologist? *American Anthropologist* 95: 671–86.

National Aboriginal Health Strategy Working Party 1989 *A National Aboriginal Health Strategy*. Canberra: Australian Government Printing Service.

Nencel, L., and Pels, P. (eds) 1991 *Constructing Knowledge: Authority and critique in social science. Inquiries in social construction*. London, Newbury Park, CA and New Delhi: Sage Publications.

Nesmith, E.L. 1995 *Health Care Architecture: Designs for the future*. Rockport MA: Rockport Publishers.

Nettleton, S. and Bunton, R. 1995 'Sociological critiques of health promotion', in R. Bunton, S. Nettleton and R. Burrows (eds) *The Sociology of Health Promotion: Critical analyses of consumption, lifestyle and risk*. London and New York: Routledge, pp. 41–58.

Northern Territory Medical Service (NTMS) 1978 *Trends in the Provision of Health Services in Aboriginal communities in the Northern Territory*. Darwin: Northern Territory Division (NTMS), Commonwealth Department of Health.

Office of Aboriginal and Torres Strait Islander Health (OATSIH) 2001 *Recommendations for Clinical Care Guidelines on the Management of Otitis Media (Middle Ear Infection) in Aboriginal and Torres Strait Islander Populations*. Canberra: OATSIH, Commonwealth Department of Health and Ageing.

O'Brien, J. 1997 *The Litmus Test: The inside story of the Port Macquarie Base Hospital Project*. Port Macquarie, NSW: Wild & Woolley.

O'Dea, K. 1991 Westernisation, insulin resistance and diabetes in Australian Aborigines. *Medical Journal of Australia* 155: 258–63.

Olivier de Sardan, J-P. 2005 *Anthropology and Development: Understanding contemporary cultural change* (English edn). London and New York: Zed Books.

Paine, R. 1977 'The nursery game: Colonizers and the colonized', in R. Paine (ed.) *The White Arctic: Anthropological essays on tutelage and ethnicity*. Newfoundland: Institute of Social and Economic Research, Memorial University of Newfoundland, pp. 76–106.

—— 1981 'When saying is doing', in R. Paine (ed.) *Politically Speaking: Cross-cultural studies of rhetoric*. Philadephia PA: Institute for the Study of Human Issues, pp. 9–23.

Palmer, G.R., and Short, S.D. 1996 *Health Care and Public Policy: An Australian analysis* (2nd edn). Melbourne: MacMillan Education Australia.

Parry, S. 1992 Disease, Medicine and Settlement: The role of health and medical services in the settlement of the Northern Territory, 1911–1939. PhD dissertation, University of Queensland.

Parsons, T. 1951 *The Social System*. Glencoe: The Free Press.

Passaro, J. 1997 'You can't take the subway to the field: "Village" epistemologies in the global village', in A. Gupta and J. Ferguson (eds) *Anthropological Locations: Boundaries and grounds of a field science*. Berkeley CA: University of California Press.

Pearce, A. 1990 Dropping Out of Sight: Social anthropology encounters post-modernism. *Australian Journal of Anthropology* 1: 18–31.

Pearson, N. 2001 On the human right to misery, mass incarceration and early death. *Arena Magazine* 56: 22–31.

—— 2005 *Welfare Reform and Economic Development for Indigenous Communities*. Sydney: Centre for Independent Studies.

Perin, C. 1998 'Making more matter at the bottom line', in G.E. Marcus (ed.) *Corporate Futures: The diffusion of the culturally sensitive corporate form*. Chicago IL and London: University of Chicago Press, pp. 63–88.

Peterson, N. and Langton, M. (eds) 1983 *Aborigines, Land and Land Rights*. Canberra: Australian Institute of Aboriginal Studies.

Pholeros, P., Rainow, S. and Torzillo, P. 1993 *Housing for Health: Towards a healthy living environment for Aboriginal Australia*. Newport Beach: Healthabitat.

Pierson, P. 1994 *Dismantling the Welfare State? Reagan, Thatcher and the politics of retrenchment*. Cambridge: Cambridge University Press.

Porter, D. 1999 *Health, Civilization and the State: A history of public health from ancient to modern times*. London and New York: Routledge.

Porter, T.M. 1995 *Trust in Numbers: The pursuit of objectivity in science and public life*. Princeton NJ: Princeton University Press.

Povinelli, E. 1993a *Labor's lot: The power, history and culture of Aboriginal action*. Chicago IL: University of Chicago Press.

—— 1993b 'Might be something': The language of indeterminancy in Australian Aboriginal land use. *Man (N.S.)* 28: 679–704.

—— 1999 Settler modernity and the quest for an Indigenous tradition. *Public Culture* 11: 19–48.

—— 2002 *The Cunning of Recognition: Indigenous alterities and the making of Australian multiculturalism. Politics, history and culture*. Durham NC and London: Duke University Press.

—— 2006 *The Empire of Love: Toward a theory of intimacy, genealogy and carnality*. Durham NC and London: Duke University Press.

Powell, A. 1988 *Far Country: A short history of the Northern Territory* (2nd edition). Melbourne: Melbourne University Press.

Power, M. 1997 *The Audit Society: Rituals of verification*. Oxford and New York: Oxford University Press.

—— 2004 *The Risk Management of Everything: Rethinking the politics of uncertainty*. London: Demos.

Preston, A., Chua, W-F. and Neu, D. 1997 The diagnostic-related group-prospective payment system and the problem of the government of rationing health care to the elderly. *Accounting, Organizations and Society* 22: 147–64.

Rabinow, P. 1992 'Artificiality and enlightenment: From sociobiology to biosociality', in J. Crary and S. Kwinter (eds) *Incorporations: Zone 6*. New York: Urzone.

Redmond, T. 2006 'Further on up the road: Community trucks and the moving settlement', in T. Lea, E. Kowal and G. Cowlishaw (eds) *Moving Anthropology: Critical Indigenous studies*. Darwin: Charles Darwin University Press, pp. 95–114.

Reid, J. 1983 *Sorcerers and Healing Spirits: Continuity and change in an Aboriginal medical system*. Canberra: ANU Press.

Riddett, L. 1987 *Sisters, Wives and Mothers: Women as healers and preservers of health in the Northern Territory during the 1930s*. Townsville: ANZAAS Congress, James

Cook University.

Riles, A. 1998 Infinity within the brackets. *American Ethnologist* 25: 378–98.

—— 2000 *The Network Inside Out.* Ann Arbor MI: University of Michigan Press.

Robertson, A.F. 1984 *People and the State: An anthropology of planned development.* Cambridge, London and New York: Cambridge University Press.

Robinson, G. 1995 Violence, Social differentiation and the self. *Oceania* 65: 323–46.

—— 1996 'Aboriginal Health: Social and cultural transitions', in G. Robinson (ed.) *Aboriginal Health: Social and cultural transitions.* Darwin: NTU Press, pp. 1–12.

—— 1997 Trouble lines: Resistance, externalization and individuation. *Social Analysis* 41: 122–51.

Rodrigues, S.B. and Collinson, D.L. 1995 Having fun: Humour as resistance in Brazil. *Organization Studies* 16: 739–68.

Rosaldo, R. 1989 *Culture and Truth: The remaking of social analysis.* Boston MA: Beacon Press.

Rowse, T. 1992 *Remote Possibilities: The Aboriginal domain and the administrative imagination.* Darwin: North Australia Research Unit, ANU.

—— 1996 *Traditions for Health: Studies in Aboriginal reconstruction.* Darwin: North Australia Research Unit, ANU.

Ruben, A.R. and Walker, A.C. 1993. A case for urgent intervention: Malnutrition in rural Aboriginal children in the Top End of the Northern Territory. *Journal of Paediatrics and Child Health* 29: 201–05.

—— 1995 Malnutrition among rural Aboriginal children in the Top End of the Northern Territory. *Medical Journal of Australia* 162: 400–03.

Rushdie, S. 1997 Notes on writing and the nation. *Index on Censorship* 26: 34–38.

Ryang, S. 1997 Native anthropology and other problems. *Dialectical Anthropology* 22: 23–49.

Sacks, H. 1984 'On doing "being ordinary"', in J.M. Atkinson and J. Heritage (eds) *Structures of Social Action: Studies in conversational analysis.* Cambridge, London and New York: Maison des Sciences de l'Homme and Cambridge University Press, pp. 413–29.

Said, E. 1985 *Orientalism.* Melbourne: Penguin.

Sandall, R. 2001 *The Culture Cult: Designer tribalism and other essays.* Boulder CO: Westview Press.

Sansom, B. 1980 *The Camp at Wallaby Cross.* Canberra: AIAS.

—— 1988 'A grammar of exchange', in I. Keen (ed.) *Being Black.* Canberra: Aboriginal Studies Press.

—— 1995 The wrong, the rough and the fancy: About immorality and an Aboriginal aesthetic of the singular. *Anthropological Forum* 7: 259–314.

Sartre, J-P. 1971 *Sketch for a Theory of the Emotions* (English translation, 1962 edn). London: Methuen & Co.

Sayers, S. and Powers, M. 1997 *Cross classification of infant size, Aboriginal infants born at Royal Darwin Hospital 1987–90.* Darwin: Royal Darwin Hospital.

Scheper-Hughes, N. 1992 *Death Without Weeping: The violence of everyday life in Brazil.* Berkeley and Los Angeles CA and Oxford: University of California Press.

Schwartzman, H. 1984 'Stories at work: Play in an organizational context', in E.M. Bruner (ed.) *Text, Play and Story: The construction and reconstruction of self and society.* Washington DC: American Ethnological Society, pp. 80–93.

—— 1981 Hidden agendas and formal organizations or how to dance at a meeting. *Social Analysis* 9: 13–24.

—— 1989 *The Meeting: Gatherings in organizations and communities.* New York: Plenum Press.

—— 1993 *Ethnography in Organizations.* Newbury Park CA, London and New Delhi: Sage Publications.

Schwartzman, H.B. and Berman, R.H. 1994. 'Meetings: The neglected routine', in T. Hamada and W.E. Sibley (eds) *Anthropological Perspectives on Organizational Culture*. Lanham MD, New York and London: University Press of America, pp. 63–93.

Scott, J.C. 1998 *Seeing Like a State: Why certain schemes to improve the human condition have failed*. New Haven CT and London: Yale University Press.

Scott, J.W. 1991 The evidence of experience. *Critical Inquiry* 17: 773–97.

Scrimgeor, D., Rowse, T. and Lucas, A. 1997 *Too Much Sweet: The social relations of diabetes in Central Australia*. Darwin: MSHR.

Senate Select Committee 1991 *What Price Health Care? Hospital Costs and Health Insurance. A report by the Senate Select Committee on Health Legislation and Health Insurance*. Canberra: The Parliament of the Commonwealth of Australia.

Sennett, R. 2003 *Respect in a World of Inequality*. New York and London: W.W. Norton & Company.

Shields, R. 1991 *Places on the Margin: Alternative geographies of modernity*. London and New York: Routledge.

Smith, M. 1977 *A Discussion Paper in response to 'A Working Paper Concerning Projections as to the Future Educational Needs of Handicapped Children in Aboriginal Communities' by T.R. Crawford, District Guidance Officer, Northern Region*. Darwin: Northern Territory Department of Education, File No 79/1175 Executive Group Meetings, ff. 49–54.

Soong, F.S. 1981 *Cultural Brokers in Western Arnhem Land: A study of the role of the Aboriginal health worker*. Diploma in Anthropology thesis, University of Sydney.

Stanner, W.E.H. 1968 'After the Dreaming', *Boyer lectures*. Sydney.

Stewart, K. 1996 *A Space by the Side of the Road: Cultural poetics in an 'other' America*. Princeton NJ: Princeton University Press.

Stoler, A.L. and Cooper, F. 1997 'Between Metrapole and Colony: Rethinking a research agenda', in F. Cooper and A.L. Stoler (eds) *Tensions of Empire: Colonial cultures in a bourgeois world*. Berkeley and Los Angeles CA and London: University of California Press, pp. 1–58.

Stoller, P. 1989 *The Taste of Ethnographic Things: The senses in anthropology*. Philadelphia PA: University of Pennsylvania Press.

Strathern, M. 1987 'The limits of auto-anthropology', in A. Jackson (ed.) *Anthropology at Home*. London and New York: Tavistock, pp. 16–37.

—— 1991 *Partial Connections. Association for Social Anthropology in Oceania Special Publications*. Savage MD: Rowman & Littlefield Publishers.

—— 2006 A community of critics? Thoughts on new knowledge. *Journal of the Royal Anthropological Institute* 12: 191–209.

Strathern, M. (ed.) 2000 *Audit Cultures: Anthropological studies in accountability, ethics and the academy*. London and New York: Routledge.

Stronach, M., Mills, K. and Ryan, M. (undated) *The Store Book: Food and nutrition guidelines for Aboriginal Community Stores*. Darwin: THS.

Sutton, P. 2001 The Inaugural Berndt Foundation Biennial Lecture: 'The politics of suffering: Indigenous policy in Australia since 1970'. *Anthropological Forum* 11: 125–74.

Tamisari, F. 2006 '"Personal acquaintance": Essential individuality and the possibilities of encounters', in T. Lea, E. Kowal and G. Cowlishaw (eds) *Moving Anthropology: Critical Indigenous studies*. Darwin: Charles Darwin University Press, pp. 17–36.

Taussig, M. 1980 Reification and the consciousness of the patient. *Social Science and Medicine* 14B: 3–13.

—— 1987 *Shamanism, Colonialism and the Wild Man*. Chicago IL: University of Chicago Press.

—— 1997 *The Magic of the State*. New York: Routledge.

—— 1999 *Defacement: Public secrecy and the labor of the negative*. Stanford CA: Stanford University Press.

Taylor, J. 2004 Social indicators for Aboriginal governance: Insights from the Thamarrurr Region, Northern Territory. *ANU e-Press* http://epress.anu.edu.au/caepr_series/no_24/mobile_devices/index.html.

Territory Health Services (THS) 1995 *Northern Territory Government Joint Agency Support for Health Infrastructure Priority Projects*. Darwin: THS.

—— 1996 *Territory Health Services 1995/96 Annual Report*. Darwin: Northern Territory Government Printer.

—— 1998 *Top End Remote Area Health Orientation Package: 'Let's work together to help fill in the gaps'*. Darwin: THS.

—— 1999 *Territory Health Services Annual Report 1998/99*. Darwin: Northern Territory Government Printer.

Thomas, D.P. 2004 *Reading Doctors' Writing: Race, politics and power in Indigenous health research, 1870–1969*. Canberra: Australian Institute of Aboriginal and Torres Strait Islander Studies.

Thompson, N. 1991 'A review of Aboriginal health status', in J. Reid and P. Trompf (eds) *The Health of Aboriginal Australia*. Sydney: Harcourt, Brace, Jovanovitch.

Thomson, G. 1998 'CURSE CLOSES REMOTE SCHOOL. Royalties demanded on tuckshop: claim', *Northern Territory News*, pp. 1–2.

Titmuss, R. 1974 *Social Policy*. New York: Pantheon.

Trice, H.M. and Beyer, J.M. 1984 Studying organizational cultures through rites and ceremonials. *Academy of Management Review* 9: 653–69.

Tsing, A.L. 2005 *Friction: An ethnography of global connection*. Princeton NJ and Oxford: Princeton University Press.

Turner, V. 1982 *From Ritual to Theatre: The human seriousness of play*. New York: Performing Arts Journal Publications.

Tyler, M.G. and Tyler, S.A. 1986 The Sorcerer's Apprentice: The discourse of training in family therapy. *Cultural Anthropology* 1: 238–56.

Van Maanen, J. 1978 'Observations on the making of policemen', in P.K. Manning and J. Van Maanen (eds) *Policing: A view from the street*. Santa Monica CA: Goodyear Publishing Company, pp. 292–308.

—— 1979 The fact of fiction in organizational ethnography. *Administrative Science Quarterly* 29: 539–50.

—— 1988 *Tales of the Field*. Chicago IL: University of Chicago Press.

Visweswaran, K. 1994 *Fictions of Feminist Ethnography*. Minneapolis MN: University of Minnesota Press.

von Sturmer, J. 1981 Talking with Aborigines. *Australian Institute of Aboriginal Studies Newsletter* New Series No. 15: 1–19.

—— 1989 Aborigines, representation, necrophilia. *Art + Text* 32: 127–39.

—— 1995 'R stands for ...': An extract from a Mabo diary. *Australian Journal of Anthropology* 6: 101–15.

Wagner, R. 1991 'The fractal person', in M. Godelier and M. Strathern (eds) *Big Men and Great Men: Personifications of power in Melanesia*. Cambridge: Cambridge University Press, pp. 159–73.

Weeramanthri, T. 2001 Autonomy, optimism, and systems: The keys to preventing and controlling chronic disease. *The Chronicle (Chronic Diseases Network NT)* 4: 8–11.

—— n.d. *Knowledge, language and mortality: Communicating health information in Aboriginal communities in the Northern Territory*. Darwin: THS.

Weiss, B. 1996 *The Making and the Unmaking of the Haya Lived World: Consumption, commoditization and everyday practice*. Durham NC and London: Duke University Press.

White, P. 2001 'Making it work means ...' *The Chronicle (Chronic Diseases Network NT)* 5: 3–5.

Wikan, U. 1994. 'Beyond the words: The power of resonance', in G. Palsson (ed.) *Beyond Boundaries: Understanding, translation and anthropological discourse, explorations in anthropology*. Oxford and Providence RI: Berg, pp. 184–209.

Williams, N. 1986 *The Yolngu and Their Laws: A system of land tenure and the fight for its recognition*. Canberra: Aboriginal Studies Press.

—— 1985 'On Aboriginal decision making', in D.E. Barwick, J. Beckett and M. Reay (eds) *Metaphors of Interpretation*. Canberra: ANU Press, pp. 240–69.

Wiltshire, K. 1987 *Privatisation: The British experience – An Australian perspective*. Melbourne: Longman Cheshire; Committee for the Economic Development of Australia.

Woollard, K., Leeder, S., Nossall, G., Hetzel, B., Stanley, F., Douglas, B., Donald, K., Matthews, J., Holman, D.A. and Ring, I. 1995 *Aboriginal and Torres Strait Islander Health – A Submission*. Australian Medical Association.

World Health Organization (WHO) 1978 *Alma Ata 1977, Primary Health Care*. Geneva: WHO.

—— 2005 *Preventing Chronic Diseases: A vital investment*. Geneva: WHO.

Wright, J. 1996 *Community X: Final Report. Evaluation of existing health care service delivery and a measured health needs analysis of a remote Aboriginal community in the Top End of the Northern Territory*. Canberra: Commonwealth Department of Health and Family Services.

Yeatman, A. 1993 Corporate managerialism and the shift from the welfare to the competition state. *Discourse* 13: 3–9.

Young, I.M. 1990 'Throwing like a girl and other essays', in *Feminist philosophy and social theory*. Bloomington and Indianapolis IN: Indiana University Press.

Zarcadoolas, C., Pleasant, A. and Greer, D.S. 2005 Understanding health literacy: An expanded model. *Health Promotion International* 20: 195–203.

INDEX

Forthcoming titles by UNSW Press

Forgetting Aborigines
Chris Healy

Locked in a cycle of forgetting, then remembering, Aborigines,
the whitefella mind is playing tricks. Is there a way off this trail of
destruction? Chris Healy offers a new way of history writing that looks
beyond the paper archive to other places where the historical sensibility
is formed: the TV screen, the embodied situation, or the heritage trail.
You emerge in the end all the wiser, for to forget 'Aborigines' is to
remember real people, in real situations. Brilliant.

– Stephen Muecke

Forgetting Aborigines explores a central paradox in Australian history:
Aborigines are often remembered as absent in the face of a continuing
and actual Indigenous historical presence. Chris Healy argues that in
the ways we remember our history, Aborigines keep disappearing. They
are present and central at certain moments but then fade from memory.
Aboriginal issues can be on the front page for weeks prompting white
Australians to ask questions like 'why weren't we told?' and then recede
again. The book examines ways in which we can stop this dishonest and
destructive cycle.

Chris Healy explores the entanglements that emerge from various
encounters between white and Indigenous people since the 1960s. The
book draws on the extraordinary cultural production emerging from
the domain of Aboriginality in painting, film, photography, exhibition,
performance, poetry, fiction and much more. Alongside key political
and social landmarks of the past 40 years, *Forgetting Aborigines* makes
personal, reflective and intellectual observations about the ways in
which we remember and forget and how we might make Aboriginality
meaningful and visible in Australia.

DR CHRIS HEALY is a senior lecturer in the School of Culture and
Communication at the University of Melbourne. His previous book is
From the Ruins of Colonialism: History as Social Memory.

ISBN 978 0 86840 884 2

Rights and Redemption
History, Law and Indigenous People
Ann Curthoys, Ann Genovese and Alexander Reilly

... An ambitious task but one that has great significance and topicality

– Antonio Buti

Exploring the tensions in the relationship between law and history, as *Rights and Redemption* does, is extremely important. Greater understanding of how the legal system can use this historical knowledge and how historians can give evidence will enhance the way in which Aboriginal and Torres Strait Islander litigants navigate the complexities of the Australian legal system.

– Larissa Behrendt

History has been central to a number of heated public debates in recent years. As Indigenous people have sought to redress through the law, the role of history in the courts has become highly charged. *Rights and Redemption* is a detailed investigation of the uses of history and historians in high-profile cases involving Indigenous litigants, something not previously attempted.

Ann Curthoys, Ann Genovese and Alexander Reilly look at cases before the Federal Court during the era of the Howard government, a time when Indigenous rights and the place of Aboriginal people in the national story were undermined in government laws and policies. They investigate how the courts have made use of historians as expert witnesses, and how the colonial past has been framed and understood by the courts.

ISBN 978 086840 807 1

Also published by UNSW Press

Australia's Welfare Wars Revisited
The Players, the Politics and the Ideologies
Philip Mendes

Over the past two decades, the Australian welfare state has been a hotly contested political terrain. In Philip Mendes' acclaimed 2003 book, *Australia's Welfare Wars,* he explicitly examined the role played by ideology and lobby groups in determining welfare state outcomes.

Now with a change of government at the federal level, Mendes has brought the book completely up to date. With specific reference to current theories about globalisation, *Australia's Welfare Wars Revisited* questions many of the key assumptions that underpin contemporary social welfare policies and argues for the reaffirmation of social democratic and welfare state ideals.

Dr Philip Mendes is a senior lecturer in Social Policy and Community Development in the Department of Social Work, Faculty of Medicine, Monash University. He has been a social work and social policy practitioner and educator for 20 years, with particular experience in the fields of child abuse and child protection, income security and illicit drugs. He has numerous publications in local and international journals, and is the author or co-author of five books including *Australia's Welfare Wars* (2003), *Harm Minimisation, Zero Tolerance and Beyond: The Politics of Illicit Drugs in Australia* (2004) and *Inside the Welfare Lobby: A History of the Australian Council of Social Service* (2006).

ISBN 978 086840 991 7